Mohammad Keyhani
The Generativity Advantage

Mohammad Keyhani

The Generativity Advantage

—

Unpredicted Innovation at Scale

DE GRUYTER

ISBN 978-3-11-079018-4
e-ISBN (PDF) 978-3-11-077963-9
e-ISBN (EPUB) 978-3-11-077979-0

Library of Congress Control Number: 2025937666

Bibliographic information published by the Deutsche Nationalbibliothek
The Deutsche Nationalbibliothek lists this publication in the Deutsche Nationalbibliografie;
detailed bibliographic data are available on the internet at http://dnb.dnb.de.

© 2025 Walter de Gruyter GmbH, Berlin/Boston, Genthiner Straße 13, 10785 Berlin
Cover image: Author; Cover design: Britta Zwarg, Berlin
Typesetting: Integra Software Services Pvt. Ltd.

www.degruyter.com
Questions about General Product Safety Regulation:
productsafety@degruyterbrill.com

———

This book is dedicated to everyone, throughout history, who ever contributed a piece of intelligent writing, art, or code to humanity, thereby helping train the AI models we have today.

Acknowledgments

My exploration of technology generativity theory and its business applications grew from collaborative research with Dr. Hamed Tajedin on firm-designed markets. This intellectual journey took a decisive turn when I encountered Satish Nambisan's suggestion that entrepreneurship scholars should engage with digital technology frameworks. His mention of Technology Generativity Theory led me to Jonathan Zittrain's pioneering work, which profoundly shaped my thinking.

The COVID pandemic provided an unexpected opportunity—my first sabbatical as a university professor allowed me to immerse myself in no-code software development, particularly on Bubble.io. This hands-on experience revealed Bubble's ecosystem as an ideal case study of generativity in practice. I'm especially grateful to PhD student Mahdieh Sarbazvatan, whose qualitative research and interviews with Bubble plugin developers yielded invaluable insights that enriched this book.

Many ideas presented here were refined through conference papers at the Academy of Management (AOM) and the Administrative Sciences Association of Canada (ASAC). The thoughtful feedback from anonymous reviewers at these conferences substantially improved the work. An early podcast interview with Hunter Hastings challenged me to reframe these concepts for a broader audience, for which I remain thankful.

My deepest gratitude goes to my family, especially my wife and intellectual sounding board, Safaneh Mohaghegh Neyshabouri, and our two children, who graciously sacrificed playtime with Dad so I could complete this project. Their patience and support sustained me throughout this journey. I also extend sincere thanks to Jaya Dalal and the team at De Gruyter Brill for their encouragement and guidance in bringing this book to fruition. Finally, I must acknowledge the role of generative AI in enhancing this manuscript—and the role of this manuscript in enhancing generative AI.

https://doi.org/10.1515/9783110779639-202

Contents

Acknowledgments —— VII

Chapter 1
Introduction —— 1
    The Messiness of Generativity —— 2
    The Saga of Laundry Buddy —— 4
    Generativity in Computer Science —— 7
    The Other Generativities —— 8
    Outline of this Book —— 9

Chapter 2
The Competitive Advantage of Generativity —— 10
    A Definition of the Generativity Advantage —— 10
    Product Generativity —— 14
    Market Generativity —— 15
    Product-Market Generativity —— 17
    The Generativity Flywheel —— 19
    Generativity as a Deliberate Strategy —— 20
    The Case of Bubble.io: Democratizing Software —— 24
        The Genesis of Generativity: From Product to Product-Market —— 25
        Navigating Strategic Trade-offs: The Tensions of Generativity —— 26
        Bubble's Generativity Flywheel: Key Mechanisms at Play —— 27
        Bubble's Path Forward —— 27

Chapter 3
Understanding Generativity: The Engine of Unpredicted Innovation —— 29
    Zittrain's Conceptualization of Generativity —— 29
    Adding Profitability to Generativity —— 30
    The Evolution of Generativity Theory —— 31
        Architectural Generativity —— 31
        Extended Generativity Theory —— 32
        Bounded Generativity —— 32
        Inverse Generativity —— 33
    Concluding Thoughts —— 33

Chapter 4
The Generativity of Products —— 34
    An Ode to Possibility —— 34
    Examples of Generative Products —— 35
    Generative Products as Sources of Surprise —— 36

Generative Products as Vehicles for Serious Entrepreneurship —— **38**
Designing Products for Generativity —— **41**
   Leverage: Empowering a Wide Spectrum of Tasks —— **41**
   Adaptability: Building Blocks for Customization and Evolution —— **42**
   Ease of Mastery: Lowering Barriers to Entry —— **43**
   Accessibility: Enabling Openness and Participation —— **43**
   Transferability: Facilitating the Spread of Innovation —— **44**
   Profitability: Taking Users Seriously as Entrepreneurs —— **45**
The Generative Properties of Digital Artifacts —— **46**
   Programmability: The Foundation of Unlimited Possibility —— **46**
   Addressability: Enabling Targeted Innovation at Scale —— **47**
   Sensibility: Creating Context-Aware Innovation —— **49**
   Communicability: Building Innovation Networks —— **50**
   Memorizability: Learning and Evolution —— **51**
   Traceability: Understanding Innovation Patterns —— **52**
   Associability: Combining and Recombining —— **53**
   Leveraging the Power of Digital for Generativity —— **54**

Chapter 5
Managing Generative Products —— 56
   The Pros and Cons of Generative Products —— **56**
   A New Mindset for Managing Generative Products —— **59**
      From Fail Fast to Patient Play —— **60**
      From Problem-Solving to Meta Problem-Solving —— **60**
      From Hypothesis Testing to Hypothesis Development —— **61**
      From Customer Feedback to User Tinkering —— **61**
      From Traditional to Thick Documentation —— **62**
   Conclusion: Reimagining Product Management for Generativity —— **63**

Chapter 6
The Generativity of Markets —— 65
   The Market as an Innovation Machine —— **65**
   Flipping the Agency Problem on Its Head —— **66**
   The Power of Large Numbers —— **66**
   The Power of Collective Intelligence —— **67**
   Markets as Learning Systems —— **67**
   On the Terminology of "Market Generativity" —— **68**

Chapter 7
Designing Markets for Generativity —— 70
    The Three-Layered Architecture —— 70
    The Allocation Layer: Building the Foundation of Markets —— 71
        Market Thickness: Building the Foundation for Generative Innovation —— 74
        Efficient Matching: Balancing Market Clearing with Discovery —— 76
        Trust and Safety: Creating a Secure Space for Innovation —— 77
        Conclusion: The Allocation Layer as Innovation Infrastructure —— 78
    The Generation Layer: Spurring Innovation at Scale —— 79
        The Power of Diversity for Innovation —— 82
        The Intellectual Orders of Generativity —— 83
        Embracing Outliers as Potential Game Changers —— 84
        Making Ideas Interactive: The Communication Infrastructure —— 85
        Social Processes and Serendipitous Discovery —— 87
        The Memory Challenge: Building Collective Knowledge —— 88
        The Experimentation Engine: From Natural Selection to Active
        Learning —— 88
        The Platform's Privileged Knowledge: Broadcasting the Frontier —— 90
        Boundary Resources and Innovation Toolkits —— 92
        Standards and Interoperability —— 94
        Enabling Organization: The Power of Teams and Organizations in User
        Innovation —— 95
        Engineering Markets for Generativity —— 97
    The Appropriation Layer: Capturing Value from Distributed Innovation —— 98
        Innovation-Friendly Pricing and Revenue Models in Generative
        Marketplaces —— 98
        Control Points and Value Capture —— 103
        The Data Advantage —— 106
        Curation and Promotion as Strategic Levers —— 107
        Ethical Considerations in Profiting from Other People's Innovations —— 109
        Capturing Value while Spurring Innovation —— 110
    External Factors: The Broader Context of Generative Markets —— 111
        Cultural Dynamics and Innovation Mindsets —— 113
        Networks and Knowledge Flows —— 114
        Educational Institutions and Learning Ecosystems —— 116
        Leveraging Urban Population Centers —— 117
        Regulatory Considerations —— 117
    Conclusion: Architecting for Generative Growth —— 118

Chapter 8
The Generativity Flywheel —— 120
    Market Incentives as Innovation Accelerant: The Power of Profit —— 120
        Sustaining Innovation Through Career-Level Commitment —— 122
    The Product-Market Generativity Framework —— 123
        Quadrant 4: High Product, Low Market Generativity —— 123
        Quadrant 3: Low Product, Low Market Generativity —— 124
        Quadrant 2: Low Product, High Market Generativity —— 124
        Quadrant 1: High Product, High Market Generativity —— 125
        Building Generative Markets from Generative Products —— 126
        Building Generative Products from Generative Markets —— 127
    The Six Stages of the Generativity Flywheel —— 128
        Stage 1: Attract Innovative Users —— 129
        Stage 2: Create Novel Applications —— 130
        Stage 3: Increase Product Value —— 130
        Stage 4: Attract More Users —— 130
        Stage 5: Enable Value Capture —— 131
        Stage 6: Expand Innovation Possibilities —— 131
    Conclusion —— 131

Chapter 9
Generativity in Practice: The Trade-offs and Challenges of Generativity —— 133
    Control Versus Generativity —— 135
        Real-World Example: Apple's Shifting Stance on iOS Development —— 136
        Potential Remedies: Balancing Control and Generativity —— 137
    Stability Versus Flexibility —— 138
        Real-World Example: Google's Android Fragmentation —— 139
        Potential Remedies: Modular Design and Versioning —— 139
    Variety Versus Utility —— 140
        Real-World Example: Video Game Consoles —— 141
        Potential Remedies: Balancing Variety and Utility —— 141
    Originality Versus Remixing —— 142
        Real-World Example: The Scratch Online Community —— 142
        Potential Remedies: Balancing Generativity and Originality —— 143
    Ecosystem Boundaries Versus Product Boundaries —— 143
        Real-World Example: LLM Platforms —— 144
        Potential Remedies: Aligning Ecosystem and Product Expansion —— 145
    Openness Versus Value Capture —— 146
        Real-World Example: The WordPress Ecosystem —— 147
        Potential Remedies: Balancing Openness and Value Capture —— 147
    Conclusion: Embracing the Paradoxes of Generativity —— 148

Chapter 10
Celebrating the Shared Potential of Humanity —— **150**
    Embracing the Unknowable —— **151**
    AI Agents and the Future of Generativity —— **153**
    A Challenge to You —— **154**

References —— **155**

About the Author —— **165**

List of Figures —— **167**

List of Tables —— **169**

Index —— **171**

Chapter 1
Introduction

On November 30, 2022 a digital product with the curious name of "ChatGPT" was released to the public by OpenAI, a company not widely known at the time. The company had been founded since 2015, bringing together an elite group of the world's top AI researchers with the goal of finding a safe way to achieve Artificial General Intelligence (Tamkin et al., 2021), an elusive holy grail of AI research, referring to highly autonomous AI systems that perform better than humans at most kinds of work (Morris et al., 2024). After ChatGPT was released, in a matter of days it broke records for the fastest widespread adoption in the history of consumer software, reaching more than 1 million users in five days and 100 million users in two months (Teubner et al., 2023).

What makes ChatGPT's story particularly fascinating is not just its explosive growth but how it exemplifies a profound pattern that is the focus of this book – one that challenges our fundamental assumptions about innovation and value creation. OpenAI created something whose applications surprised even its own creators. As users worldwide began sharing their ChatGPT experiences on social media, they revealed uses that no one at OpenAI had anticipated. Mira Murati, then Chief Technology Officer at OpenAI, captured this phenomenon in an interview (Lynch, 2024):

> It's one thing to statistically predict the performance of the model, it's another thing to actually see the capabilities when you test them across different domains and see that the models can rhyme, they can do extremely well in biology or math tests," she states. "That is completely different, when you actually bring it in the real world and see how the statistical performance translates into actually solving hard problems.

As you will see throughout this book, product creators being surprised by their own products is a common theme in a pattern we refer to as generativity: a system's ability to channel unpredicted innovations from a vast variety of contributors.

The artificial intelligence technology behind ChatGPT is not limited to the ChatGPT user interface. In fact, even before ChatGPT was released as a consumer product, OpenAI was selling the services of its models to developers through Application Programming Interfaces (APIs) which OpenAI has made incredibly easy to use. As of late 2024, around 3 million software developers around the world were building their own tools with these models or using the services of the OpenAI models in existing software tools (Metz, 2024). Because each developer uses a unique API key to access the AI models, API usage is tracked by OpenAI, and the company charges a rate for each individual API call.

The nature of OpenAI's products allow the company to profit from the innovations of others on a massive scale, without having to manage or even know much about those innovations internally, let alone make any predictions about their success. This mechanism, which we refer to as the generativity advantage, is an incredi-

https://doi.org/10.1515/9783110779639-001

bly powerful engine of value creation and profit that has been the key driver of success for some of the world's most valuable companies in the digital era. Surprisingly however, generativity as a driver of competitive advantage has remained severely underappreciated in discussions of business strategy and entrepreneurship. Youngjin Yoo, a world-leading scholar of information systems, argued years ago that the "age of generativity" is upon us and that it calls for new management practices, as well as new theoretical models and frameworks to guide those practices (Yoo, 2013). It is time for the world of business strategy to catch up.

This is the gap addressed by the present book. While the book is mostly geared toward businesses that can be described as "digital platforms," many of the arguments apply to other types of businesses as well. By digital platforms, I mean digital products that facilitate the interaction of multiple stakeholders whose contributions can extend or increase the value of the product (de Reuver et al., 2018).

The core arguments of this book are as follows: a) the properties of generative technologies conceptualized in technology generativity theory can be viewed as intentionally achievable outcomes or design choices that can be pursued with strategic intent as features of generative products; b) the properties of dynamic markets conceptualized in economic theories of knowledge-generating economies can be pursued with strategic intent as design parameters or features of generative marketplaces; c) generative products and generative marketplaces, especially in combination with each other where generative marketplaces form around generative products, allow firms to tap into the generativity advantage: the mechanism of profiting from the distributed innovations of others on a massive scale. This involves taking user-innovators seriously as profit-generating entrepreneurs and helping them succeed and build sustainable businesses around your platform; and d) the implementation of a strategy to intentionally pursue a generativity advantage is not for everyone and is far from trivial: the path sometimes requires specifically going against certain approaches that are considered "best practice" in strategy and entrepreneurship and often involves strategic trade-offs along the way. These core arguments form the organizing logic of the chapters in this book.

Throughout the book, many anecdotes and cases are referred to that either illustrate examples of generative products and marketplaces, or illustrate certain product or marketplace features that can be conducive to generativity.

The Messiness of Generativity

The generativity advantage is fundamentally different from traditional approaches to innovation that rely on the company's own innovative capacity or its ability to identify and acquire promising innovations from others. A generativity advantage derives from creating the conditions for an entire ecosystem of external innovators to generate value in ways that benefit the platform owner, without requiring the owner to anticipate or directly manage those innovations.

The implications of this approach are profound. Traditional strategic thinking emphasizes control, prediction, and direct management of innovation. But the generativity advantage flips this logic on its head. It suggests that in certain contexts, the most powerful competitive advantage comes from deliberately creating conditions for unplanned, distributed innovation. This is not merely about "open innovation" or "crowdsourcing" – it is about architecting systems of uncontrolled distributed value creation, and channeling a fair amount of that value back to the platform creator.

However, this lack of control over the innovations that happen around your product is not without its costs. Generativity is often messy and noisy, and is not always desired. An example of a non-generative digital platform is Uber. You need it to do something specific (get from point A to point B), and you would rather that the app does this reliably and predictably, rather than for the app to introduce and encourage all sorts of unpredictable innovations from its drivers. Even for a product as generative as the smartphone, a loss of control is not always an intuitive goal to pursue. Steve Jobs was famously against allowing third-party apps on the iPhone, initially resisting what has hence become Apple's greatest money-making machine (Stier, 2024).

OpenAI has had to deal with its own share of the messiness that comes with generativity. The first method in which OpenAI opened its ecosystem to external innovations was through the API. But many entrepreneurs and innovators who started building with the API were ridiculed for building simple "GPT Wrappers," a term used in a somewhat derogatory way to mean that these products were not adding much value beyond what ChatGPT could do itself, and were not really sophisticated or hard-to-build accomplishments to be proud of. Nevertheless, many entrepreneurs who persisted and moved fast were able to profit handsomely from such products, although there was and continues to be uncertainty around which applications will be replaced by features in OpenAI's own products and which applications will continue to provide unique value.

By early 2025 after the release of the DeepSeek models that pointed toward a rapid commoditization and severe cost competition at the model layer of generative AI, it became apparent that much of the profit margin was going to be in the application layer, where there is much more room for diverse and unique ideas. Pieter Levels, the famous indie entrepreneur who profited handsomely with his PhotoAI product at the application layer, tweeted[1] in reaction to the DeepSeek developments that "I can't believe we all accidentally betted right on making GPT Wrappers, even though everyone trolled us for it for years, and are now living The Good Life™." But the story around the messiness of masses of external innovations got even more interesting when OpenAI opened up the ecosystem to non-developers.

---

[1] https://x.com/levelsio/status/1885316855801209067

The Saga of Laundry Buddy

In its first attempts to create a managed marketplace around its products that went beyond APIs, on the occasion of OpenAI's first developer day in November 2023, Sam Altman announced the possibility to create "Custom GPTs" and make them available to everyone (Stokel-Walker, 2023), later saying that they were looking at implementing some sort of revenue-sharing arrangement with the creators of Custom GPTs (which still has not materialized as of early 2025). Such marketplaces that go beyond APIs and Software Development Kits (SDKs) are crucial milestones for gaining a generativity advantage, because they extend to a larger population of potential innovators on your platform beyond software developers, tapping into the creativity and ideas of the general public. If they could make this work, it would be a big win for OpenAI.

However, generativity is easier said than done. First, OpenAI failed to clearly define and offer the incentive mechanism for innovators to create custom GPTs. A vague promise of potential revenue-sharing arrangements in the future was not enough for most serious innovators, and they were hesitant to exert too much effort into building custom GPTs. In fact, it turned out that this hesitancy was well founded because months later, as of the time of writing, the revenue sharing mechanism still seems to be a work in progress. However, this was not a complete deal-breaker and users eventually found third-party methods to add paywall or payment mechanisms to custom GPTs (Do Rosario, 2024). Still, it was an indication that OpenAI was not taking its non-developer user-innovators seriously as entrepreneurs.

Second, the somewhat unpredictable and fuzzy behavior of LLMs themselves created unanticipated difficulties for innovators to be able to protect their innovations on the platform. A key advantage of building a custom GPT was that the functionality of ChatGPT could be extended and improved for specific use cases by giving the original LLM additional instructions and documents that the average user may not have or may not find it easy to give the LLM. If the platform could allow innovators to conceal and protect these custom instructions and additional documents, it would allow them to protect their intellectual property and incentivize them to participate in this market. However, soon users learned that it was relatively easy to trick or manipulate a custom GPT to reveal its instructions and even provide its custom documents for download. This issue again created an incentive problem preventing innovators from considering custom GPTs as a serious profit opportunity. OpenAI could potentially address this problem by, for example, adding a protector agent in the workflow of users interacting with custom GPT that would check if the custom GPT was about to reveal too much, and prevent it from doing so. The company already has such mechanisms to prevent ChatGPT from re-producing large pieces of copyrighted text. But unfortunately, as of the time of writing, the company has not made a similar effort to protect the intellectual property of custom GPT creators.

A clue as to why the custom GPT marketplace has received such little love from OpenAI developers may be found in the now infamous saga of Laundry Buddy. Laundry Buddy was the name of one of the examples of a custom GPT that was displayed in Altman's developer day presentation. It was a custom version of ChatGPT instructed to focus on laundry care advice. After Altman's presentation, Laundry Buddy became a point of controversy, ridicule, and expressions of disappointment among some of the users and developers of the OpenAI ecosystem.

The concept of Laundry Buddy quickly became fodder for jokes and memes across social media platforms. Someone on the OpenAI community forum wrote that "These are just placeholder apps (GPTs) to fill space. Obviously nobody needs a "laundry buddy" GPT."[2] Many viewed Laundry Buddy as a symbol of underwhelming innovation and a loss of direction, especially given the high expectations surrounding artificial general intelligence (AGI). This sentiment was captured in a popular quote: "We were promised AGI and got laundry buddy." For example, Jeremy Howard, a prominent figure in the field of artificial intelligence and machine learning, posted this tweet about the announcement of custom GPTs[3] (see Figure 1.1):

> I could barely watch the keynote. It was just another bland corp-speak bunch of product updates. For those researchers I know that were involved from the beginning, this must have felt nausea-inducing. The plan was AGI, lifting society to a new level. We got Laundry Buddy.

The Laundry Buddy saga demonstrates that pursuing a generativity strategy is not easy, and not always well understood or appreciated. While at first glance it may seem "beneath" a team of the world's greatest AI researchers earning exorbitant salaries to produce Laundry Buddy, the point of custom GPTs like this was exactly that anyone, anywhere, especially those outside of OpenAI, and especially non-developers, could now build and innovate with ChatGPT, and they could build things as seemingly distant from the work of OpenAI as a laundry assistant. We are already used to this in other contexts of more established generative marketplaces. For example, a simple game app like Flappy Bird that was made in just 2–3 days by a lone developer could be considered as not up to par with the standards of world-leading software engineers who work at Apple Inc., but everybody is comfortable with the fact that the entire point of the App Store is to allow for innovations from people who do not work for Apple (Keyhani, 2023).

The Laundry Buddy controversy illuminates a crucial paradox at the heart of generativity strategies. Those who dismissed it as trivial missed its profound strategic significance. In the digital economy, true power often comes not from creating the most sophisticated applications but from enabling others to create applications of any sophistication level, even applications that seem mundane, boring, useless, or not up to par with the grand vision or standards of a leading edge company. This principle—that generativity is messy and that is what makes it powerful—has driven the success

---

2 https://community.openai.com/t/custom-gpt-prompts-can-be-recovered-publicly/491424
3 https://twitter.com/jeremyphoward/status/1725712222629081547

Figure 1.1: Jeremy Howard's tweet in disapproval of custom GPTs like Laundry Buddy.

of platforms from the Apple App Store to WordPress, where simple innovations like Flappy Bird can coexist with sophisticated enterprise software. The story of Laundry Buddy suggests that this idea is not something to be taken for granted.

OpenAI continues to struggle with the messiness of generativity. On January 14, 2025 the company announced a new "Tasks" feature for ChatGPT, and users found many of the use cases to be unsophisticated, once again attracting widespread mockery. For example, one user wrote in mocking tone "this is chatgpts [sic] true purpose"[4] in a tweet with a screenshot of ChatGPT sending a reminder to check the oven in 5 minutes. Another user wrote "so nothing actually useful. But im [sic] sure wall street

---

4 https://x.com/nicdunz/status/1879338590125351158

[sic] loves this."[5] But one user wrote an appropriate response to this tweet, which captures the point I am trying to make here: if seeing some mundane use cases for a new generative feature makes you dismiss the product as useless, "you must have zero imagination."[6]

Generativity in Computer Science

The launch of ChatGPT marks an early milestone in the generative artificial intelligence (AI) revolution, which is set to bring advances even greater than previous industrial revolutions (Dohmke et al., 2023; Eloundou et al., 2023; Zarifhonarvar, 2024). The "generativity" that is the topic of this book is mostly unrelated to the "generativity" of generative AI in the computer science sense of the word. But it just so happens that generative AI is also an incredibly generative technology in the technology theory sense of the word that is the topic of this book, making ChatGPT a perfect case study. It may help to clarify the different notions of generativity before we move on.

ChatGPT is based on a technological breakthrough in machine learning, using neural networks to build Large Language Models (LLMs), which essentially learn patterns from everything humans have ever written, to generate new writing on demand based on user queries (Minaee et al., 2024).

The "GPT" in ChatGPT alludes to the particular architecture of the neural network and machine learning setup that was able to achieve a performance leap in Large Language Models, making them so intelligent that they rendered the famous Turing Test[7] irrelevant almost overnight (Tikhonov & Yamshchikov, 2023). The acronym GPT stands for Generative Pretrained Transformer. A transformer in machine learning is a specialized neural network architecture designed to process sequential data, particularly excelling at understanding the relationships between elements in a sequence like words in a text. Unlike previous approaches that processed sequences linearly, transformers can attend to all elements simultaneously through a mechanism called "self-attention," allowing them to identify complex patterns and dependencies regardless of how far apart elements appear in the sequence (Vaswani et al., 2017). The "pretrained" component indicates that the model undergoes an initial training phase on vast amounts of data before being fine-tuned for specific applications. This pretraining allows the model to develop a broad understanding of patterns in language

5 https://x.com/MWalters1017/status/1879286033906626803
6 https://x.com/JGisSatoshi/status/1879385718897975614
7 The Turing Test is a protocol suggested by Alan Turing (1950) to test the level of intelligence achieved by a computer. The test evaluates artificial intelligence by having a human judge engage in separate text conversations with both a computer and another human, without knowing which is which. If the judge cannot reliably identify which conversation partner is the machine based on their responses, the computer is considered to have passed the test.

or other sequential data that can then be applied to particular tasks. The "generative" aspect refers to the model's ability to generate new sequences by predicting what elements should come next given a starting point.

Before generative AI, prediction was the main task that AI was used for. But if you just put together the next prediction with the next prediction with the next prediction and so on, you can effectively generate new content. For Large Language Models, these predicted elements are small strings of text called "tokens," not exactly words, but you could think of the process as guessing the next word in a sentence, and the next word, and the next word, until you have a meaningful piece of writing (Ouyang et al., 2022).

More generally, in the context of AI, the words "generative" or "generativity" typically refer to the ability of a system to create new content – whether text, images, code, or other media – that resembles human-created work. This AI-based generation happens through statistical pattern recognition on a massive scale, where the system learns to predict likely sequences of words, pixels, or code based on the patterns it has observed in its training data. LLMs and diffusion models (for images and video) and other forms of generative artificial intelligence have turned "Generative AI" into ubiquitous terminology.

The Other Generativities

Generativity is a concept that is used in different ways in other contexts. The term "generativity" carries distinct meanings across various disciplines, each enriching our understanding of creation and contribution.

In the domain of psychology, Erik Erikson introduced "generativity" in his theory of psychosocial development (Erikson, 1963), defining it as the concern for establishing and guiding the next generation. In another usage of the term, psychologist Robert Epstein's Generativity Theory (Epstein, 1999) offers a framework for understanding how novel ideas and behaviors emerge. It posits that creativity results from the interaction of established behavioral repertoires, leading to new combinations and innovations. In linguistics, "generativity" refers to the capacity of grammar to produce an infinite number of sentences from a finite set of rules (Chomsky, 1961). This concept, central to Noam Chomsky's theory of generative grammar, highlights the innate human ability to generate and understand novel sentences, reflecting the creative aspect of language use. But these meanings of generativity are not the focus of this book.

Generativity, in the context of technology theory, represents the capacity of systems to drive unanticipated innovation through the contributions of broad, varied, and often uncoordinated audiences. This notion, prominently articulated by Jonathan Zittrain (2006, 2008), describes the ability of a system to empower and incentivize others—be they users, developers, or other external actors—to innovate and contribute back to it in ways that are valuable, and sometimes unexpectedly so. This interplay fosters an environment where innovation flourishes, often arising from surprising directions and producing outcomes that were neither predicted nor controlled by the original creators. When leveraged strategically, this sense of generativity creates exponential value by harnessing the distributed creativity of millions of minds, each building upon and extending the work of others in ways that would be impossible to centrally coordinate or predict. This is the meaning of generativity that is the focus of this book.

Outline of this Book

The premise of *The Generativity Advantage* centers on the transformative power of generativity as a core driver of competitive advantage in the digital era. Chapter 2 summarizes the core arguments of the book and introduces the case of Bubble.io, a no-code software development platform that I have both used and studied extensively, and frequently use for illustrative purposes throughout the text. Chapter 3 provides a deep dive into the concept of generativity, as formulated by Zittrain and augmented in this book (by adding a profitability dimension). The chapter also reviews some more recent developments in the generativity literature, although this content is not a pre-requisite for the remainder of the book. Chapter 4 applies generativity theory to the unit of "product" and focuses on the notion of a generative product. The chapter provides suggestions on how to go about designing products to be intentionally generative. Chapter 5 explores some ways in which managing a generative product could involve deviations from common practices in product management.

Chapter 6 applies the notion of generativity to the unit of "market" although here it is not so much generativity theory we are building on as it is theories from the economics literature on dynamic innovation-generating economies. Chapter 7 builds on the premise that many digital platforms have enough flexibility and control over their marketplaces to intentionally design them for optimal generativity. The chapter suggests a three-layered architecture for generative markets, and dives deep into the attributes of each layer: allocation, generation, and appropriation.

Chapter 8 explores the idea of putting product generativity and market generativity together and benefiting from the synergies therein. Chapter 9 provides a review of some of the challenges involved in implementing a generativity advantage in practice. Specifically, a number of tensions or trade-offs are considered that organizations are likely to face when pursuing a generativity advantage. Chapter 10 concludes the book by reflecting on generativity as an approach to business that is based on the timeless idea of empowering others to innovate, and more broadly as a celebration of the shared potential of humanity.

Chapter 2
The Competitive Advantage of Generativity

As discussed in the previous chapter, the idea of "generativity" has been defined by Harvard law scholar Jonathan Zittrain as "a system's capacity to produce unanticipated change through unfiltered contributions from broad and varied audiences" (Zittrain, 2008, p. 70).[1] An alternative way to describe generativity is a mechanism that allows for a massive increase of participation into the value creation process and allows for the conversion of this participation into a massive increase of innovation. This key mechanism has been recognized as one of the most consequential affordances of digital technology (Yoo, 2013). However, it has remained largely underappreciated from a business perspective as a source of competitive advantage. Despite some suggestions (Nambisan, 2017), none of the major theories of strategic management and competitive advantage such as the resource-based view (Barney, 2001) or the theory of dynamic capabilities (Teece et al., 1997) covers the generativity mechanism in any useful manner. This is quite a glaring omission as the generativity pattern can be found at the heart of the business models that produced many of the major giants of the digital era, including Alphabet (Google), Apple, Microsoft, Amazon, Facebook, and Alibaba. In this chapter we explicitly conceptualize generativity as a source of strategic and competitive advantage, and provide a summary of the arguments that will be elaborated on in the remainder of the book. The next chapter goes deeper into the generativity concept itself.

A Definition of the Generativity Advantage

The generativity mechanism of competitive advantage can be defined in simple terms as the mechanism of profiting from the unpredicted innovations of others on a massive scale. It is helpful to break down this definition word by word (see Figure 2.1).

Others, not yours. No matter how many and how smart your employees are, most of the best ideas will come from outside your company. This has been pointed out by open innovation researchers for years (Chesbrough, 2006). The trick is in the tools and incentives, or how to enable and motivate masses of people outside your organization to innovate in ways that benefit your organization and allow you to share in the fruits of their innovations. For example, Apple and Google benefit—and take a revenue cut—from many innovative mobile apps on their app stores, developed by people around the world who do not work for these companies. If these companies were to hire ten times the number of employees they currently have and put together

---

1 See p. 70 in Zittrain, J., 2008. *The future of the internet–and how to stop it*. Yale University Press.

https://doi.org/10.1515/9783110779639-002

all their brain power, they still could not possibly conceive of the number and range of innovative apps available now or in the future on their app stores. Even if Apple hired every top software developer in Silicon Valley, they still couldn't match the creative output of millions of developers worldwide working on countless different problems and opportunities. The power lies not just in numbers but in diversity of knowledge, perspective and motivation.

Innovations, not just ideas. Ideas are a dime a dozen, and not all of them prove to be valuable. To profit from generativity there must be mechanisms in place to not only attract a large number of ideas and experiments but also help turn participant ideas into value-creating innovations. For example, Google and Apple both provide extensive application programming interfaces (APIs), software development kits (SDKs), and documentation to help people learn how to build apps for their platforms. Google provides various toolkits such as Firebase, Google App Engine, Android Studio, as well as various APIs to other Google services such as Google Gemini, Google Maps, and Google Cloud Machine Learning to help developers build apps. As a result, numerous apps are released every day. However, the population of developers who can use APIs and SKDs is still a limited group compared to the general public. A common way in which organizations fail to take full advantage of generativity is to limit participation to developers and software companies. While this can be seen as a form of filtering or quality control, the most generative platforms are the ones that truly empower the everyday innovator and tap into the distributed ideas among the general public. Third party no-code tools like Flutter, Adalo, and others allow non-developers to build on top of the Google ecosystem and for the Android marketplace, these tools expand the population of innovators. As of the time of this writing, every single day more than 1200 apps are released on each of these app stores, and about 2 million apps are available for download on both platforms.[2]

The word "unpredicted" is perhaps the most counterintuitive yet most crucial aspect of generativity advantage. Traditional strategic thinking emphasizes prediction and control. But what if the greatest opportunities are precisely those you couldn't have predicted? The emphasis on unpredictability highlights the relatively undirected nature of knowledge search enabled by generative systems (Tajedin et al., 2019). Generativity is a mechanism to unchain knowledge search from the limitations of the searcher. This unchaining frees the search process not only from the organizational capacity and cognitive capacity limits of the searcher but also from their prejudices, biases, and blind spots (a.k.a. "unknown unknowns"). Generative competitive advantage arises from mechanisms that result in the organization benefiting from future innovations it cannot and need not predict or conceive of on its own. It is not necessarily the case that all such innovations are unpredictable, although many may be. The point is to remove the need to predict them as a condition to benefit from them.

---

2 https://42matters.com/stats

For example, when the low production quality mobile game "Flappy Bird" became a sensation, making tens of thousands of dollars of daily revenue in 2014, Apple and Google took a large cut of this revenue without having had to conceive of this idea or predict whether or not it would work. If their employees had been forced to predict, they would reasonably have predicted that the app would be a failure due to its low production quality (it was developed by a lone developer in the course of 2–3 days). The game's crude graphics and simple mechanics seemed to violate every principle of good game design. Yet it captured something in the zeitgeist that no focus group or market analysis could have revealed.

An emphasis on massive scale refers to the capability of digital technologies to automate processes and distribute information at zero or close-to-zero marginal costs of production (Shapiro & Varian, 1999). Leveraging these technologies through their products, organizations can effectively engage in practically unlimited interactions with unlimited people in parallel without being bound by human and organizational capacities. The massive scale of engagement allows organizations to tap into the activity that goes on in a large network of uses, with the creation of ideas, contributions, and innovations of others building on each other and enabling even more ideas, contributions, and innovations. Once "Flappy Bird" was released, it was virtually costless for Apple and Google to instantly distribute the app to countless number of people, and to allow any number of people to download and pay for the app instantly at any time. It also came at no significant cost to Apple or Google for Flappy Bird's creator to learn and get ideas from other mobile games in order to come up with this idea, and for countless later games to learn and get ideas from Flappy Bird and its game mechanics.

Lastly, the word "profiting" emphasizes the need to find ways to channel innovations into a path that ultimately benefits the organization. While the generativity mechanism may drive innovation and value creation on a massive scale, it does not necessarily turn into a driver of competitive advantage for any particular firm if that firm does not have any method of systematically profiting from those innovations. For example, no one company[3] has been able to substantially appropriate value from the immense generativity created around the WordPress content management system, estimated to be used by 43% of all websites on the internet.[4] However, Apple and Google take substantial cuts from all the revenue generated through their app stores. Other examples of success in both value creation and value capture from generativity include the game platforms Minecraft (Mojang Studios) and Roblox.

Another key element of profitability in the generativity advantage is that in order for you (the platform owner) to profit, your user-innovators must profit. To do that,

---

3 Except maybe Google (which was not the creator of WordPress) because so many of those websites find their audience through Google Search and monetize through Google Ads.
4 https://w3techs.com/technologies/details/cm-wordpress

you must take your user-innovators seriously as profit-generating entrepreneurs. This is why I advocate for a profit-driven approach to generativity in this book. The most powerful way to drive sustained innovation is to enable users to build viable businesses and careers around the platform, turning occasional contributions into long-term commitment. By enabling users to capture value, the product harnesses a powerful incentive, driving the scale and sophistication of innovation in ways that other incentives cannot.

Yet another important aspect of profitability in generative advantage is to avoid bearing significant costs resulting from failed experiments and unproductive or value-destroying ideas. For example, if a mobile app is costly to build but ends up being a flop, making no revenue once released, Apple or Google do not incur any substantial costs for this failed experimentation. These companies benefit from all the successes and incur virtually no cost from the failures. This is an underappreciated benefit of relinquishing direct control over innovation.

Components of Generativity Advantage

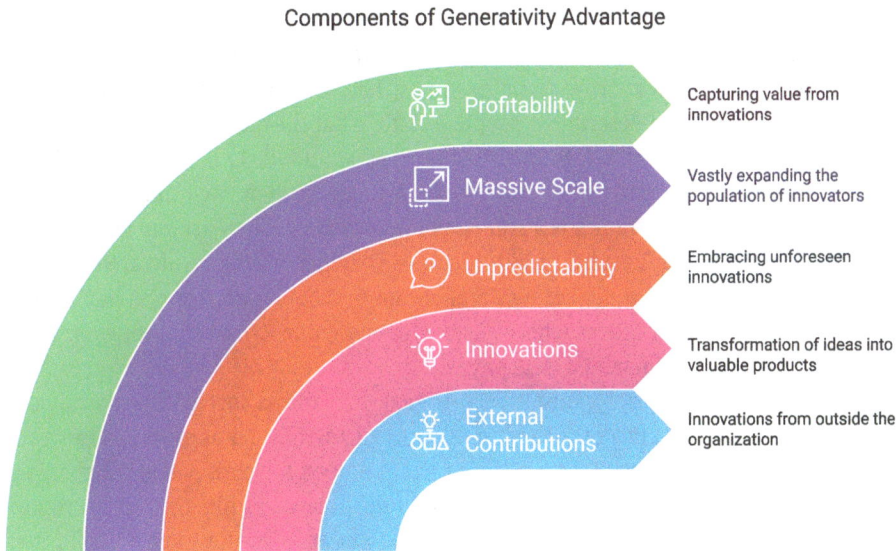

Figure 2.1: The Components of Generativity Advantage.

There are two powerful devices through which firms can pursue and gain a generativity advantage: through products and through markets. It is also possible, and immensely potent, to benefit from a generativity advantage through both products and markets, a phenomenon I refer to as the "generativity flywheel." I describe each of these below.

Product Generativity

Zittrain (2008) offers five key characteristics of a generative system or technology. In simplified terms, these are: leverage (the number of things it can do), adaptability (how easily it can be modified to do new things), ease of mastery (how easy it is to learn and build on it), accessibility (how easily it is to access and use it), and transferability (how easy it is for innovations to be shared and build on each other). In this book we add a sixth element: profitability (how easy it is to profit from innovations with it). See the next chapter for a more detailed discussion.

Consider how these characteristics played out in the evolution of the smartphone. When the iPhone was first released, who could have predicted it would become a platform for everything from mental health therapy to autonomous drone control? Its generativity emerged from the combination of these six elements – powerful capabilities, endless adaptability, relative ease of use, broad accessibility, the ability for innovations to build upon each other, and the ability of innovators to profit from their innovations.

Generative products are more like general-purpose toolkits that could be put to many uses rather than narrow-scope products that accomplish a limited number of tasks. It is often hard to describe to people exactly what they do, and even if the product creator tried to describe it in exact terms, they would likely be doing the product a disservice by limiting its description to the bounds of their own imagination. For example, SparkFun Electronics is a company that offers products around very generative platforms like the Raspberry Pi which are very generative hardware products. The company has made a deliberate decision not to label its products as having specific uses, because of instances where customers were able to find uses for their products that they had not imagined (Murphy, 2014).

The ambiguity around generative products presents a fascinating paradox in business strategy and entrepreneurship. Almost all established approaches to strategic planning and business planning emphasize the need for clear value propositions and defined use cases. Think of popular tools and frameworks like the Value Proposition Canvas (Osterwalder et al., 2015) or the notion of an "elevator pitch." Yet for generative products, this clarity can be counterproductive. When personal computer products were first released, their creators faced a dilemma: how do you market a tool whose most valuable uses haven't been invented yet? It was hard to describe to people exactly what they're good for until certain "killer apps" were found that demonstrated their practical value to most users (Zynda, 2013). One of those killer apps was spreadsheet software (e.g., VisiCalc), which is itself a highly generative product.

It often takes a long time for generative products to really take off. Building and managing generative products is tricky, as some of the existing "best practices" in entrepreneurship and product management do not assume generativity by default. Profiting from generative products requires an extraordinary amount of patience, as time is required to allow large numbers of users to "play" with a product and learn what they can do with it that is valuable to them.

The ambiguity tolerance and patience requirements of generativity make certain environments hostile to generative products. The more a system requires you to have to convince others before you build something (such as academic peer reviewers, granting agencies, investors, incubators, funding bodies, etc.), and the more a system rewards short-term results instead of long-term plays, the less nourishing it will be for generativity. The more you have to be specific about exactly what problem you are solving (instead of being given the flexibility to solve classes of problems at a meta level), and the more you are forced to provide specific plans and timelines, the farther you are getting from an environment that nurtures generativity. For these reasons, managing for generativity often requires practices that may run counter to commonly recognized best practices.

Not all products should be designed for generativity, and generativity is not always desirable. But when it works well it can be an extremely powerful mechanism because it essentially embeds knowledge search and opportunity discovery into the product itself, so that these processes are no longer limited by the existing employees or organizational capacity of the company, and no longer constrained by the preexisting knowledge, biases, and blind spots of those employees. Because the product itself encourages and enables play and innovation, the burden of engendering these innovations is largely lifted from the shoulders of the organization.

Importantly, generativity is, to a large extent, a feature of the technology itself, not just a way to manage or organize around digital technologies. In other words, it is a way to get the technology to do some of the hard work of organization for you. This autonomous aspect of generativity unleashes an incredible level of scalability which is perhaps the key reason behind the success of today's digital behemoths. However, this does not mean that organizational techniques cannot be leveraged to enhance the generativity advantage.

The range of opportunities that the firm can benefit from through product generativity is much larger than those that could be discovered through direct search by the firm itself. However, the search range afforded by product generativity is still bounded by the features of the product. No product, even a highly generative one like the mobile phone or spreadsheet software, can be put to unlimited uses.

Chapters 3, 4, and 5 of this book provide a deeper dive into the characteristics of generativity and how to design and manage products for generativity.

Market Generativity

Markets are essentially knowledge-generating mechanisms that enable and incentivize distributed innovations without any coordination or prediction required by a central organizer. It has taken a long time for economists to truly appreciate this knowledge-generating and innovation-producing feature of markets (Warsh, 2006) and un-fortunaltey the traditional view of markets as purely resource allocation mechanisms (Backhouse & Medema, 2009) still looms large.

Granted, some markets should be focused on resource allocation only, and we do not need the noisiness of generativity and unpredicted innovation in them. These include for example various "matching" markets such as the matching of interns to hospitals, organ donors to recipients,[5] and drivers to riders (e.g., Uber). In such markets, we often prefer efficiency, predictability, and reliability over new knowledge and innovation. But most general-purpose markets and economies are powerful and noisy engines of innovation, and this has been the main source of advancement in our societal well-being and prosperity over the course of history (Phelps, 2013; Phelps et al., 2020).

The beauty of market generativity lies in its ability to harness what Friedrich Hayek (1945, p. 521) called "the knowledge of particular circumstances of time and place" – the scattered bits of insight and opportunity that no central planner could ever fully grasp. When Apple created the App Store, they didn't need to predict that ride-sharing would revolutionize transportation or that mobile gaming would become a multi-billion dollar industry. They simply needed to create conditions where entrepreneurs could discover and exploit such opportunities, while ensuring they captured a share of the value created. A firm that enjoys market generativity does not have to know or predict much about the specifics of the problems on the demand side or the solutions on the supply side, other than the general domain knowledge necessary to engage with that market as a business model. For example, Amazon may have some general knowledge about the business of books but does not need to know exactly what content needs to be written in a book for it to sell. For a more detailed discussion of the benefits of markets as a mechanism that can be strategically deployed, see Chapter 6.

Firms can gain a market generativity advantage by tapping into the generativity of markets they design and govern themselves (a.k.a. "firm-designed markets"), tapping into the generativity of markets managed by others, or tapping into the generativity of the entire economy. Essentially, market generativity advantage involves figuring out ways to "tax" or otherwise profit from the distributed and unpredicted innovations that occur in a market on a massive scale. This advantage is greater if the firm can effectively enable and incentivize these innovations, especially those it can profit the most from. While generativity is often driven by curiosity and play, the notion of market generativity emphasizes profit incentives that are known to be a powerful mechanism of distributed coordination.

---

5 These allocative markets are the types of markets frequently studied in the market design branch of economics, and the subject of study for multiple winners of the Nobel prize in economics (Rochet & Tirole, 2003; Roth, 2008).

As I have written elsewhere, my definition of successful entrepreneurship is the creation of self-sustaining value-creating systems (Keyhani, 2023) where value creation refers simply to achieving more preferred states for all affected stakeholders. To successfully launch and operate a generative marketplace we need to make sure that it is both value-generating and self-sustaining, and that its user-entrepreneurs are also empowered to create self-sustaining value-creating systems around their innovations on the platform.

Firms like Apple and Google profit from app marketplaces that they themselves design and govern. These marketplaces are complements to—and dependent on–specific products owned or controlled by the two companies, such that the products (apps) bought and sold on these marketplaces only have value in relation to the products owned and controlled by Apple and Google. Therefore the success of user-entrepreneurs and the platforms are interlinked.

In designing a marketplace, aiming specifically for generativity can be a conscious strategic decision. These design choices and decisions are covered extensively in Chapter 7. The default mental model of what a market is and does is that of resource allocation and matching, so it takes deliberate mental effort to think in terms of market generativity. As noted above, optimizing for innovation and knowledge generation may involve trade-offs with allocative efficiency and reliability. Some implementation challenges of generativity are discussed in terms of trade-offs in Chapter 9.

Product-Market Generativity

One of the key arguments in this book is that generative products are most powerful in combination with generative markets. Instead of concepts like community, ecosystem, or crowds, I emphasize markets specifically because of the high-powered incentives. Market incentives prove uniquely powerful in driving sustained, sophisticated innovation. When people can build viable businesses and careers around a generative platform, they invest in ways that transcend occasional contribution. If you have only one takeaway from this book let it be this: if you have a generative product, take your users seriously as innovators who can generate profit, and empower them as entrepreneurs. Go beyond the idea of looking at user-innovators as novelties or interesting phenomena that illustrate how surprisingly valuable your product is. Acknowledge that in fact the most important sources of value from your product may be discovered by those users and that they deserve to profit from such discoveries.

The mapping of market generativity on product generativity creates four distinct patterns:

1. Traditional Products and Markets (Low Product, Low Market Generativity): Companies like Uber and Netflix that focus on efficient matching and delivery rather than enabling external innovation

2. Generative Products Without Markets (High Product, Low Market Generativity): Platforms like early Notion or Raspberry Pi that enable extensive user customization but initially lack formal marketplaces for sharing innovations
3. Innovation Marketplaces (Low Product, High Market Generativity): Platforms like Etsy that create vibrant markets for innovation without particularly generative core products
4. Full Generative Systems (High Product, High Market Generativity): Platforms like mobile app marketplaces or Roblox that combine generative products with robust markets for innovation

Many successful platforms begin with highly generative products and later evolve to build marketplaces around them—a natural progression as user innovations create opportunities for formal exchange. The relationship between generative products and marketplaces is almost magnetic—generative products naturally attract and almost demand the formation of marketplaces around them. This is no coincidence. The very features that make a product generative—its adaptability, extensibility, and capacity to enable diverse innovations—create perfect conditions for marketplace formation. When users can create novel solutions with a product, they inevitably want to share and monetize these innovations.

This natural affinity helps explain why so many successful generative products eventually evolve to incorporate formal marketplaces, and why OpenAI wanted to create the market for custom GPTs. The marketplace is the logical completion of the product's generative potential. If the product creator doesn't establish an official marketplace, unofficial ones often emerge organically to fill this vacuum. Consider how users of Microsoft Excel, in the absence of an official template marketplace, have turned to platforms like Etsy and Gumroad to sell their spreadsheet innovations. The generative potential of Excel created such a strong pull toward market formation that users found alternative channels when no official marketplace existed. Similarly, before Notion created a template marketplace on its own website, users were already buying and selling templates outside of the platform, and informal marketplaces like Notionery.com had launched to organize these transactions. Consider this conversation between Ivan Zhao (founder of Notion) and Natsuki Zihnioglu (DNX Ventures) showing their interest in this phenomenon (Zihnioglu & Zhao, 2020):

> **Natsuki**: So there are these Notion "pro" people, consultants who are not Notion employees, but independently creating a bunch of templates and selling them and stuff. They are all quite creative, and so helpful for those who find it difficult to create something from scratch. Just like you envisioned, it's getting even easier to create a new way of workflow.
>
> **Ivan**: Indeed, now the community of users is taking the "Lego" pieces to places that you never imagined, right? So there's the Lego convention, where plenty of enthusiasts showcase their creations. So it is with Notion users. They share their template, work setups on Reddit, on Twitter,

and some people are selling them and making a great business for themselves. Maybe I should quit my job, and start selling Notion templates (laughs).

This magnetic attraction between generative products and marketplaces points to a crucial strategic insight: companies with highly generative products will do better to proactively build and manage marketplaces rather than leaving this natural evolution to chance. Chapter 8 provides a more detailed discussion of product-market generativity and the idea of the generativity flywheel, which we discuss next.

The Generativity Flywheel

The synergy between product and market generativity creates what we might call a "generativity flywheel." A generative product attracts innovative users who create novel applications. These applications make the product more valuable, attracting more users and developers. Meanwhile, the marketplace surrounding the product enables value capture and provides incentives for continued innovation. The innovations not only increase the value of the product but open entire new possibilities for further innovations. This virtuous cycle explains why companies that master both forms of generativity – like Apple and Google, and even Amazon – have become some of the most valuable enterprises in history.

Consider how this dynamic unfolded in Apple's ecosystem. The iPhone's product generativity – its capacity to be reprogrammed and extended through applications – attracted developers eager to experiment with its capabilities. Early innovative applications like Instagram and Uber demonstrated novel uses of the device's cameras and location services, expanding people's understanding of what a smartphone could do. This attracted more developers who now had new ideas for apps based on the newfound examples. These innovations in turn attracted more users to the platform, increasing the potential market for developers' applications.

Simultaneously, the App Store's market generativity provided clear pathways for value capture, ensuring that successful innovations could be monetized. This economic incentive drew more developers, who brought diverse expertise from fields Apple had never considered – from medical imaging to autonomous navigation. Each new application potentially opened up new use cases, attracting specialized user segments who might not have otherwise seen value in a smartphone.

The flywheel gains additional momentum through spillover effects – where one successful application inspires related but distinct innovations. When Uber succeeded with ride-sharing, it sparked innovations in food delivery, courier services, and other on-demand marketplaces, to the extent that many new business models were referred to as "Uber for X." Each of these innovations further enhanced the platform's value proposition while generating revenue that the platform owner could share in.

Crucially, this flywheel effect is more than just a network effect. Traditional network effects make a product more valuable as more people use it – like a telephone network or social media platform (Katz & Shapiro, 1994). The generative flywheel goes further: each turn not only increases value through greater adoption but also expands the possibility space for future innovations. Today's successful application might enable tomorrow's breakthrough by demonstrating new technical capabilities or user behaviors that entrepreneurs can build upon.

This compound innovation effect helps explain the remarkable durability of platforms that successfully harness both product and market generativity. While individual applications might rise and fall in popularity, the platform's generative capacity continues to enable new waves of innovation, maintaining its strategic relevance and value-creation potential.

But it is not just the behemoths like Google and Apple that can benefit from the generativity flywheel. Bubble.io's competitive advantage lies not solely in its core platform but in its capacity to empower a diverse user base to innovate and contribute. As a no-code platform, Bubble's initial offering was already highly generative, allowing users to build a wide array of applications. However, the introduction of a plugin marketplace, which allowed users to create and share reusable components, amplified this generativity. This move was not a simple feature addition but a strategic shift to leverage the creativity of the broader Bubble community, turning them into an extended R&D arm for the platform. This allowed Bubble to scale its innovation capacity without the need for equivalent growth in internal development resources, something that is characteristic of a company that leverages the power of generativity

Understanding the generativity flywheel provides crucial strategic insights for platform creators. It suggests that early design choices should prioritize not just immediate functionality but the potential for unforeseen innovation. Similarly, marketplace design should balance value capture with the need to maintain incentives for continued experimentation and innovation. Success requires careful orchestration of both dimensions of generativity, creating conditions where each reinforces and amplifies the other.

Generativity as a Deliberate Strategy

The notion of a generativity advantage is premised on the idea that the patterns of generativity can be intentionally leveraged by companies and turned into a source of competitive advantage. The generativity flywheel effect described earlier helps explain why this advantage, once established, can become nearly unassailable. When product generativity combines with market generativity, it creates self-reinforcing cycles of innovation and value creation that extend far beyond what any single organization could achieve through traditional means.

Some of the world's most valuable companies have achieved their positions by mastering this dynamic, benefiting greatly from the unpredicted innovations of others on a massive scale. Their success demonstrates that while the path to generative advantage may be slower and less predictable than traditional competitive strategies, its potential for value creation is virtually unlimited. The generativity flywheel, once properly established, can continue spinning and accelerating long after traditional competitive advantages would have eroded.

While it may be possible to benefit from generativity by accident (for example by accidentally realizing that your users are putting your products to many uses you didn't design them for), it is prudent to think about how to be deliberate in one's pursuit of a generativity advantage.

The most important factor to consider in the pursuit of a generativity advantage is that signs of success can be dispiritingly slow to appear. The natural ambiguity of generative products and the requirement to wait to see what other users can do with them rather than determining their scope yourself are aspects to this kind of business that are not easy to handle managerially, and make it difficult to pitch the product to investors and other stakeholders. Similarly, generative markets often suffer from the famous chicken-and-egg problem in the early stages (Tiwana, 2013). Furthermore, the slow growth processes involved in generativity cannot easily be sped up with injections of cash and resources, as the processes of getting masses of people to play with and innovate with a product cannot easily be time-compressed (Dierickx & Cool, 1989). However, there are at least three key reasons for why pursuing a generativity advantage could be well worth the trouble: the sheer amount of the advantage can be colossal, the advantage is likely to be highly sustainable, and the strategy can take competitors by surprise.

Successfully gaining a generativity advantage can be like an electricity generator tapping a wire directly into the Sun when everyone else is trying to draw power from a coal power plant.[6] Obtaining a generativity advantage means removing the constraints of profiting only from your own ideas and innovations, and being unshackled from your own knowledge of where to search for ideas and opportunities. Digital technology allows companies to profit from the innovations of others on a massive scale in incredibly short time periods and with almost zero expenditure of organizational resources relative to the value of innovations produced. Furthermore, the mechanisms of the generativity advantage allow the firm to benefit from the fruits of successful experiments while bearing almost no costs for the failed ones.

A generativity advantage typically involves the creation of large communities of users and enthusiasts upon whom the good part of many traditional burdens of organization are distributed. Users are more likely to feel invested in a generative product

---

6 This analogy is inspired by Schumpeter's comparison of "bombardment" with "forcing a door" in Schumpeter (2013).

because they typically have to invest time and effort to learn to work with it and have a sense of ownership over the ideas and innovations they produce with it.[7] These large communities fuel network effects, increase switching costs and result in forms of "lock-in" to the organization's ecosystem, thereby creating a formidable competitive "moat" (Parker et al., 2016).

The sustainability of generativity advantage comes from its distributed nature. Unlike traditional competitive advantages that depend on a company's internal resources and capabilities, generativity advantage draws its strength from an entire ecosystem of independent innovators. This distributed agency means that the system's innovative capacity is not limited by any single organization's knowledge or resources. The flywheel effect ensures that each successful innovation makes the platform more attractive for future innovations, creating a self-reinforcing cycle that becomes increasingly difficult for competitors to replicate or disrupt.

Generative products are often described as taking on "a life of its own" because so much of the agency in their value creation is distributed and located beyond the focal firm. This means that the generativity advantage becomes largely independent of the firm's own knowledge, resources, and capabilities and thus immune to the obsolescence of those resources and capabilities. Cultivating a vibrant community of users and developers is crucial. This involves fostering communication channels, promoting knowledge sharing, and recognizing and rewarding contributions. A thriving community becomes a collective engine for driving innovation and value creation.

A key argument in this book is that the most powerful way to incentivize this "community" is the market mechanism. Rather than relying on community goodwill or volunteerism, I argue that user-innovators must be taken seriously as entrepreneurs: people who can generate profit from their innovations. The market unburdens the organization's resources in the process of engendering user innovations and appropriating value from them.

For each innovation conceptualized as a problem-solution match, the firm's employees need not identify the problem nor the solution, nor spend any resources building and deploying the solution (Tajedin, Madhok, & Keyhani, 2019). But throughout this process the focal firm that created the generative product being innovated with in the first place must be humble enough to realize that it is not the center of the universe, and that a user innovation may end up being more valuable than any of the company's own innovations. A true hallmark of a company that has embraced generativity is that it is entirely prepared for one of its users to find a use case for its product that the company itself had not imagined, and is prepared to help this user profit immensely from such an innovation, even more than the company does.

A generative marketplace allows the firm to access and profit from innovations for which it did not have to actively search for. Therefore, the mechanism protects

---

7 Psychologists and economists refer to this as the "endowment effect" (Knetsch, 1989).

against uncertainty and lack of knowledge, because the burden of knowledge is removed from the shoulders of the organization and distributed in the market. For example, a popular mobile app for architects, interior designers, and real estate professionals on the iOS App Store is RoomScan Pro, which uses the smartphone's cameras to generate a floor plan of a property. Apple takes a large cut from sales of this app, and yet no employee in Apple needs to know anything about architecture or be in the real estate business for this benefit to accrue automatically.

However, generativity is not just a protection against a *lack* of knowledge, but also a protection against the wrong kind of knowledge. Those cases where an organization mistakenly thinks it knows something but doesn't, or is otherwise blind to its own ignorance, can be even more dangerous than a simple "lack of information" type of uncertainty (Levinthal & March, 1993; Smithson, 1989).

Another benefit of generative firm-designed markets is that the firm appropriates value from all successful experiments in the marketplace, and yet generally loses nothing or incurs no significant costs from the failed experiments. If RoomScan Pro had been a failure, Apple would not lose anything. Overall, a generative firm-designed market allows the firm to systematically and autonomously profit from the ideas and innovations of others on a massive scale, and this is the main reason why these markets are such powerful drivers of competitive advantage in the digital era.

Observers have noted that each individual company is limited in the extent to which it can prepare for the future and innovate using traditional organizational methods. The dynamism of the market has undermined hope in the possibility of sustainable competitive advantage (D'Aveni et al., 2010), whereas the market system itself continues to thrive, produces innovations regularly, and maintains its dynamism. Beinhocker (2007, p. 334) goes as far as to say: "companies don't innovate, markets do." For him:

> Businesses play the role of interactors in the evolutionary system of market economies. From the market's point of view, each business is an experiment in Business Plan space; some succeed and are amplified, while others fail and disappear . . . the process of differentiating, selecting, and amplifying Business Plans works better at the level of the market than inside the walls of most companies . . . Companies have an inherent disadvantage in that they can never have the same diversity of Business Plans as contained in the market as a whole. Nor can they ever perfectly mirror the selection pressures of actual markets or have the nearly infinite resources of the capital markets to invest in amplifying and scaling up Business Plans that succeed. From the unsentimental perspective of the evolutionary algorithm, businesses are just experimental grist for the evolutionary mill.

Beinhocker is echoing a similar sentiment from Foster and Kaplan (2011, p. 20):

> Markets, on the other hand, lacking culture, leadership, and emotion, do not experience the bursts of desperation, depression, denial, and hope that corporations face. The market has no lingering memories or remorse. It has no mental models. The market does not fear cannibalization, customer channel conflict, or dilution. It simply waits for the forces at play to work out . . .

the market simply removes the weak players, and in removing them, improves overall returns. Lacking production-oriented control systems, markets create more surprise and innovation than do corporations.

By building a generative marketplace on top of a generative product, companies can harness the power of markets that these authors are talking about to their own advantage. In addition, due to the boundless nature of new ideas that could be produced by various people in a large population, once a generativity advantage takes off there is often no limit in sight. Unlike allocative markets where the most efficient possible allocation of resources can be envisioned as the "limit" to growth, generative markets typically do not have such limits to speak of, because their mechanisms of growth are similar to the mechanisms enjoyed by an entire economy. This is why I have suggested elsewhere that generativity is a mechanism that can indeed lead to sustained competitive advantage, despite growing skepticism about whether any competitive advantage can be sustained in the long term (Keyhani, 2023).

Not only can it be a source of sustained advantage, but it can also have another key feature of good strategies (Rumelt, 2011): generative advantage can really take competitors by surprise. Precisely because generative products are hard to describe and understand, and because their full value is still unrevealed (even to their creators) in their early stages, they are also easier to dismiss as competitive threats. This allows them to go under the radar for quite a while, and when they suddenly take off and reach the exponential growth that typically comes with network effects, competitors are blindsided and find it difficult to respond. If the founders themselves can be surprised by user innovations, so can competitors.

A generativity perspective on business and entrepreneurship emphasizes the idea that success often comes not from predicting the future, nor from controlling the future (Sarasvathy, 2001), but from creating environments where unpredictable innovations can flourish. This insight challenges traditional strategic thinking, which emphasizes planning and control. Instead, platform leaders need to master what we might call "structured serendipity" – creating conditions that make valuable accidents more likely to happen.

The Case of Bubble.io: Democratizing Software

In 2012, Emmanuel Straschnov and Josh Haas embarked on a mission to democratize software creation. Their creation, Bubble.io, emerged as a pioneering platform in the burgeoning "no-code" movement. Bubble's core promise was simple yet powerful: to enable individuals without formal programming training to build sophisticated web applications. This case study explores how Bubble's approach to generativity has fueled both its success and its challenges, providing crucial insights for other platforms aiming to harness the power of distributed innovation.

Bubble is a platform that I have both personally used extensively and studied extensively. In collaboration with doctoral student Mahdieh Sarbazvatan, we have collected extensive archival data from podcasts, blogs, forums, and other sources as well as conducted original interviews with Bubble power users and plugin developers. Therefore, anecdotes from this case study appear frequently throughout the book.

The Genesis of Generativity: From Product to Product-Market

Bubble's initial value proposition was deeply rooted in accessibility. By abstracting away the complexities of coding, the platform empowered a diverse range of users to transform their ideas into functional applications. Bubble users and developers we interviewed noted that it was able to attract "less sophisticated users" to software development or that it allowed entrepreneurs to overcome the bottleneck of having to find a technical co-founder to bring their ideas to life: "they have an idea, they're non-technical themselves, can't find a co-founder or can't find a technical co-founder. So one day, they decided they're going to roll up their sleeves and build it themselves" (anonymous, personal communication).

Unlike traditional software development tools that required specialized expertise, Bubble offered a flexible, open-ended environment where users could experiment and build a variety of applications. This inherent flexibility was key to its product generativity, allowing the platform to be applied in ways that even its founders had not imagined. One professional Bubble developer that we interviewed said about his conversations with the Bubble team, "So, in almost all the interactions that I've had with the team and bubble . . . they realize that . . . when they built bubble, they had no idea that it could be used for these type of applications" (anonymous, personal communication).

The platform's initial general-purpose nature created ambiguity, which paradoxically became a catalyst for user-driven innovation. Users began to build applications spanning a broad spectrum of use cases, from simple productivity tools to complex business systems. One notable example was the development of a companion app for mothers during the pandemic, a use case that highlighted the platform's versatility and unforeseen potential. This application attracted health care-focused developers, who then created specialized plugins for medical data handling, further expanding the platform's capabilities and attracting even more users and developers.

However, Bubble's transformation into a truly generative ecosystem was not solely due to its initial architecture. A key turning point was the introduction of plugin and template marketplaces. These marketplaces, which emerged organically over time, provided avenues for third-party developers to share and sell custom functionalities and application designs. The decision to open the platform to third-party contributions was strategic, fostering an environment where the collective ingenuity of the user base became a central driver of platform growth. As a result, Bubble transitioned from a product-centric platform to a dynamic product-market system, where the platform's value was constantly being enhanced and extended by its users.

Navigating Strategic Trade-offs: The Tensions of Generativity

As Bubble evolved, the company faced a series of strategic trade-offs inherent in managing a generative platform. The first was the tension between openness and control. While encouraging user contributions, the platform had to grapple with the problem of quality control. The lack of stringent review processes in the plugin marketplace led to the proliferation of low-quality or "copycat" plugins that added little value. This created a delicate balancing act between encouraging broad participation and ensuring a high-quality user experience.

Another critical trade-off involved balancing ease of use for beginners with advanced features for power users. While Bubble's no-code interface was designed to be accessible, the increasing complexity of the platform presented a steep learning curve for new users. The platform attempted to address this by introducing features such as version control and reusable elements, but these also added to the platform's overall complexity.

Platform lock-in was also a significant strategic consideration. Because users do not own the code of their applications, they are heavily reliant on the platform for their continued functionality. Bubble's easy-to-use interface, paradoxically, is a feature that locks users into the platform. This presented a risk for users who were concerned about the long-term viability of the platform.

Moreover, pricing strategies presented a considerable challenge. Bubble experimented with different pricing models for both the platform and the marketplace, trying to find the right balance between sustainability and accessibility. Controversial price changes ignited strong reactions from the user community, revealing the need for transparent and equitable pricing mechanisms.

Finally, community engagement became a vital element of the platform. Bubble recognized the value of its user community, using it as a source for new ideas and talent. The company worked to foster a supportive environment and encouraged community members to contribute to documentation and platform improvements. This symbiotic relationship with the community was essential for Bubble's continued growth and innovation, while the company also had to manage the community to prevent it from becoming a source of low-quality information or a venue for negative interactions.

Bubble's Generativity Flywheel: Key Mechanisms at Play

Bubble's success in establishing a generative ecosystem can be attributed to several key mechanisms that promote innovation and growth.

First, the platform's core architecture is inherently generative, exhibiting key characteristics such as accessibility, modularity, extensibility, transferability, and profitability (although initially integrating a payment platform like Stripe into Bubble apps was not that easy). Bubble's no-code approach ensures that a broad range of users can engage with the platform. The plugin architecture and reusable elements allow for a high degree of modularity, while the marketplace provides an avenue for extending the platform's capabilities through third-party contributions. The ability to share and reuse templates ensures knowledge transfer and the efficient scaling of innovation. The platform's version control allows users to experiment and track changes safely. But perhaps most importantly: profitable software businesses have been built on Bubble. The platform has proven itself as more than just a prototype-making tool. There are now many cases of profitable businesses as well as startups that successfully raised millions of dollars built with Bubble, and the company showcases many of these on their website. Examples include Synthflow AI, Qoins, Dividend Finance, Teaddl, Hive Health, Fishburners, Fairie, Flexibple, BluBinder, Messly, and others. Just in 2024, over $850 million dollars was billed through apps made on Bubble.[8]

Second, the platform's marketplaces act as generative markets, exhibiting thickness, efficient matching, trust and safety mechanisms, diversity of ideas, interactivity, and opportunities for experimentation (see Chapter 7). The large number of users and developers creates a vibrant marketplace, where ideas are exchanged and tested. The platform facilitates matching buyers and sellers but also allows for the discovery of unexpected opportunities. Trust and safety mechanisms, while imperfect, are crucial for a thriving marketplace. And the marketplace is a place where diverse ideas can be exchanged freely, fostering innovation and growth. The platform's marketplace is rich enough that entire companies like Zeroqode have been established to develop and sell Bubble plugins and templates.

These core mechanisms work together, forming a generativity flywheel. The platform's generative properties attract users and developers who, in turn, contribute to the ecosystem. This flywheel is further fueled by the marketplace, the active community, and continuous feedback loops, with the platform constantly evolving in response to user needs.

---

8 https://x.com/estraschnov/status/1929981930528768133

Bubble's Path Forward

Bubble's journey as a generative platform offers valuable lessons for entrepreneurs and managers interested in harnessing the power of distributed innovation. The platform's success lies in its core mission of democratizing software creation. The introduction of the plugin and template marketplaces has further extended the reach of the platform by harnessing the creativity of the user community.

However, Bubble must also address its weaknesses to ensure long-term viability. Improving quality control in the marketplace, managing platform lock-in, simplifying the learning curve, providing better tools to plugin developers, and addressing security concerns are all crucial areas for improvement. The company also needs to continue engaging its community and to foster an equitable and transparent marketplace.

The rise of AI and no-code competitors presents both opportunities and challenges. As one developer noted, the integration of AI has the potential to transform the platform. However, AI coding platforms like Lovable.dev, Bolt.New, and Replit are rapidly taking market share away from no-code platforms like Bubble, while providing users with full access to their codebase. Bubble has responded by announcing a vision for AI visual development where the power of AI coding will be augmented with no-code visual development.[9]

Bubble has established itself as a key player in the no-code movement, and its approach to generativity provides valuable lessons for other platforms seeking to leverage distributed innovation. Its approach to accessibility, community, quality control, platform governance, and the tension between openness and control offer important insights for businesses aiming to create truly generative ecosystems.

Ultimately, Bubble's journey highlights a key paradox in the management of generative platforms: the very openness that enables external innovation also requires careful orchestration to ensure quality and sustainability. Bubble's future success will depend on its ability to manage this paradox and to foster an environment where both the platform and its community can thrive. The key, as always with generative systems, will be to empower the many rather than rely on the few.

---

9 https://www.youtube.com/watch?v=lIykj1C0lr8

Chapter 3
Understanding Generativity: The Engine of Unpredicted Innovation

The mechanism of generativity lies at the heart of some of the most transformative technologies of our time. From the Internet's astounding growth to the unexpected uses of personal computers, generative technologies have repeatedly demonstrated their power to drive innovation in ways that their original creators could never have anticipated. But what exactly makes a technology generative, and how does this characteristic enable unpredicted innovation on a massive scale?

Zittrain's Conceptualization of Generativity

The concept of generativity in technology was developed by Jonathan Zittrain, who defined it as "a system's capacity to produce unanticipated change through unfiltered contributions from broad and varied audiences" (Zittrain, 2008, p. 70). The concept captures a profound insight about how certain technologies enable innovation. Generativity is about a system's ability to channel unexpected innovations from diverse contributors who may not be working in concert.

Zittrain identified five key factors that make a technology generative:
1. Leverage: How extensively the system can make difficult tasks easier
2. Adaptability: How easily the system can be modified for different purposes
3. Ease of mastery: How readily new contributors can learn to use and build upon it
4. Accessibility: How easily people can access and use the technology
5. Transferability: How easily modifications can be shared with others, particularly non-experts

Generative technologies invite people to tinker with them. By design, they accept, improve, and grow through any contribution that follows a basic set of rules, and thereby unshackle their growth from the constraints of traditional managerial control over the innovation process. These factors help explain why some technologies become powerful platforms for innovation while others remain limited in scope. For example, the early personal computer and the Internet both exhibited these characteristics strongly, allowing them to overcome more controlled, proprietary alternatives like standalone word processors and closed online services such as CompuServe and AOL (Zittrain, 2008).

Generative tools are not always inherently better than their non-generative counterparts. Appliances are often easier to use and can be safer and more effective. Gen-

https://doi.org/10.1515/9783110779639-003

erative technologies need not produce forward progress. They invite disruption—along with the good things and bad things that can come with such disruption.

Adding Profitability to Generativity

In this book I suggest adding a sixth element to generativity in order to emphasize the incentives for distributed innovations to occur on a massive scale. This sixth element is profitability and the overall augmented model can be called a profit-driven model of generativity (see Figure 3.1). A truly generative system not only empowers users to create and innovate but also enables them to capture value from those innovations. This involves creating mechanisms that allow users to build viable businesses and careers around the platform. By taking users seriously as entrepreneurs and providing them with the tools and opportunities to profit from their contributions, a system can unlock a far greater level of sustained innovation. This profit-driven approach ensures that innovation in a generative ecosystem is not treated just as side-projects or curiosities but as serious endeavors.

The power of profit-driven innovation becomes clear when we contrast it with other approaches. While open source projects and community platforms can generate enthusiastic participation, they often struggle to sustain professional-grade innovation over time. Even sophisticated ecosystem approaches that rely primarily on strategic partnerships or intrinsic motivation rarely match the scale and sophistication of innovation that emerges when participants can build viable businesses around a platform.

When users can construct sustainable careers and businesses around a platform, their relationship transforms from occasional contributors to deeply committed innovators. This career-level commitment enables crucial dynamics such as the development of deep platform expertise, long-term planning, and sustained investment in sophisticated solutions. Furthermore, the market mechanism acts as a massive parallel search process, using price signals to guide both the direction and intensity of innovation efforts.

This emphasis on profitability requires platform leaders to fundamentally shift their mindset. Rather than viewing the ability of users to profit from their innovations on the platform as merely happy accidents, they must intentionally and seriously pursue the opening of paths to entrepreneurial success for their users. This necessitates implementing comprehensive support mechanisms – from clear monetization pathways to robust infrastructure for business growth – that enable users to translate their creativity into tangible economic gains.

Elements of Product Generativity

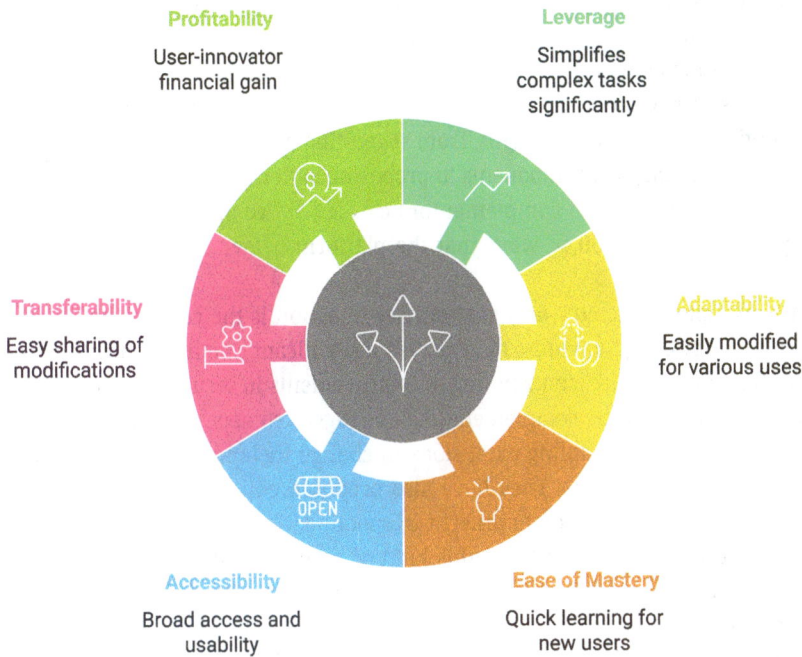

Figure 3.1: An Extended Model of Profit-Driven Generativity.

The Evolution of Generativity Theory

As scholars have built upon Zittrain's foundation, our understanding of generativity has become more nuanced and multifaceted. In this section we review some of the more recent literature and conceptual developments in the theory of generativity. Helpful reviews of this literature have been provided by others (Eck et al., 2015; Eck & Uebernickel, 2016; Thomas & Tee, 2022). Here we discuss a select number of ideas that better relate to our discussion in this book.

Architectural Generativity

The paper by van der Geest & van Angeren (2023) highlights the concept of "architectural generativity," referring to the process of actively soliciting and selectively incorporating contributions from complementors—third-party developers and innovators—to help evolve the platform's architecture in unanticipated ways. It is not just about building on the platform but about shaping the underlying structure that enables innovation.

Complementors play a crucial role in this process. They possess a unique understanding of the platform's capabilities and limitations, having worked intimately with its architecture to develop their own complementary innovations. As such, they can offer valuable insights into how the platform can be improved, enhanced, and secured. Their contributions can take many forms, from suggesting new ways to facilitate access to the platform's technological components to proposing better ways to control and configure the platform. In essence, complementors can act as "co-architects," helping to shape the platform's evolution in ways that the platform owner may not have envisioned.

A prime example of architectural generativity in action is the case of the Mozilla Firefox web browser. Complementors have played a significant role in shaping the evolution of Firefox's architecture, contributing to improvements in security, performance, and functionality. For instance, complementors have suggested new ways to access platform components, such as enabling extensions to change the appearance of the user interface on a per-window basis. They have also proposed enhancements to security, such as adding a special permission to prevent UI spoofing.

The Coda.io ecosystem also exhibits this kind of architectural generativity. "Most SaaS companies provide a solution. But we're letting you take control in shaping Coda, blurring the line between product and community," explains the company. "When growth like this is driven by and for our makers, everyone wins" (Jaume, 2022).

Extended Generativity Theory

Fürstenau et al. (2023) have proposed some extensions to generativity theory. They suggest an integrative view of two distinct lenses found in the generativity literature: The Social Interaction View emphasizes the role of social interactions between platform providers and complementors in driving innovation. Meanwhile the Product View focuses on the expansion of a platform's functionalities through the addition of new components and features. In their paper Fürstenau et al. (2023) propose two new concepts for generativity theory: bounded generativity and inverse generativity.

Bounded Generativity

It is generally recognized that generativity allows platforms to evolve in unexpected ways, generating new value and attracting an ever-growing user base. However, the prevailing assumption that generativity always leads to unbounded growth may be an oversimplification. In some cases, generativity can be bounded, meaning that the growth it generates eventually stabilizes. This can occur due to several factors, such as the maturing of the platform, the limited pool of potential complementors, or the strategic decisions of platform owners.

Inverse Generativity

Interestingly, the relationship between generativity and growth can also be reversed. In some cases, growth can lead to generativity, a phenomenon termed "inverse generativity." This means that as a platform's user base expands, it can attract more complementors and generate more innovation. This relates to the notion of the "Generativity Flywheel" discussed in this book.

The growth of Bubble.io provides an example of "inverse generativity," where an expanding user base attracts more complementors, and in turn fuels further innovation. As Bubble's user base grew, it attracted more plugin developers and template creators, each bringing unique skills and perspectives. New users learned to use Bubble in new ways which led to a richer ecosystem, with more diverse functionalities and solutions. As the platform grew, the community became more active, creating a powerful "generativity flywheel." This is evidenced by the emergence of companies dedicated to Bubble plugin development and maintenance, further enhancing the platform's value for users and its overall generative capacity.

Concluding Thoughts

In this chapter we have reviewed the concept of generativity as conceptualized by Jonathan Zittrain, as well as more recent developments in the literature that has flourished around the concept among scholars of technology and innovation. From here we move on to more practically minded chapters that deal with the design and management of generative products (Chapters 4–5), followed by chapters that get deeper into the idea of generative markets (Chapters 6–7).

Chapter 4
The Generativity of Products

The premise of this chapter is that it is not only broad "technologies" that can be generative but also specific products developed by specific companies and organizations. Not all products are or should be generative, but when it is desirable to purposefully design for generativity, there are certain guidelines that can help us do so.

An Ode to Possibility

A generative product is not a finished creation but rather a beginning – a spark that ignites countless other sparks. As described by Lehmann & Recker (2019), they are "offerings that are ever-in-the-making." Like a seed containing the blueprint of a mighty tree, it holds within itself the latent potential for a thousand unexpected blooms.

Consider the humble spreadsheet. On the surface, it presents itself as a grid of empty cells awaiting numbers. Yet in the hands of millions of users, it becomes financial models, project schedules, interactive games, works of pixel art, and takes on countless other forms, beyond what its original creators could have imagined.

The true magic of generative products lies in what they enable others to create. They could be more akin to languages than to tools – flexible grammars through which users can express solutions to problems that the original designers never conceived. The early personal computer was not valuable because it could run VisiCalc; it was valuable because it could run anything that clever humans could dream up and translate into code. VisiCalc was a manifestation of that vast possibility space.

This is why describing generative products can feel like trying to capture smoke in your hands. The moment you define them by their current uses, you have already limited their potential. They resist categorization precisely because their essence is to transcend categories, to shape-shift according to the needs and imagination of their users.

Yet this ambiguity, this resistance to definition, is their greatest strength. They can evolve and be repurposed and reimagined as new challenges and opportunities emerge. They grow through both careful cultivation by their creators, and through the distributed creativity of their users, each adding to the collective pool of possibilities.

To create a generative product is to release control while maintaining influence – to set in motion a process of innovation that takes on a life of its own. It requires the humility to acknowledge that the most valuable uses of your creation may come from directions you never anticipated, and the wisdom to design for that beautiful uncertainty.

https://doi.org/10.1515/9783110779639-004

In the end, a generative product is a platform for possibility, a stage for serendipity, an invitation to innovation. And in that invitation lies perhaps the most profound truth about generative products: they are meta-products that solve the problem of empowering others to solve problems we have not yet imagined.

Examples of Generative Products

Zittrain's own examples of "generative technologies" that were the focus of his book were the internet and the personal computer: "both were generative: they were designed to accept any contribution that followed a basic set of rules (either coded for a particular operating system, or respecting the protocols of the Internet). Both overwhelmed their respective proprietary, non-generative competitors" (Zittrain, 2008, p. 3). In general, the concept of generativity is relative rather than binary. It is helpful to think of any product as being on a continuum of generativity, although the position of a product on this continuum is often determined relative to its alternatives that appear in practice. For example, Zittrain considers a hammer to be more generative than a jackhammer, Lego bricks more generative than a prefabricated dollhouse, and a knife more generative than a potato peeler. The smartphone is certainly more generative than the dumbphone, but the Android operating system and Apple's iOS have each been generative in different ways (Eaton et al., 2011; Remneland-Wikhamn et al., 2011).

In the software world, a prime example of a highly generative product is the spreadsheet. Users of spreadsheet software found so many different value-creating uses for it that many consider it to be the first ever "killer app" and the main reason behind the rapid adoption of personal computers (Zynda, 2013). Another example is the WordPress content management system (Um et al., 2013).

Other examples of modern cloud software products that have proved to be highly generative include the Slack.com messaging software, the AirTable.com cloud database software, API connector tools such as Zapier.com and Make.com, no-code app development tools such as Bubble.io, Retool.com, and Adalo.com, as well as the new generation of dynamic content management systems such as Notion.so and Coda.io. These are just a few examples of highly generative cloud software products currently available, and most of them fast-growing as of the time of writing. Given that Lego bricks are a well understood manifestation of generativity, it is pertinent to consider how Ivan Zhao, the founder of Notion, describes their product as a "Lego for Software" (Zihnioglu & Zhao, 2020):

> For those who don't know what Notion is, it's something you can think of as a combination of notes, documents, wiki, project management, all in one product. For many teams and companies, Notion can be the collaboration tool to replace email, Slack, Google Docs, Asana, Trello, Evernote, and it's also great for personal use, I've probably used it more for personal use as well as for work. So it's extremely flexible. You can almost mold it into any types of tool you want for yourself. We call it a Lego for software.

As of the time of this writing, a new kind of generative technology, which happens to have another meaning of the word "generative" in its title, is taking the world by storm and allowing generative products to become even more so by integrating generative AI into their features (Keyhani & Mohaghegh-Neyshabouri, 2025). The companies that built the first frontier Large Language Models (LLMs) have many paths ahead of them in terms of how they evolve their products. A key question they face is to what extent they should add features themselves and to what extent they should allow the market to build products using their APIs.

A hallmark of generative products is their ability to open a particular category of tools previously used only by specialists, to a broader population of people. For example, no-code tools opened up software development to non-developers, and generative AI coding or "vibe coding" tools are again doing that in a new way. AI coding tools like Cursor, v0, Replit, Bolt.New and Lovable.Dev are opening software programming to the masses like never before. Users constantly post about amazing things they have been able to build with these products, at much lower costs than they had been quoted from professional developers.[1] Even children are empowered to build software with these tools.[2]

Generative Products as Sources of Surprise

Due to their nature, generative products often lead to surprises: user innovations that no one anticipated before, including the creators of the generative product, and also potential competitors. There are many cases of such surprises. For example, years after launching, Bubble co-founder Emmanuel Straschnov shared a new application built by a Bubble user that he said "didn't think was even possible!!" (see Figure 4.1).[3]

There are many such cases of surprise among no-code platforms and other generative products. Shishir Mehrotra, CEO and co-founder of Coda, describes how he and others are regularly surprised by what Coda can do (Mehrotra, 2024):

> Coda has incredibly diverse use cases that would surprise many people. We have millions of users and tens of thousands of teams using Coda in innovative ways—from Qualtrics running their engineering, product, and design resource planning to Tonal streamlining their operations. I've met some very surprising Coda customers as well, like the team behind the Sphere in Las Vegas managing their video content to professional football and basketball teams planning their plays and drafts with Coda to some of the world's most popular YouTubers managing their fast-growing YouTube channels.

---

1 https://x.com/amasad/status/1871411257322127584
2 https://x.com/rickyrobinett/status/1825581674870055189
3 https://www.linkedin.com/posts/straschnov_okay-this-may-be-the-most-advanced-implementation-activity-6944956421549568000-Rd9r/

Okay, this may be the most advanced implementation i've seen in Bubble to date... It's a visual canvas built entirely without code on Bubble. It's quite awesome to see people being able to do things that I didn't think was even possible!!

https://lnkd.in/gYXqPtBv

Figure 4.1: The co-founder of Bubble being surprised by a user's innovation.

Ivan Zhao, the founder of Notion, describes a company culture at Notion that embraces learning from user innovations. When asked what the most surprising uses of Notion have been for him, he replied (Zihnioglu & Zhao, 2020):

> Notion roughly can be used as four different products: notes, document, wiki, and project management. It's just a general-purpose database workspace. And so far, plenty of people use Notion for those four uses on the consumer side or on the enterprise side. On both consumer and enterprise sides, there're so many interesting uses, for example, because Notion can be notes and document tools on the internet, so plenty of people use Notion as a lightweight web page or a publisher. And on the enterprise side, many companies put up jobs' pages or publish releases in Notion directly. They don't have to set up their blog, they can just use Notion directly without using a CMS or anything.

> It's amazing how complex people's project management workflows are. A lot of companies say Notion actually gives people a database, where you can customize for any way to run a competent team. Some of the customers would talk about how they have set up very intricate workflows on their project management for their companies. And that has been eye-opening, which also ties back to our mission of "The people should lead the software, and it should flow into the company and not the other way around."

Wade Foster, co-founder and CEO of Zapier, said in response to a similar question (Yang & Foster, 2021):

> *I still remember very vividly, very early on, maybe a year or two in, we got an email from a customer that was like, hey, your product is great. I built an entire business off the back of this thing in a weekend. . . . and it sort of made me go, huh, what is that business? . . . There's actually two of them. One is called Seinfeld Quotes, and the other is called Kanye Text . . . the idea is you go to this landing page, you put in a phone number for a friend, and you pay either $5, $10, or $20 . . . Based on the phone number you put in, it texts that person various quotes at a delay . . . so he built this little app in a weekend on Zapier . . . so that, to me, was the first time where I realized, wow, the possibilities of what you can build with Zapier far exceeds these simple little integrations. We're actually talking about folks who can build full-on applications, who can automate full-on different things. It's not just about simple integrations anymore. It's about empowering people to build stuff that they didn't think they could do before.*

More recently, the rise of generative AI powered by Large Language Models, multi-modal models, and diffusion models (for image and video) has been a story full of surprises at every turn. In a first study of GPT-4, Microsoft researchers documented numerous "remarkable capabilities" including the ability to draw graphical images, despite being only trained on text (Bubeck et al., 2023). Beyond researchers, regular users around the world regularly share prompts with each other, illustrating how they got an LLM to do something interesting or useful. On the flip side, users also regularly share stories of how an LLM chatbot said something terrible, incorrect, biased, racist, sexist, or in some other way wrong or inappropriate. Researchers have found every bias imaginable in the behavior of LLMs (Gupta et al., 2024; Kamruzzaman et al., 2024; Navigli et al., 2023) and the companies that make them, have been hard at work trying to minimize or mitigate these issues (Jaech et al., 2024). The entire story of humanity learning how generative AI works and how to use it, is a process of collective discovery full of surprise after surprise (Keyhani et al., 2023).

Generative Products as Vehicles for Serious Entrepreneurship

A highly generative product is not one where surprises happen by accident; they are deliberately nourished as a natural part of a platform for entrepreneurial opportunity. While characteristics such as leverage, adaptability, ease of mastery, accessibility, and transferability lay the groundwork for distributed innovation, it is the possibility of profit that transforms this potential into sustained and scalable value creation. A generative product, therefore, should be designed to empower users not merely as innovators but as entrepreneurs. This necessitates a fundamental shift in mindset, urging platform leaders to recognize that the most significant sources of value derived from their products may indeed be discovered by the users themselves, provided they are enabled to profit from these discoveries. This perspective acknowledges that the most potent driver of sustained innovation lies in empowering users to construct viable businesses and careers around the platform, thereby converting occasional contributions into long-term commitments.

There have been cases where creators of generative products have failed to see the full potential of what they have made. They view user contributions as supplementary or secondary to the core functionalities designed by them. However, when a product is designed with generativity in mind, the user transitions from being a mere consumer to a potential entrepreneur. User entrepreneurs should not be limited to "accidental" ones (Shah & Tripsas, 2007). If users see that they are being taken seriously as entrepreneurs, they start to view their innovations on the platform as not merely side-projects but serious endeavors that can result in significant economic and social value.

The concept of a generative product as a platform for serious entrepreneurship is related to the principle of "residual claimancy" (Alchian & Demsetz, 1972), a term economists use to describe the right of innovators to capture a significant portion of the value they create. This concept is crucial because it relates to how the incentives of the platform's users align with the platform's overall success. Digital platforms have evolved hybrid forms of residual claimancy that differ fundamentally from traditional firm structures. While classical firms concentrate ownership rights in a single residual claimant (i.e. the shareholders), platforms typically feature a split structure where user-contributors may also have residual claimancy, at least in relation to their own contributions (Nicoli & Paltrinieri, 2019). This creates a complex dynamic where platforms must balance value capture through their control of coordination mechanisms while ensuring sufficient returns flow to users to maintain innovation incentives. The success of platform entrepreneurship thus depends heavily on finding an optimal distribution of residual claims – too much value capture by the platform can stifle user innovation and participation, while too little may fail to sustain the essential platform infrastructure and coordination services. This balance is particularly critical because platforms compete not just with other platforms but with the possibility of users bypassing intermediaries entirely for un-intermediated exchange, placing natural limits on how much value platforms can extract from coordination services (Brousseau & Penard, 2007).

When innovators are confident that they will be the primary beneficiaries of their efforts, they are more likely to invest time, resources, and creativity into developing novel solutions. A well-designed generative platform must not only enable innovation but must also ensure that innovators can effectively translate their creativity into tangible economic gains. A generative product creates expansive possibility spaces for innovation, while profit potential directs sustained investment toward valuable opportunities within those spaces.

To truly empower user-innovators as entrepreneurs, platforms must implement comprehensive support mechanisms. These go beyond APIs and SDKs or innovation toolkits (Von Hippel, 2001) that allow people to build with the platform. Examples of these mechanism include:

Clear Monetization Mechanisms: A critical requirement is to offer clear, straightforward ways for user-innovators to monetize their work. This could involve the creation of app stores, marketplaces, or direct revenue-generating features within the product itself. The key is that the platform must clearly establish and communicate how users can transform their innovations into a source of income. For instance, a platform could allow users to create and sell templates, plugins, or custom features to other users, establishing a clear link between effort and reward.

Reasonable Platform Fee Structures: While platform owners need to sustain their operations, they must also ensure that the fee structures are reasonable and do not unduly burden innovators. Overly aggressive value capture can stifle innovation, while too little can make the marketplace unsustainable. A balanced approach is crucial, allowing the platform to capture sufficient value while leaving innovators with enough profit margin to justify their continued efforts. This may involve lower fees for early-stage innovators, tiered fee structures that scale with success, or revenue-sharing models that align the platform's success with that of its users.

Intellectual Property Protection: A robust system for protecting intellectual property is paramount to encouraging innovation. Innovators need to be confident that their creations will not be copied or exploited without their consent. The platform should provide mechanisms for users to secure ownership of their innovations, such as licensing agreements or copyright protection. This not only motivates innovation but also establishes trust in the platform's commitment to safeguarding the rights of its contributors.

Support for Premium Pricing: Generative platforms should enable users to offer premium options for high-value or specialized solutions, allowing them to monetize their expertise and specialized capabilities. Premium plugins for WordPress, for example, command prices from hundreds to thousands of dollars annually per customer. The ability to set premium prices allows innovators to offer differentiated products and services, enabling them to capture a larger share of the value they create and also invest in developing sophisticated solutions.

Infrastructure for Recurring Revenue: Providing the tools for recurring revenue through subscriptions or memberships is vital for ensuring sustained income streams. This is particularly important for innovators who provide ongoing services or updates. Subscription models provide predictable income for innovators, enabling them to invest in long-term development and improvement.

Tools for Customer Relationship Management (CRM): The most successful platforms recognize that building a business goes beyond creating a product; it also requires building relationships with customers. Platforms should equip their innovators with the necessary CRM tools, such as features for customer communication, support, feedback collection, and user analytics. This allows user-innovators to build a business and brand by establishing direct relationships with their customers and also to improve their products based on customer feedback.

Payment and Subscription Handling: Finally, seamless and reliable systems for processing payments and handling subscriptions are essential for removing the complexities involved in managing financial transactions. Handling some of the complexities around payments centrally allows creators to focus on innovation rather than logistics. By managing these complexities, the platform allows users to focus on what they do best: creating and innovating. For example, Gumroad recently announced that it is becoming a "merchant of record" and will be able to handle all tax obligations for its users.[4]

In summary, a generative product that aims to be a vehicle for serious entrepreneurship must be designed with the intent of empowering user-innovators to build sustainable businesses around the platform. By ensuring residual claimancy, providing clear monetization mechanisms, reasonable fee structures, intellectual property protection, support for premium pricing, infrastructure for recurring revenue, effective CRM tools, and seamless payment handling, generative platforms become catalysts for innovation and economic value creation. This is how a platform truly embraces its users not just as consumers but as valued and empowered entrepreneurs. Platform leaders who truly understand this do not just tolerate participant profits – they actively help their ecosystems build profitable, sustainable businesses and careers.

Designing Products for Generativity

Designing for generativity means intentionally crafting products with features that empower and encourage the unpredicted innovations of others on a massive scale. This section dives deeper into the practical aspects of design for generativity, focusing on the specific features that can unlock a product's generative potential. Software products being "digital artifacts" have an exceptionally high potential to be designed for generativity if so desired. This is because the inherent characteristics and features of digital technology (such as combinatory capacity and reprogrammability) are a great fit for generativity. But many of the arguments in this book may apply to non-software products as well (such as Lego building blocks).

The section is organized around a mapping of the characteristics of generativity onto a number of more detailed design patterns.

Leverage: Empowering a Wide Spectrum of Tasks

A key principle of design for generativity is maximizing a product's capacity for leverage, meaning its ability to enhance user productivity across a broad spectrum of tasks. This goes beyond optimizing for a narrow set of predetermined functionalities and demands a more expansive perspective on potential use cases, even those not explicitly anticipated by the designers.

---

4 https://gumroad.gumroad.com/p/gumroad-is-becoming-a-merchant-of-record-more-updates

Consider the example of the mobile phone. Its initial purpose was voice communication, but its generative potential became evident as developers and users discovered its capacity for diverse tasks like messaging, photography, navigation, and mobile computing. This expansion of functionalities was fueled by the phone's underlying architecture and software, which allowed for reprogramming, customization, and the integration of new applications.

To design for leverage, consider the following questions:

- **Beyond the Obvious:** What are the non-obvious tasks users might want to accomplish with this product?
- **Versatility:** How can the product's core functionalities be designed to support a wide range of potential applications?
- **Emergent Uses:** How can we design the product to enable and support uses and applications we have not yet imagined?

Adaptability: Building Blocks for Customization and Evolution

A hallmark of generative products is their inherent adaptability, meaning their capacity to be readily modified and reconfigured to accommodate new tasks and evolving user needs. This principle is deeply intertwined with modularity, enabling users to break down the product into constituent components and recombine them in novel ways. The notion of architectural modularity or "decoupling" is key to most generative products. For example, the decoupling of software and hardware has been key to the generativity of computers: "The essence—and genius—of separating software creation from hardware construction is that the decoupling enables a computer to be acquired for one purpose and then used to perform new and different tasks without requiring the equivalent of a visit to the mechanic's shop" (Zittrain, 2008, p. 14).

The success of platforms like WordPress and Shopify lies in their modular design, empowering users to customize their online presence through a wide array of themes, plugins, and extensions. This adaptability allows these platforms to continuously evolve and cater to diverse user needs, fostering a vibrant ecosystem of developers and users.

Key considerations for designing adaptability include:

- **Modularity:** Can the product be broken down into reusable components that can be easily reconfigured?
- **Interfaces:** Are the interfaces between components well-defined, allowing for seamless integration and customization?
- **Openness:** Does the product's architecture allow for the incorporation of external components and modifications?

Ease of Mastery: Lowering Barriers to Entry

For a product to truly unleash its generative potential, it needs to be accessible to a broad audience, not just a select group of experts. This necessitates a focus on ease of mastery, meaning the relative effort required for users of varying skill levels to learn, understand, and effectively utilize the product.

The intuitive interface of the Apple iPhone, combined with its comprehensive app store and readily available learning resources, exemplifies this principle. This ease of mastery played a crucial role in attracting a massive user base and fostering a thriving ecosystem of app developers. In addition, users of the iPhone were eager to show each other what they can do with their device and how to do it. This community-driven learning can be even more powerful than having proper documentation.

Designing for ease of mastery involves:

- **Intuitive UX:** Is the product's user experience intuitive and easy to navigate, even for novice users?
- **Documentation and Support:** Is comprehensive and user-friendly documentation readily available? Are there accessible learning resources and support channels?
- **Community-Driven Learning:** Can we foster a community where users can share knowledge, tutorials, and best practices? Are there ways to motivate users to teach other users?

Accessibility: Enabling Openness and Participation

A fundamental principle of generative design is ensuring accessibility, meaning removing barriers, both technical and social, to building upon, extending, and modifying the product. This can involve a range of strategies, from offering open APIs and providing access to source code to fostering a culture of open collaboration.

The open-source nature of the Android operating system, combined with its readily available software development kit (SDK), showcases this principle. This openness has led to a diverse and vibrant ecosystem of devices and applications, far exceeding what Google, the platform's originator, could have achieved alone. Furthermore, no-code app builders became easier to build for third-party developers for Android compared to iOS due the more open nature of Android.

Key considerations for designing accessibility include:

- **Open APIs and SDKs:** Does the product offer well-documented and readily accessible APIs and SDKs that allow developers to integrate with its functionalities?
- **Intuitive No-Code Interfaces for Non-Specialists:** Does the product allow non-specialists (especially non-developers) to innovate with the product?
- **Open Source:** Is the product, or at least parts of it, open source, enabling users and developers to directly modify and extend its codebase?

– **Community Platforms:** Are there platforms and channels that facilitate communication, collaboration, and knowledge sharing among users and developers?

Transferability: Facilitating the Spread of Innovation

The ability to readily share, disseminate, and build upon modifications and innovations is critical for fostering a product's generative potential. This principle of transferability ensures that individual contributions can be easily replicated, adopted, and further enhanced by others, creating a powerful network effect where each innovation adds to the collective value. While the emphasis in discussions of generativity is often on change and adaptability, it is also very important to emphasize that widespread participation and creative contributions to a product are only possible if the product has a well-designed, well-functioning, stable core, around which various innovations can be developed (Baldwin & Woodard, 2009). Without the necessary standardization and stability at the core of a product ecosystem, the system as a whole becomes too unreliable and thus users are not incentivized to "invest" time, effort, and resources in contributing to it.

The success of platforms like GitHub is deeply rooted in their ability to facilitate the transfer of code snippets, solutions, and best practices across a vast network of developers using standardized protocols. Any open code repository on GitHub can easily be cloned and "forked" for another direction of development. Many repositories have thousands of forks. This seamless transferability fuels a virtuous cycle of collaborative innovation, accelerating the pace of development and expanding the platform's capabilities.

Furthermore, while the emphasis in discussions of generativity is often on the "uncoordinated" and "unfiltered" nature of contributions, it must also be emphasized that the way in which an organization governs the processes by which external contributions are solicited, incentivized, and disseminated makes a great deal of difference in the ultimate generativity that is achieved by the product and its ecosystem. This governance role has been extensively studied in the literature on software platforms, where it is often referred to as an "orchestrator" role (Helfat & Raubitschek, 2018).

Designing for transferability involves:

– **Reusability:** Are modifications and innovations possible to transfer and reuse by others in different contexts through methods such as cloning or forking?
– **Standardized Formats:** Are there standardized formats and protocols that facilitate the sharing and integration of contributions?
– **Community-Driven Dissemination:** Does the platform offer mechanisms for users to easily share, discover, and adopt innovations created by others?

Profitability: Taking Users Seriously as Entrepreneurs

Product creators should strategically integrate profitability into the very fabric of their generative products. This integration is not a mere afterthought or a secondary consideration; rather, it is a foundational element of a successful generative ecosystem. A truly generative product should be designed to be not only a powerful tool for creativity and problem-solving but also a robust platform for entrepreneurship, where users can confidently build sustainable businesses and flourishing careers. This perspective recognizes that user profitability is not just a happy accident but a key design target.

The financial success of a generative product is inextricably linked to the success of its user-innovators. Therefore, by consciously designing with the financial goals of user-innovators in mind, product creators can activate a powerful positive feedback loop: as users achieve financial success through their creative outputs, they become more invested in the platform, which in turn attracts more users and innovations, thus leading to a virtuous cycle of growth.

To achieve this, product creators must ask themselves some crucial questions about how the design of their product will impact the profitability of their users:

- **Monetization Pathways:** Are there clear, built-in mechanisms for users to transform their innovations into revenue streams?
- **Value Distribution:** Does the fee structure ensure innovators capture a fair share of the value they create while maintaining platform sustainability?
- **Business Infrastructure:** Does the product provide the necessary tools and infrastructure for users to build and scale sustainable businesses?
- **IP Protection:** Are there robust mechanisms to protect user innovations and intellectual property rights?

By embracing these six pillars of generative design, companies can create products that not only fulfill immediate needs but also serve as platforms for continuous evolution and unforeseen innovation. These principles, however, are not a rigid formula but rather a framework for approaching product development with a generative mindset. The specific implementation will vary depending on the product's nature, target audience, and the strategic goals of the organization. However, the underlying aim remains consistent: to create products that thrive on change, empower users, and unlock a sustainable competitive advantage by tapping into the distributed unanticipated innovations of others at scale.

As argued earlier, digital products have a particularly high potential for generativity. In the next section we investigate this idea in more detail.

The Generative Properties of Digital Artifacts

To understand how digital products are particularly well suited for generativity, we must first understand their fundamental properties. Yoo (2010) identifies seven key properties that distinguish digital artifacts from traditional physical products: programmability, addressability, sensibility, communicability, memorizability, traceability, and associability (see Figure 4.2). Understanding these fundamental properties is crucial because they form the technical foundation that makes generativity possible in digital products. Below, we explore how these properties can be specifically harnessed to create generative potential.

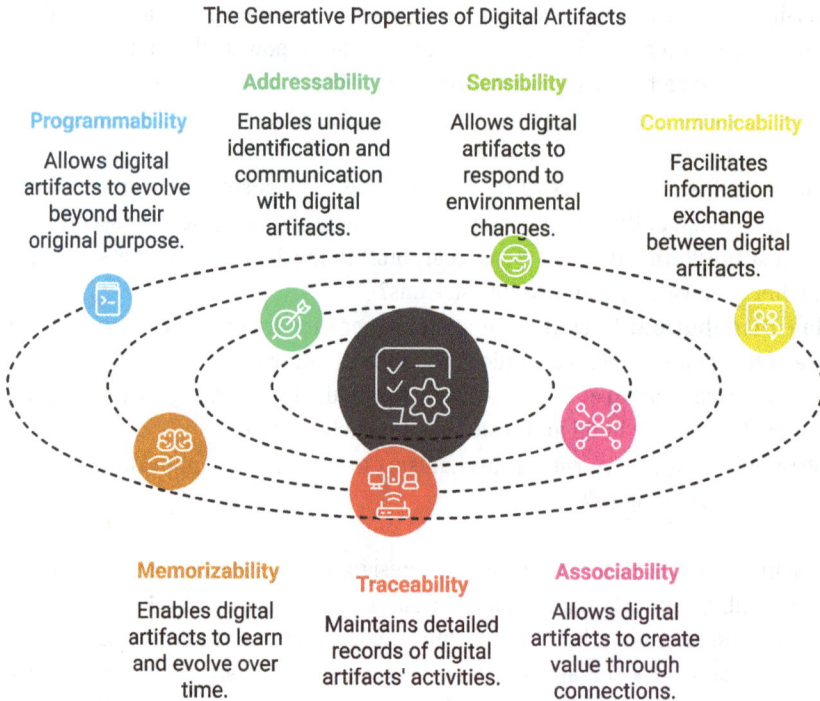

Figure 4.2: Yoo's Seven Properties of Digital Artifacts.

Programmability: The Foundation of Unlimited Possibility

Programmability means that a digital artifact can accept new instructions that modify its behavior. Unlike physical products whose functionality is fixed at manufacture, programmable artifacts can be fundamentally transformed through software changes. The case of Notion illustrates this transformative power perfectly.

When a product is truly programmable, three key characteristics emerge that enable generativity:

First, it can modify its behavior based on new instructions. Unlike a physical tool with fixed functionality, a programmable artifact can be taught entirely new patterns of operation. When Notion launched in 2016, it offered basic document editing capabilities. However, its deeply programmable nature meant that users could essentially create their own productivity tools within the platform by programming new behaviors and interactions. What began as a simple text editor could be instructed to behave like a database, a project management system, or a customer relationship tool – all through the modification of its underlying programmatic rules. The company itself was often surprised by what users created – reflecting how programmability enables products to evolve beyond their creators' imagination.

Second, it can implement conditional logic and decision-making. Rather than following a single fixed path, programmable products can evaluate conditions and respond differently based on context. This ability to embed sophisticated decision trees allows users to create complex, responsive tools that adapt to different scenarios. When Notion introduced its database capabilities, users could program rich conditional behaviors – showing different information to different team members, automatically updating related records, or triggering specific actions based on data changes.

Third, it enables behavioral composition – the ability to combine multiple programmed behaviors into more sophisticated ones. Users can layer instructions to create increasingly complex functionality, similar to how simple programming functions can be combined into more powerful applications. This composability means that each new programmed behavior becomes a building block for even more sophisticated capabilities.

Generative platforms do not try to anticipate every possible behavior. Instead, they focus on making their core functionality as programmable as possible, then let their users define new patterns of operation. This approach requires a fundamental shift in product strategy: rather than trying to build every behavior yourself, focus on building a foundation that enables others to program behaviors you haven't even imagined.

Addressability: Enabling Targeted Innovation at Scale

Addressability refers to the ability to uniquely identify and communicate with individual instances of a digital artifact. While this may seem like a purely technical feature, it enables a profound shift in how innovation can occur and scale. Unlike physical products which exist as identical copies, addressable digital artifacts can be individually recognized and modified – enabling precise targeting and customization at massive scale.

Consider how Amazon's marketplace leverages addressability to drive innovation. Every product, seller, customer, and interaction has a unique digital identity, enabling the platform to create highly personalized experiences. Sellers can test new product variations with specific customer segments, dynamically adjust pricing based on individual buying patterns, and create targeted bundles for different user groups. This granular level of control allows for a kind of distributed experimentation that would be impossible with traditional retail.

Three key mechanisms make addressability particularly powerful for generativity:

First, it enables precision experimentation. Every digital instance can be uniquely tracked and measured, allowing innovators to run sophisticated A/B tests, gather granular feedback, and iterate rapidly based on specific user responses. Spotify uses this capability to test new music recommendation algorithms with select user groups before broader rollout, learning from detailed interaction patterns to refine their innovation before scaling.

Second, it allows for dynamic adaptation. Digital products can modify their behavior based on the specific identity and context of each user interaction. Netflix's recommendation system demonstrates this power – the same core platform delivers radically different experiences to each viewer based on their unique viewing history, preferences, and behavior patterns.

Third, it enables network-driven innovation. When every interaction is addressable, platforms can identify and amplify emerging patterns of value. When every interaction in Roblox is uniquely identifiable and trackable, the platform can detect emerging patterns across millions of gaming sessions that no individual developer could discover alone. For instance, when players across different demographics consistently engage longer with games featuring specific collaborative mechanics, Roblox can identify this pattern as valuable. The platform then amplifies these successful innovations through multiple channels. It might highlight these games in recommendations, feature them in discovery feeds, or provide insights to developers about what's resonating. For example, when a small studio created a novel approach to team-based obstacle courses that showed unusually high retention rates among teenage players, Roblox could detect this pattern and elevate it.

The strategic implication is that digital platforms often do not have to rely on "one size fits all" solutions, and can foster an ecosystem of targeted innovations (by themselves and by their users) that serve specific niches exceptionally well. This enables a long tail of specialized solutions that collectively create more value than a few broadly targeted ones ever could. More importantly, addressability allows platforms to learn from and amplify the most successful innovations, creating a kind of distributed learning system that becomes more intelligent with every interaction.

Sensibility: Creating Context-Aware Innovation

Sensibility describes a digital artifact's ability to monitor and respond to its environment through various forms of sensors and inputs. It is about the capability of digital products to understand and interact with their surroundings. Modern digital artifacts can detect location, motion, temperature, light, sound, and numerous other environmental factors, and then use this sensory information to adapt their behavior or trigger specific responses.

The evolution from basic inputs to rich environmental awareness has dramatically expanded the possibilities for digital innovation. While early computer interfaces could only sense keyboard strokes and mouse clicks, today's multimodal AI systems demonstrate the transformative power of enhanced sensibility. Multimodal Large Language Models (LLMs) can analyze images, interpret technical diagrams, read handwritten text, understand spatial relationships, and even follow your computer interactions by watching your screen. This rich sensory capability enables products to understand and respond to their environment in increasingly sophisticated ways, creating rich data streams that inspire new applications.

The smartphone provides an earlier illustration of how enhanced sensibility drives waves of innovation. Each new sensor added to phones has catalyzed entirely new categories of applications. GPS sensors enabled the creation of navigation apps and location-based services, fundamentally changing how we move through physical space. Accelerometers gave birth to motion-controlled games, transforming how we interact with mobile entertainment. Biometric sensors created new possibilities for health and fitness applications, allowing phones to become personal wellness monitors. Camera improvements enabled augmented reality experiences, blending digital and physical worlds in novel ways.

The strategic significance of sensibility lies in its ability to create contextual awareness that can trigger innovative responses. A digital product with rich sensory capabilities becomes a platform for innovations that were not previously possible. Moreover, these sensors generate streams of data that entrepreneurs can leverage to create entirely new types of value. The key is not just adding more sensors, but thoughtfully considering how enhanced sensibility can enable new forms of interaction and value creation.

This suggests that when designing potentially generative products, leaders should think carefully about what types of environmental awareness would enable the most valuable innovations in their context. Sometimes, adding a single new type of sensor can unlock entirely new categories of possible applications. The goal is not necessarily to maximize the number of sensory inputs but to identify the specific types of sensibility that will enable the most valuable forms of innovation for your particular ecosystem.

Communicability: Building Innovation Networks

The ability of digital artifacts to exchange information with other artifacts and systems represents a fundamental shift in how innovation can spread and combine. While physical products exist as isolated units, digital artifacts can communicate through standardized protocols and interfaces, enabling them to work together, share resources, and coordinate actions. This communication can be synchronous or asynchronous, local or remote, and can involve the transfer of data, instructions, or even capabilities.

The story of Zapier illustrates how communicability can transform entire digital landscapes. The company began with a deceptively simple insight: what if we could make different web applications talk to each other? This vision of universal communicability has led to thousands of apps being able to interact in millions of different combinations. Any user of Zapier can engage in combinatorial innovation (Varian, 2010) with every software that has a Zapier integration, essentially turning web and mobile applications into building blocks through a no-code interface.

Consider how this property has revolutionized workplace productivity. A customer email can automatically create a task in project management software. A calendar event can trigger team notifications in Slack. A form submission can update multiple databases simultaneously. Social media posts can be coordinated across platforms. Each of these capabilities represents not just automation but the potential for novel combinations and workflows that weren't possible before.

Zapier builds on the fact that so many software applications now have Application Programming Interfaces (APIs). But even before Zapier, the rise of APIs was already demonstrating the power of communicability. Stripe's payment processing API made complex payment infrastructure accessible through simple communication protocols, leading to thousands of innovative applications and allowing many innovators to profit more easily from their innovations by adding a stripe integration. Each new application doesn't need to reinvent payment processing – it can simply communicate with Stripe's infrastructure.

Three key mechanisms make communicability particularly powerful for fostering innovation. First, it enables products to work together in novel ways, creating value that no single product could deliver alone. Second, it creates ecosystems where innovations can build on each other, with each new capability becoming available to the entire network. Third, it facilitates the rapid spread of innovative solutions, as successful innovations can be quickly integrated into other products through established communication channels.

This suggests that when designing for generativity, leaders should think carefully about their communication protocols. The goal is to enable rich exchange of data and services, and to open up possibilities for unexpected combinations and interactions. The most generative platforms tend to have well-documented, accessible APIs that make it easy for others to build on their capabilities.

Memorizability: Learning and Evolution

Memorizability refers to the capacity of digital artifacts to store and retrieve information about past states, interactions, and events. But this property goes far beyond simple data storage – it enables systems to learn from experience and continuously evolve. Through machine learning, digital artifacts can transform accumulated memories into sophisticated patterns of behavior, allowing them to improve and adapt their functionality over time.

Machine learning has proved to be a powerful tool to incorporate memorizability in digital products. Netflix refines its recommendations by analyzing not just what users watch but how they watch – tracking pauses, rewinds, and viewing sessions to understand engagement at a deeper level. Spotify's Discover Weekly playlist learns each user's unique music taste by examining subtle patterns in listening behavior, from skips to song completion rates. Social media platforms like Instagram and TikTok have mastered the art of learning from rapid-fire user interactions, using every scroll, pause, and like to tune their content algorithms. These systems actively learn from user behavior, developing increasingly sophisticated models of user preferences and behavior.

Three key mechanisms make memorizability particularly powerful for innovation:

First, it allows products to learn systematically from usage patterns. Google Search exemplifies this through its ability to remember which results users click on, how long they spend on different pages, which queries lead to refined searches, and regional and temporal search patterns. The search algorithm continuously improves by learning from billions of interactions, understanding not just what people search for but why they search and what makes a result valuable to them.

Second, it enables adaptive intelligence through memory-driven learning. Rather than following fixed rules, systems can develop increasingly sophisticated behaviors by analyzing patterns in their stored experiences. ChatGPT demonstrates this through its memory feature and fine-tuning capabilities. The system can maintain context throughout conversations, building on previous exchanges to provide more relevant responses. Through fine-tuning, it can even learn new patterns of interaction that modify its behavior – learning to write in specific styles, follow particular formats, or handle specialized tasks based on curated examples.

Third, it creates compounding intelligence through transfer learning. Knowledge gained in one context can be applied to novel situations, enabling unexpected innovations. When an LLM learns a new capability through fine-tuning or by seeing a new document, it often discovers creative ways to combine this new knowledge with its existing knowledge. This combinatorial learning can lead to emergent behaviors that were not explicitly programmed.

The strategic implication is that memorizability opens new doors as to how products can evolve. Rather than relying solely on deliberate design decisions, products can learn and adapt based on actual usage patterns. This creates powerful feedback loops where each interaction potentially contributes to future improvements. For leaders seeking to create generative products, this suggests the importance of building robust systems for capturing and processing experiences, while ensuring these systems respect user privacy and security. More importantly, it highlights how memory-driven learning can create products that grow more valuable through use, developing capabilities that might surprise even their creators.

Traceability: Understanding Innovation Patterns

Traceability means that digital artifacts can maintain detailed records of their activities and transformations over time. Every interaction, modification, or event can be logged with precise timestamps and contextual information, creating a comprehensive audit trail that shows not just what happened but when, how, and in what sequence.

Git, the version control system used by millions of programmers around the world, demonstrates how traceability can transform collaborative innovation. Every change to the code is tracked with multiple dimensions of context: who made the change, when it was made, why it was made (through commit messages), how it relates to other changes, and what problems it solved or created. This comprehensive traceability has enabled software development to scale globally in ways that would have been impossible without such detailed change tracking.

GitHub built upon this foundation to create what is essentially a "social network for code," where traceability enables entirely new forms of collaborative innovation. When every change is traceable, developers can learn from others' solutions, understand how successful projects evolve, identify patterns in software development, and build upon others' innovations. This creates a powerful learning network where each contributor's work becomes a potential building block for future innovations.

Three key mechanisms make traceability particularly powerful for fostering innovation:

First, it enables rapid experimentation with safety. Because every change is tracked and reversible, innovators can experiment boldly knowing they can always roll back to previous working versions. This reduces the risk of innovation and encourages more adventurous exploration.

Second, it facilitates learning from history. By examining the trace of changes that led to successful outcomes, innovators can understand not just what works but how and why certain approaches evolved. This creates a rich context for learning and improvement.

Third, it supports complex collaboration at scale. When every change is traceable, large groups can work on the same project without creating chaos. Different paths of innovation can proceed in parallel, with the ability to merge successful approaches back into the main project.

Traceability's impact on innovation extends far beyond software development. New AI-powered tools like Cursor, Replit, Bolt.New, and v0.dev are bringing Git-style version control to a broader audience. These tools allow writers, designers, and other creators to track the evolution of their work with the same precision that developers use to track code. A writer can explore different plot directions while maintaining the original story. A designer can try radical changes knowing they can always return to previous versions. When combined with AI assistance, this traceable history becomes even more powerful – the AI can analyze successful patterns in the history to suggest promising new directions. This democratization of traceability means that complex, collaborative innovation is no longer limited to technical domains.

Associability: Combining and Recombining

Associability enables digital artifacts to discover and leverage meaningful relationships between different elements in a system. Associability is about understanding the links between things – how they relate, why they matter together, and what new value their combination might create.

Consider how Spotify creates value through musical associations. The platform understands patterns of musical similarity, listening context, and emotional resonance. It can recognize that while two songs might be from completely different genres, they often appear together in user-created workout playlists. Or that certain songs, while sonically different, evoke similar moods and work well for focused work. These rich associations enable the platform to create personalized experiences that transcend traditional music categorization.

Coda demonstrates a different kind of associability through its relational databases. Users can create sophisticated webs of interconnected information where changes ripple intelligently through the system. A project timeline can be associated with team capacity data, which connects to individual workload tracking, which links back to project priorities. These associations help teams understand and manage complex workflows. When someone updates their capacity, all related views and dashboards automatically reflect the implications of that change.

Three key mechanisms make associability particularly powerful:

First, it enables semantic understanding. Digital products can recognize not just that things are connected but how they are connected. Amazon's recommendation engine, for instance, understands that buying a tent suggests an interest in sleeping bags not just because they are both camping items, but because they are complementary tools for the same activity.

Second, it supports contextual relevance. The same elements can have different associations depending on context. Google Photos can recognize that the same person appearing in different photos might be relevant for a family album in one context, a work presentation in another, and a vacation memory in a third.

Third, it creates emergent knowledge. By analyzing patterns of association across many users and interactions, systems can discover entirely new categories of relationship. LinkedIn's skill endorsements, for example, have revealed unexpected combinations of expertise that characterize successful careers in emerging fields.

The power of associability lies in its ability to create new value from existing relationships. Associative systems help us understand why connections matter and what they mean. This transforms raw data and simple links into rich networks of meaning that can drive innovation in unexpected directions.

Leveraging the Power of Digital for Generativity

The seven fundamental properties of digital artifacts – programmability, addressability, sensibility, communicability, memorizability, traceability, and associability – work together to create unprecedented potential for generative innovation.

Bubble.io demonstrates how these properties enable generativity in practice. Through its plugin system, small independent components can be programmed, combined, and modified. Different parts of the system can evolve independently while remaining connected. Users can reconfigure the platform for diverse applications, from e-commerce sites to project management tools. The platform tracks usage patterns to improve over time, while making all this power accessible to non-technical users.

Several key insights emerge from examining these properties through a generativity lens. First, these properties are mutually reinforcing. Programmability becomes more powerful when combined with communicability to share new capabilities. Sensibility gains value when paired with memorizability to learn from environmental data. Traceability amplifies associability by making patterns of successful combinations visible.

Second, these properties do not automatically create generativity – they must be intentionally designed and exposed to enable innovation by others. Simply having the technical capability for programmability or communicability is not enough. Leaders must carefully consider how to make these properties accessible and usable by their broader ecosystem of potential innovators. As we have seen in cases like Notion, Bubble, and Coda, the most successful platforms find ways to make sophisticated technical properties approachable to non-technical users.

For leaders seeking to harness the generative potential of digital products, this suggests several key strategic priorities:
1. Design for extensibility: Make core properties accessible and usable by others.
2. Enable experimentation: Create safe spaces for testing new innovations.
3. Reduce friction: Make it easy to share and build upon successful innovations.
4. Foster connections: Help innovators find each other and combine their work.
5. Learn systematically: Build capabilities to understand and amplify emerging patterns of innovation.

The properties of digital artifacts make new forms of innovation possible. They help users discover, create, and build upon each other's ideas. When digital products make good use of these properties, they create environments where innovation can come from anywhere. Over time, this leads to a rich ecosystem of distributed creativity that becomes increasingly valuable for everyone involved.

Chapter 5
Managing Generative Products

When designing and managing products with generative potential, traditional product management "best practices" may not always apply. The conventional wisdom around entrepreneurship, innovation, and product development often needs fundamental reconsideration when dealing with generative products. There really is something different when you're building a product like Notion, Coda, Bubble, Adalo, Zapier, AirTable, and other highly generative tools, as I am sure the entrepreneurs who took these products to market will attest to.

There is not much guidance to be found in the literature specifically on managing generative products, so this chapter opens the conversation by exploring what makes these products uniquely powerful – and challenging – to oversee. We will examine their key advantages and limitations, while highlighting the fundamental shifts in thinking required to manage them effectively.

Generative products exhibit distinct patterns of spontaneous, self-directed evolution. These patterns allow both the product and its surrounding ecosystem to develop along unexpected trajectories with limited centralized oversight. While such unplanned developments can manifest within the product itself, they more commonly emerge through novel applications and value creation enabled by the product. What makes generative products particularly powerful is their capacity to harness the collective knowledge, creativity, and innovative potential of users outside the organization – enabling possibilities far beyond what the original product creators could have conceived or implemented alone.

While complete relinquishment of control rarely appeals to product creators, the relationship between control and generativity involves careful calibration (see Figure 5.1). Increased generativity typically requires decreased control from product creators (Cennamo & Santaló, 2019), which can affect the security and reliability guarantees they can provide to users. However, even highly generative products remain bound by their foundational architecture – their initial design, features, and capabilities establish the parameters within which evolution can occur. The scope for original innovations by users depends on the creative latitude permitted by the product and the supporting infrastructure of tools, standards, and guidelines made available to users (Remneland-Wikhamn et al., 2011).

The Pros and Cons of Generative Products

Generative products are often described as taking on "a life of their own" which can either sound like a treasure trove of autonomous growth, or a quagmire of noisy mess, depending on how you look at it. Making products generative isn't always the

https://doi.org/10.1515/9783110779639-005

Should a company prioritize generativity or control in product development?

Generative Products

Specific-Use Products

Foster innovation but risk chaos and ambiguity

Ensure stability and control

Figure 5.1: Generative products vs. specific-use products.

right choice (see Figure 5.2). While powerful when implemented successfully, generative products face three fundamental challenges: managing chaos, dealing with ambiguity, and requiring significant time to mature. Interestingly, these very challenges can become competitive advantages for companies that successfully navigate them at scale.

Many products are better served by maintaining a specific, controlled purpose rather than opening themselves up as platforms for innovation. This is especially true when reliability and stability are paramount – qualities that could be compromised by increasing generativity. In these cases, product creators need to maintain tight control over functionality, something that modern cloud software architectures make increasingly feasible.

Even in cases where generativity makes sense strategically, loosening control carries risks. User innovations aren't universally beneficial – some can actively destroy value. Consider the emergence of computer viruses, which appeared almost immediately after networked computing became possible, creating widespread disruption. Such negative innovations can severely damage the experience for all users.

Generative products also face a fundamental challenge of ambiguity, particularly in their early stages before a community of users has discovered and shaped their primary applications. Describing exactly what these products do proves surprisingly difficult, and being too prescriptive risks constraining their potential by imposing limited interpretations. SparkFun Electronics encountered this directly with their Raspberry Pi-related products – after seeing customers discover unexpected uses, they deliberately stopped defining specific use cases for their products (Murphy, 2014).

This inherent ambiguity creates significant practical challenges, particularly around communicating value to stakeholders – from investors to customers to internal teams. The personal computer's early days illustrate this perfectly: in the 1970s, explaining its value proposition remained difficult until "killer apps" like VisiCalc's spreadsheet software emerged to demonstrate its practical utility (Zynda, 2013).

The struggle to define and describe highly generative products creates fascinating – and sometimes amusing – challenges for technology journalists and marketers.

Generative Products

Pros   VS   Cons

Nearly boundless potential   Chaos

Competitive moat   Ambiguity

Vibrant user community   Time-consuming

Autonomous Growth   Loss of control

Negative user innovations

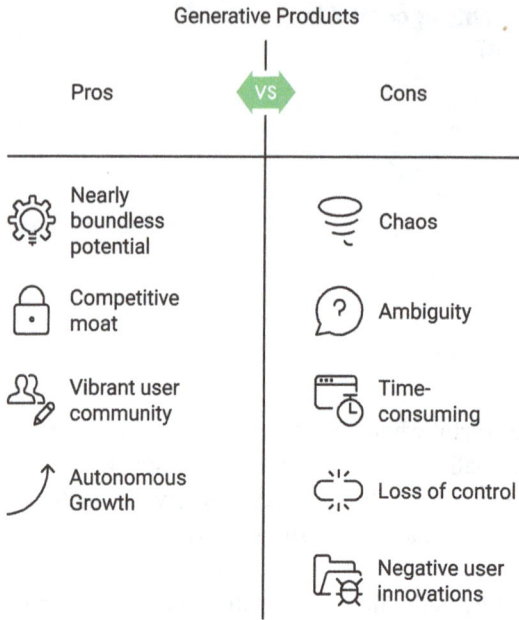

Figure 5.2: Pros and cons of generative products.

Early coverage of these products often reveals a striking confusion about their fundamental nature and purpose. Consider the illuminating case of Coda.io: examining five different articles referenced in its Wikipedia entry reveals that various authors decided on entirely different metaphors to capture what the product actually does (Wikipedia Contributors, 2025). One describes it as a way to turn "docs into apps," another as a spreadsheet alternative, another as an automation tool, one as "Minecraft for docs," and another as a rethinking of documents (see Table 5.1). The diversity of these descriptions is so pronounced that just from the headlines one might reasonably conclude they were discussing entirely different products altogether.

Time represents another significant challenge for generative products. Their path to widespread adoption tends to be gradual and methodical, requiring sustained patience. This extended timeline stems from the multi-layered process of user engagement: individuals must experiment with the product, master its capabilities, learn to innovate within its framework, share their discoveries with others, and build upon collective insights. Typically, a dedicated community of early adopters and innovators must emerge to articulate the product's value in terms that resonate with mainstream audiences before broader market acceptance becomes possible.

However, this temporal barrier carries an interesting strategic advantage for companies that successfully scale their generative products. The time investment, combined with the emergence of vibrant user communities, creates formidable competitive moats. These communities of enthusiasts generate tremendous value for the

Table 5.1: Examples of how a generative product (Coda.io) is described in the press.

Metaphor for describing Coda.io	Reference (as found on the Wikipedia entry for Coda.io)
A document-based app–builder tool	McCracken, Harry (2019-02-05). "Coda, which wants to turn docs into apps, is now generally available." Fast Company. Retrieved 2019-11-19.
A new kind of spreadsheet software	Newton, Casey (2017-10-19). "Coda is a next–generation spreadsheet designed to make Excel a thing of the past." The Verge. Retrieved 2019-11-19.
Rules-based automation platform	"Coda's rules–based Automations feature automates repetitive tasks." VentureBeat. 2018-11-16. Retrieved 2019-11-19.
A document builder tool ("Minecraft for docs")	Flynn, Kerry. "A startup is taking on Google and Microsoft with a 'Minecraft for docs'". Mashable. Retrieved 2019-11-19.
A new kind of document editor	"Two Google alums just raised $60M to rethink documents." TechCrunch. Retrieved 2019-11-19.

product owner through their collective efforts in exploration, innovation, and knowledge creation. Moreover, they often shoulder significant portions of the financial and developmental risks associated with innovation. These user communities naturally evolve into powerful engines of marketing, promotion, and knowledge dissemination. Perhaps most significantly, users who participate in these communities tend to develop deeper emotional investment in the product, driven by their active role in its evolution and their sense of ownership over their contributions to its ecosystem.

A New Mindset for Managing Generative Products

The distinctive nature of generative products demands a fundamental reimagining of how we approach product development and management. Traditional "best practices" in entrepreneurship and innovation, while valuable for conventional products, often prove insufficient or even counterproductive when applied to generative offerings. At the heart of this challenge lies what (Garud et al., 2009) identifies as the inherent "incompleteness" of generative products – they are fundamentally open-ended, with possibilities that extend far beyond their initial conception.

This section explores the critical mindset shifts required to effectively shepherd generative products toward success. We identify five pivots from conventional product thinking, each accompanied by practical strategies and guidelines for implementation (see Figure 5.3).

From Fail Fast to Patient Play

The temporal dynamics of generative products demand a rethinking of traditional product development cycles. The conventional wisdom around rapid iteration and quick feedback loops (Cagan, 2017; Ries, 2011), while powerful for standard products, requires significant adaptation when generativity enters the equation.

The popular "fail fast" mantra (Hall, 2007) proves doubly problematic for generative products. The inherent ambiguity of these offerings makes both "failure" and "speed" difficult to meaningfully assess. Organizations often find themselves navigating extended periods where their generative product shows mixed signals – neither clearly succeeding nor failing by traditional metrics. This reality demands extraordinary patience, though not infinite tolerance. While clear performance thresholds still matter, they tend to be broader and more nuanced than those applied to conventional products.

Perhaps most crucially, organizations launching generative products must embrace a fundamental uncertainty about their creation's full potential. Rather than dictating specific uses, they must cultivate the patience to watch users explore, experiment, and collectively discover applications through organic play and collaborative innovation. This represents a profound shift from traditional product management – one that requires both humility and strategic restraint.

From Problem-Solving to Meta Problem-Solving

Managing generative products requires a shift from addressing specific challenges to creating tools that solve entire categories of problems. These platforms might better be understood as "meta-products" – tools that enable problem-solving at a higher level of abstraction. This elevated perspective naturally leads to product descriptions and visions that can seem frustratingly abstract, challenging the conventional wisdom about clear, specific value propositions.

This abstract nature creates an interesting paradox in communication: while fewer potential stakeholders may immediately grasp the concept, those who do understand it often recognize its transformative potential. Rather than addressing a single pain point, these products tackle entire problem spaces. This broader vision particularly resonates with individuals comfortable with abstract meta-cognitive thinking (Metcalfe & Shimamura, 1996). Alan Turing exemplifies this meta-level problem-solving brilliance: when faced with the challenge of decrypting enemy messages during World War II, he didn't just create a solution for breaking current codes – he developed an algorithmic framework that could adapt to evolving encryption methods (Hodges, 2014). This ability to solve problems at a meta-level, while harder to communicate initially, ultimately enables far greater impact than narrowly-focused solutions.

From Hypothesis Testing to Hypothesis Development

Traditional product development frameworks, as outlined by Blank and Dorf (2020), rest on three key assumptions: that teams can identify their target users, understand the specific problems they are solving, and quickly validate product utility through user observation. With generative products, these foundational assumptions require reconsideration.

Instead of jumping straight to hypothesis testing, generative products demand more focus on the more exploratory phase of hypothesis formation. This shift mirrors an important distinction in research methodology: while quantitative hypothesis testing proves invaluable for validating specific ideas, the early "fuzzy front end" of innovation often demands more qualitative, exploratory approaches. In research terminology, this crucial preliminary phase focuses on "hypothesis development" or "hypothesis generation" (Hartwick & Barki, 1994) – creating the intellectual space to discover what questions we should be asking in the first place.

This reframing transforms how we approach product testing in three crucial ways:
1. Rather than targeting narrow user segments, we expose the product to diverse populations without preconceived notions about who might find it valuable.
2. Instead of defining problems upfront, we allow users to discover novel applications and use cases organically.
3. Rather than seeking quick validation, we provide users the time and resources to explore, experiment, and naturally discover the product's utility.

In essence, the early stages of generative product development require fewer "user testers" and more "problem hunters" – individuals who can help uncover entirely new domains where the product might generate unexpected solutions. This approach acknowledges that with generative products, we're not just validating predetermined hypotheses – we are discovering what hypotheses are worth exploring in the first place.

From Customer Feedback to User Tinkering

Generative products demand a fundamental reimagining of the problem discovery process. While conventional products benefit from the rapid validation cycles championed by the lean startup methodology (Blank & Dorf, 2020; Ries, 2011), generative platforms require a more expansive and patient approach. The traditional drive to quickly establish and capitalize on a narrow product-market fit gives way to something more fluid and expansive – a broader, more nuanced conception of how products create value.

This shift requires embracing a different rhythm of discovery. The clear, immediate feedback signals that typically validate market segments prove more elusive with generative products. Instead, organizations must cultivate the patience to watch users explore, experiment, and gradually uncover possibilities. This "tinkering" approach stands in marked contrast to the rapid validation emphasized in lean startup thinking. Where Blank and Dorf (2020, p. 214) suggest that meaningful validation comes from seeing "pupils dilate" in immediate recognition of value, generative products often inspire a quieter initial response – one of curiosity and intrigue rather than instant delight. Our research with Bubble.io users revealed that transformative "aha moments" typically emerged only after sustained engagement – after completing tutorials and extensively testing the platform's capabilities against their creative visions.

To nurture this exploratory process, organizations need to provide two crucial infrastructural elements: modular integrations and robust knowledge bases. Modular integrations, facilitated through APIs and flexible component architectures, enable users to engage in combinatorial innovation – mixing and matching elements to discover novel solutions. Meanwhile, comprehensive knowledge bases support collective learning, allowing users to build upon each other's discoveries and best practices.

From Traditional to Thick Documentation

One of the challenges in managing generative products is capturing and learning from the rich web of interactions that emerge as different participants engage with them. Schoffelen and Huybrechts (2013) introduce the concept of "thick documentation" – an approach that goes beyond simply recording features or user experiences to capture the complex socio-material assemblies where people and objects mutually shape each other.

Thick documentation aims to reveal what Schoffelen and Huybrechts call the "hidden exchanges" – the often invisible ways that different participants (makers, users, designers, engineers) interact with and influence each other through the product. For example, when documenting a multitouch table project, thick documentation would capture not just the technical specifications and user interface, but also how art professionals interact differently with it compared to general audiences, how engineers' decisions affect designers' possibilities, and how users' unexpected applications lead to new features.

Implementing thick documentation requires creating spaces and mechanisms for multiple perspectives to emerge:
- Live gatherings where participants can demonstrate and discuss their different uses and interpretations
- Collaborative mapping tools that visualize relationships between people, objects, and contexts

- Open documentation platforms where participants can build on each other's contributions
- Guidelines that encourage documenting not just what was done but why and how decisions emerged

Making visible the hidden connections and possibilities in a product, inspires new interpretations and adaptations. Of course, this approach faces key challenges in practice. Motivating busy participants to invest time in documentation can be difficult, and treating documentation as composed of dynamic, messy, constantly changing material can cause confusion. It is not trivial to find the right balance of documentation thickness.

Reimagining Product Management for Generative Products

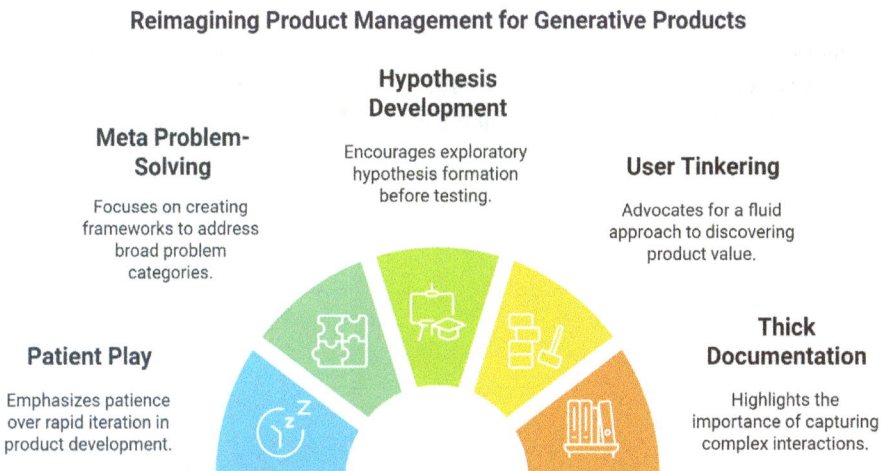

Hypothesis Development
Encourages exploratory hypothesis formation before testing.

Meta Problem-Solving
Focuses on creating frameworks to address broad problem categories.

User Tinkering
Advocates for a fluid approach to discovering product value.

Patient Play
Emphasizes patience over rapid iteration in product development.

Thick Documentation
Highlights the importance of capturing complex interactions.

Figure 5.3: A new mindset for managing generative products.

Conclusion: Reimagining Product Management for Generativity

While generativity is not universally desirable or appropriate for all products, it has emerged as a powerful source of competitive advantage among today's most successful technology companies. Yet despite its demonstrated importance, we lack robust frameworks for understanding and managing generative products. The unique dynamics of these products demand fresh thinking about product management – thinking that moves beyond traditional frameworks and best practices.

Generative products fundamentally challenge our assumptions about organizational agency and control. Where traditional product management assumes centralized direction from the product-creating organization, generative products distribute agency in fascinating and often unpredictable ways. The product itself becomes an

actor in organizational processes, particularly around knowledge discovery and innovation.

However, this shift toward distributed agency doesn't eliminate the need for
thoughtful organizational oversight – it transforms it. Product-creating organizations
must develop new capabilities and mindsets to effectively shepherd generative products toward success. This involves mastering temporal patience, embracing strategic
ambiguity, and creating environments that nurture user exploration and innovation.

This chapter represents an initial expedition into the emerging landscape of product management for intentionally generative products. By highlighting the distinctive
challenges and opportunities of generative products, I hope to encourage other scholars and practitioners to develop more sophisticated frameworks for managing these
powerful but complex offerings.

In the next chapter we move from product to a somewhat different unit of analysis: markets. However, in many ways this is a continued discussion of the generative
product because creators of generative products can orchestrate user innovations in
marketplaces intentionally built around the generativity of their product.

Chapter 6
The Generativity of Markets

The Market as an Innovation Machine

When most people think about markets, they imagine systems for matching buyers with sellers – like Uber connecting riders with drivers, or Amazon matching shoppers with products. This view of markets as primarily allocation mechanisms has dominated both business thinking and economic theory for centuries, conjuring Adam Smith's famous "invisible hand" metaphor emphasizing the autonomous matching capability of markets as their most valuable feature. But this perspective captures only a fraction of what markets actually do.

When Nobel laureate Paul Romer revolutionized economic thinking in the 1990s, he made a simple but profound observation: ideas are fundamentally different from physical resources. While traditional resources get used up when consumed, knowledge can be used by anyone without diminishing its value for others. Romer called this the "non-rival" nature of ideas (Romer, 1990, n.p.), and this insight helped explain something that had puzzled economists for centuries: how do economies keep growing despite limited physical resources?

The answer lies in the extraordinary ability of markets to generate new knowledge and ideas. Unlike physical resources that get depleted with use, knowledge builds upon itself, creating what economist Edmund Phelps calls "self-refueling systems" of innovation (Phelps, 2013, n.p.). Think about how the invention of the smartphone created possibilities for millions of mobile apps, each of which in turn created new possibilities for other innovations. This is the essence of generative growth, where each innovation opens doors for countless others.

Hence, the true power of markets lies not just in resource allocation but in their ability to function as innovation generators, systematically incentivizing the distributed generation of new knowledge and the opening of possibilities across all market participants in a way that no single organization or central planner could do on their own. As economist William Baumol argued, free markets are powerful "innovation machines" that continuously enable and incentivize breakthroughs by their participants (Baumol, 2002), thereby functioning as self-refueling systems (Jacobs, 2000). This view challenges traditional economic thinking that viewed markets purely as mechanisms for efficient resource allocation (Backhouse & Medema, 2009).

Consider the contrast between Uber and Apple's App Store. Uber's marketplace is masterfully designed for allocation – efficiently matching drivers with riders in real-time. But it is intentionally not designed for generativity. Uber doesn't want its drivers innovating with new types of services or experimenting with different business models. The company maintains tight control over the core transaction, optimizing for reliability and predictability.

https://doi.org/10.1515/9783110779639-006

The App Store, on the other hand, is explicitly designed for generativity. While it provides basic allocation functions (connecting app developers with users), its real power comes from enabling and incentivizing countless developers to create applications that Apple itself could never have conceived. When the creators of RoomScan Pro developed their innovative floor-planning app that uses iPhone sensors to automatically generate property layouts, Apple did not need to know anything about architecture or real estate to profit from their innovation. The company simply created conditions where such innovations could emerge and flourish.

Flipping the Agency Problem on Its Head

What makes generative marketplaces particularly powerful is their ability to transform traditional organizational challenges into advantages. Consider the classic "agency problem" in business – the challenge that arises when one party (the agent) has more information than another (the principal). In traditional organizations, this information asymmetry is seen as a problem to be solved through monitoring and incentives (Eisenhardt, 1989; Fama, 1980; Ross, 1973).

But generative marketplaces flip this dynamic on its head. Instead of trying to overcome information asymmetries, they leverage them. The fact that potential innovators know more about their own capabilities and ideas than the platform owner becomes an advantage rather than a liability. When you reframe what agency theory would call "adverse selection" (Akerlof, 1970, n.p.) as self-selection, the agency problem becomes an agency opportunity, and the threat of cheating is turned into the possibility of learning, or even the possibility of profiting without needing to learn at all.

This self-selecting power of markets becomes particularly potent at scale, because it automates knowledge discovery by distributing it to all market participants. Rather than having to identify and approach potential innovators (an impossible task when you don't know what innovations you need), generative marketplaces allow those with relevant knowledge to self-identify and step forward. This process bypasses what economists call "meta-uncertainty" or the idea of "unknown unknowns" – the problem of not even knowing what it is that you do not know (Tajedin et al., 2019).

The Power of Large Numbers

As participation in a marketplace grows, it develops what economists call a "law of large numbers" effect. Individual errors or failed experiments get absorbed by the system, while successful innovations rise to the top. When market scale is large enough, the competition mechanism brings about necessary adjustments by inducing others "to fill the gap that arises when someone else does not fulfill the expectations" (Hayek, 2002, p. 18). This effect manifests in several ways: failed experiments are balanced by successful ones, poor quality offerings are outcompeted by better alternatives, manipulation attempts are diluted by honest participation, knowledge gaps are filled by diverse participants, and innovation dead-ends are offset by breakthrough discoveries.

Consider how this plays out in the App Store. While many apps fail to gain traction, the system as a whole continues to thrive and generate value. The platform's scale means that even if the majority of experiments fail, the successful ones can still create enormous value. And crucially, Apple bears virtually no cost from the failed experiments while automatically capturing value from every success. On the contrary, as of the time of this writing, Apple takes a minimum $99 annual fee just to grant the developer account the privilege to publish apps on the App Store, regardless of their performance.

The Power of Collective Intelligence

Beyond their role as innovation engines, generative markets serve as powerful knowledge aggregation systems. Austrian economist Friedrich Hayek was among the first to recognize this property, noting how markets effectively mobilize and coordinate fragmented knowledge dispersed among countless individuals (Hayek, 1945).

Consider prediction markets, where participants effectively "bet" on future outcomes. The aggregated prices in these markets often prove remarkably accurate at forecasting everything from product launches to election results (Wolfers & Zitzewitz, 2004). This demonstrates what James Surowiecki (2004) famously called "the wisdom of crowds" – the remarkable ability of large groups to collectively achieve outcomes that elude even expert individuals.

In fact, the price signal has long been viewed by economists as the central coordination mechanism of markets, enabling the efficient matching of supply and demand (Smith & Butler-Bowdon, 2010). The sufficiency of the price signal has also been used in arguments favoring deregulation and smaller government (Friedman, 2009). But today's generative marketplaces go far beyond simple price signals in aggregating knowledge, and owners of digital platforms typically have much more control points to leverage than a national government trying to influence an economy. To view the price signal as "enough" of a coordination mechanism for a firm-design marketplace would be to miss an enormous opportunity to nurture a more dynamic economy on your platform.

Markets as Learning Systems

Perhaps the most powerful aspect of generative markets is their ability to function as autonomous learning systems. Unlike traditional organizations where learning is often centralized and directed, generative markets create distributed learning networks where:

Failed Experiments Create Value: Even unsuccessful innovations generate valuable learning. As Phelps (2013) notes, failed ideas aren't wasted – they indicate where not to look further and often spark insights that lead to eventual successes.
Knowledge Builds Cumulatively: Each innovation becomes a foundation for future innovations. When mobile game developers discovered the power of "freemium" business models, that knowledge quickly spread and evolved across the entire app ecosystem.
Cross-Pollination Accelerates Learning: Solutions from one domain often inspire breakthroughs in others. The success of Uber's matching algorithm has influenced everything from food delivery to home services.
Learning Spreads Automatically: Successful innovations naturally propagate through the system as profit incentives drive others to observe, adapt, and improve upon them.

The power of this learning system becomes clear when we examine how mobile app marketplaces have evolved. The first iPhone apps were relatively simple utilities and games. But as developers learned from each other's successes and failures, they collectively discovered:
- New business models (subscriptions, freemium, in-app purchases, etc.)
- Novel user interface patterns (such as Tinder's swipe mechanism)
- Creative uses of device capabilities (such as using the phone's camera to scan barcodes or QR codes)
- Innovative marketing techniques (like allowing users to unlock features by watching ads)
- Breakthrough application categories (such as "disappearing content" apps and features inspired by Snapchat)

On the Terminology of "Market Generativity"

When economists like Hayek, Romer, and Phelps discussed the dynamic, innovative power of markets, they didn't use the term "generativity." Instead, they spoke of markets as discovery processes, innovation machines, or self-refueling systems. Yet when we examine what makes markets so powerful at generating new possibilities, we find it maps perfectly onto Jonathan Zittrain's definitions of generativity. Recall for example, "a system's capacity to produce unanticipated change through unfiltered contributions from broad and varied audiences" (Zittrain, 2008, p. 70).
　　Think about how this definition applies to dynamic marketplaces:
- "Unanticipated change" – Like when the App Store enables innovations Apple never imagined
- "Unfiltered contributions" – Direct participation without central control

- "Broad and varied audiences" – Diverse participants bringing different perspectives
- "System's capacity" – The market's built-in mechanisms for enabling innovation

Hayek captured this essence when he noted that market discoveries can be "unpredictable and on the whole different from those which anyone has, or could have, deliberately aimed at" (Hayek, 2002, p. 10). This is very much in line with Zittrain's notion of generativity, even though Hayek didn't explicitly use that term.

There is another crucial reason why "generativity" is a term I apply to markets in this book: in the digital age, marketplaces aren't just organic phenomena that emerge naturally – they are products that we intentionally design and build. When economists wrote about markets as innovation machines, they were typically describing naturally occurring markets in the broader economy. But today's digital platforms give us unprecedented control over marketplace architecture and operation.

This shift from observing markets to designing them changes everything. We are no longer just trying to understand how markets generate innovation; we are actively creating systems to maximize their generative potential. Just as a product designer might optimize a smartphone for durability or a car for fuel efficiency, we can now optimize marketplaces for generativity. Since the previous chapters of this book applied the notion of generativity to the unit of product, and marketplaces can essentially be designed as products, the idea of marketplace generativity seems like a natural extension of product generativity.

The next chapter goes deep into ways in which we can intentionally design and orchestrate markets for generativity.

Chapter 7
Designing Markets for Generativity

Most of our thinking about how to design and operate marketplaces is still stuck in an older paradigm that views markets primarily as allocation machines – efficiently matching buyers with sellers. As argued in the previous chapter, while this allocation function is important, it captures only a fraction of what marketplaces can do. The distinction between allocative and generative markets matters because the architecture needed to support the allocation function is not by itself sufficient to support generative marketplaces. The traditional focus on the features that market design economists have identified for improved allocation such as "thickness, non-congestion, and safety" (Roth, 2008), while important, is insufficient. As Edmund Phelps noted in his analysis of innovative economies, we need to consider other crucial elements such as "the desire of people to attempt innovation, peoples' capabilities at innovating, and the latitude society gives to innovators" (Phelps, 2015, p. 256).

In this chapter our focus is to review a variety of practical design choices and managerial decisions that go into the design and management of marketplace platforms where the ultimate goal is not just allocation but also generativity, in a way that leads to a self-refueling value-creating system.

The Three-Layered Architecture

I suggest that we view allocation as only one layer—albeit a crucial one—in a full architecture for generative marketplaces, and that we add a generation layer to prioritize the kinds of features that drive distributed innovation. However, since we know that profiting from distributed innovation is far from trivial, I suggest adding a third layer to the architecture focusing on value capture or appropriation. Therefore, the recommendations for market design in this chapter are organized around an architecture for generative marketplaces with three distinct but interconnected layers:
1. An allocation layer that provides the basic market functions such as matching buyers and sellers, processing transactions, maintaining order and safety, and creating incentives for participation.
2. A generation layer that enables and encourages innovation by providing the tools and environments needed for innovation: knowledge sharing systems, collaboration channels, development tools, and community spaces.
3. An appropriation layer that ensures value can be sustainably captured, such as business models that allow the platform owner to collect fees or "tax" the system in a way that is deemed reasonable enough to continue incentivizing participation.

https://doi.org/10.1515/9783110779639-007

Getting this architecture right is critical because generative marketplaces can become extraordinarily valuable assets for companies that successfully build and operate them. They are essentially knowledge search devices that aren't limited by the cognitive or organizational capacity of their owners. Unlike traditional research and development that requires directed search, generative marketplaces can facilitate the discovery of opportunities that their creators never even thought to look for.

The true power of a generative marketplace comes from how these layers reinforce each other. A well-designed allocation layer creates incentives that drive activity in the generation layer. The generation layer produces innovations that create value, which the appropriation layer can then help distribute value in ways that keep the entire system sustainable and encourage more innovation.

Think about how these layers work together in the App Store:
- The allocation layer connects developers with users and handles transactions
- The generation layer provides tools, documentation, and APIs that enable innovation
- The appropriation layer ensures both Apple and developers can capture value

The appropriation layer is particularly tricky because overly aggressive value capture can stifle innovation, while too little can make the marketplace unsustainable. Apple's long-running troubles and legal battles over its commissions, platform fees, and rules around in-app purchases is a perfect illustration of how hard this balancing act can be.

Beyond these three internal layers, generative marketplaces are also profoundly shaped by their broader context – the economic, social, cultural and institutional environments in which they operate. While marketplace designers cannot directly control these external factors, understanding how to influence, leverage and adapt to them can be conducive to success. From economic institutions that provide fundamental frameworks for property rights and transactions to cultural attitudes that enable or inhibit innovation, to the concentrated knowledge networks of urban centers, these contextual elements can either amplify or constrain a marketplace's generative potential.

In the following sections, we will examine each layer in detail, as well as additional external or contextual factors (see Figure 7.1). While some of the concepts that will be discussed have deep roots in economic theory, our focus will be practical and centered on one key question: how can business leaders create and manage marketplaces that are self-refueling systems (Jacobs, 2000) and innovation machines (Baumol, 2002) rather than just matching mechanisms?

The Allocation Layer: Building the Foundation of Markets

Before we can enable breakthrough innovations or foster creative experimentation, we need to build a rock-solid foundation that makes basic market functions possible. This foundation is what I call the allocation layer. In traditional marketplaces, this

Knowledge Spillover
Inflows

Knowledge Spillover
Outflows

External Factors
Economic, Political, Educational Institutions
Cultural Dynamics
Population Centers
Regulatory Environment

Appropriation Layer
Innovation-Friendly Pricing and Revenue Models
Control Points, Lock-in and Switching Costs
Data Advantage
Curation and Promotion
Ethical Distribution of Profit

Generation Layer
Range and Diversity of Ideas, Interactivity of Ideas, Intellectual Orders
Embracing Outliers, Experimentation Engine, Knowledge Broadcasts
Social Dynamics, Structured Serendipity, Memory Mechanisms
Boundary Resources, Innovation Toolkits
Standards and Interoperability
Enabling Organization among Innovators

Allocation Layer
Market Thickness (Participation Mechanisms and Incentives)
Efficient Matching (Structured Discovery)
Trust and Safety

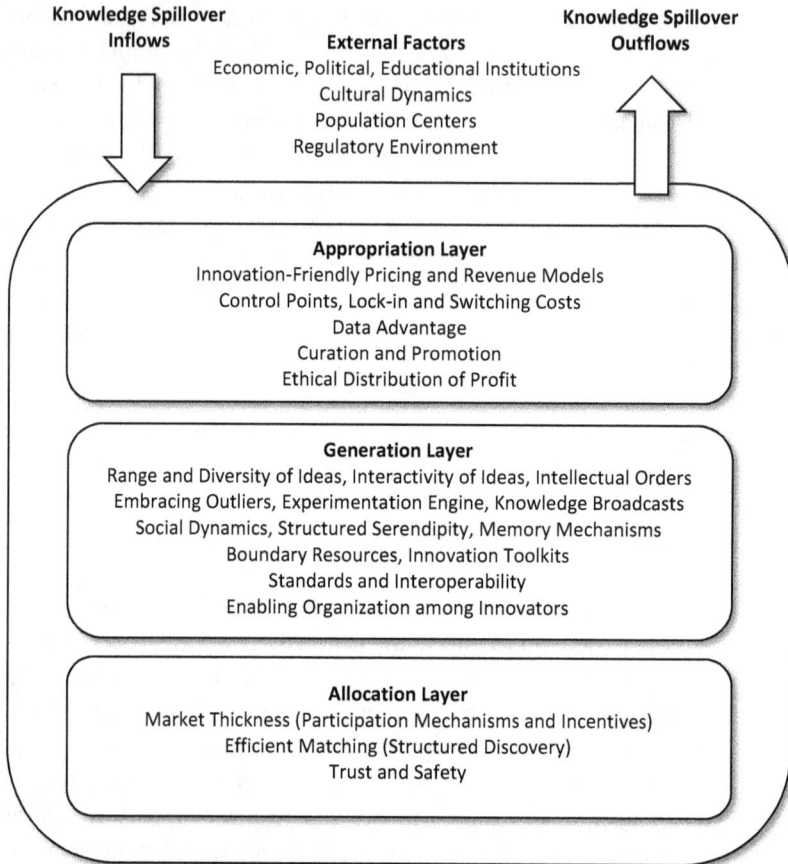

Figure 7.1: A suggested Architecture for Generative Marketplaces.

layer focuses solely on efficiency—matching buyers with sellers, processing transactions, and maintaining order. Think of how Uber's marketplace relentlessly optimizes for quick, reliable matches between riders and drivers. It is true that Uber is not a generative marketplace (because it doesn't do much beyond allocation), but allocation is something that every market needs to get right, regardless of whether or not it is designed to be generative. Therefore, even generative marketplaces have something to learn from allocative marketplaces like Uber.

The allocation layer rests on three fundamental pillars referred to in the market design literature as thickness, non-congestion, and safety (Roth, 2008). Here, we use slightly different labels to capture the core ideas: market thickness, efficient matching, trust and safety. See Table 7.1 for a summary of the ideas in this section.

Table 7.1: Components of the Allocation Layer in the Architecture of Generative Marketplaces.

Element and Purpose	Challenges	Key Strategies	Examples
Market Thickness: Ensures enough participants on all sides of the marketplace to enable reliable matching, reduce transaction uncertainty, and foster innovation.	– Solving the "chicken-and-egg" problem where each side waits for the other. – Attracting the right participants who contribute to and benefit from innovation.	– Start with a focused niche to build initial density. – Offer standalone value before network effects emerge. – Partner with established brands and complementary platforms.	– Bubble leveraged professional developers and plugin creators to reduce user uncertainty. – Facebook initially targeted Ivy League schools before scaling. – Webflow built its niche in professional U.S. web designers.
Efficient Matching: Balances speed in market clearing with enough time for participants to discover, evaluate, and pursue innovative matches.	– Maintaining "productive friction" for discovery without slowing transactions. – Balancing transactional efficiency with creative exploration needs.	– Implement "innovation-friendly friction" to allow for evaluation and comparison. – Use layered search and recommendation tools to surface unexpected options. – Enable discovery for novel connections.	– Uber allows driver bidding for optimized matches. – Upwork supports portfolio evaluations and detailed proposal comparisons. – Coda's marketplace provides efficient yet deep documentation for innovative use cases.
Trust and Safety: Builds secure systems that foster confidence among participants to transact, experiment, and innovate while mitigating abuse and risk.	– Balancing openness with sufficient security to encourage participation. – Establishing robust trust mechanisms without discouraging creativity or raising barriers to entry.	– Layered infrastructure: reputation systems, verification, and community moderation. – Combine automation (e.g., AI monitoring) with human oversight. – Provide clear rules and supportive standards.	– Notion handles financial transactions centrally for user protection. – Adalo prioritizes robust creator verification. – Coda's Pack marketplace combines openness with trusted usage mechanisms.

Market Thickness: Building the Foundation for Generative Innovation

The first crucial pillar of the allocation layer is market thickness – having enough participants on all sides of the marketplace to enable reliable matching and transactions. This challenge is particularly acute for generative marketplaces because they need to attract participants who might not immediately see the relevance of the market to their needs. Thickness essentially reduces transaction uncertainty – with enough active participants, both sides gain assurance that they can find matches, or find alternative matches if any particular transaction fails.

Relative market thickness has been a key advantage for the Bubble no-code platform compared to other no-code platforms, given its head start in this market. With many potential users of no-code software development platforms being hesitant to adopt this new approach to software development, Bubble enjoys the advantage of having enough professional developers, freelancers, and plugin developers available to provide options for users, and conversely enough users to incentivize the developers. Over time, this moat becomes deep enough that new players will have a difficult time competing with Bubble, even if they have some other highly desirable features.

In order to create thickness, almost every marketplace faces what observers have called the "cold-start problem" (Chen, 2021, n.p.) or the chicken-and-egg dilemma: participants on each side will only join if there are enough participants on the other side (Parker et al., 2016). However, building a marketplace on top of an already generative product is often feasible because a community of innovators has already been attracted to the product as users, and they are often curious to learn from other users and eager to monetize their own innovations with the product. This can be seen for example in the community of users who started building custom GPTs as soon as this feature was made available in OpneAI's ChatGPT product. In what follows we discuss some of the strategies that can be used to help build market thickness, despite the chicken-and-egg problem.

Strategic Approaches to Building Thickness
One crucial strategy involves ensuring the platform provides immediate value even without a marketplace having formed around it, a.k.a. "single player mode" (Rachitsky, 2023). This can be achieved through core features that provide standalone value, educational content and resources, tools that help participants prepare for marketplace activity, and data or insights that benefit early participants. Notion exemplifies this approach with their template marketplace. Before launch, they built a powerful core product that attracted millions of users. When they launched the marketplace, they not only had a built-in audience but ensured template creators could use their own templates internally even if no one purchased them. This meant creation had immediate value regardless of marketplace success.

Sometimes the platform itself needs to act as a market participant initially to ensure that the model works and to kindle the supply side in order to attract users on the demand side. Uber famously used this approach in their evolution from a taxi fleet provider to a marketplace matching riders and drivers. Apple's App Store launched with a suite of Apple-created apps, ensuring users had immediate value while third-party developers came on board. When Coda launched their Packs marketplace, they created several essential Packs themselves to demonstrate the platform's potential while attracting third-party creators.

Successful platforms often leverage existing networks by partnering with established brands and communities, working with influencers who can bring their followers, building integrations with complementary platforms, and creating cooperative relationships with existing market players. Webflow exemplifies this through their partnerships with design communities and agencies. They worked with prominent design firms and educators who already had audiences interested in web design, helping them quickly build marketplace participation.

Building Robust Participation Mechanisms

One of the most powerful architectural choices involves enabling participants to play multiple roles in the marketplace. Notion's users naturally move between creating and consuming templates, customizing them for their needs, and sharing modified versions back to the marketplace. Even large organizations both consume templates and share their workflow templates back to the community. This fluidity between roles helps build marketplace activity organically.

Successful marketplaces create non-monetary incentives beyond direct financial rewards, using reputation systems, gamification, and community recognition to drive participation. Adalo's marketplace, for instance, highlights successful creators through their showcase section and community spotlights, creating social incentives for participation.

Managing Strategic Growth

Successful marketplaces often start small and focused rather than trying to serve everyone immediately. Consider Facebook's early strategy of focusing exclusively on college campuses – first Harvard, then other Ivy League schools, before eventually opening to everyone. This concentrated approach helped them build the density needed for network effects to take hold. Similarly, while many digital marketplaces can theoretically serve global markets immediately, successful ones often focus geographically at first.

Another important tool that can be leveraged by marketplace owners is to use strategic subsidies or incentives. For example, it often makes sense for a platform owner to lose money on at least one side of the market (provide services at a cost) just to increase the user base for a period of time (Rochet & Tirole, 2003, 2006). This is common practice in many platform businesses. For example, video game consoles are often sold at below cost so that the platform can later make money by "selling" its large user base to game developers through royalties and licensing fees. Ad-supported business models from newspapers to various websites all provide their software to users for free so that they can grow one side of the market such that the other side (advertisers) are willing to pay for their attention.

Innovation contests can also be leveraged (Terwiesch & Xu, 2008). When Coda launched their Packs marketplace in 2022, they implemented a $1 million "Maker Fund" to incentivize early creators. But importantly, they didn't just offer money – they provided development support, promotional opportunities, and special access to beta features. This comprehensive approach helped attract not just developers but domain experts who could create specialized tools.

By establishing a strong foundation of market thickness – through strategic focus, standalone value creation, robust participation mechanisms, and careful evolutionary growth – platforms create the conditions necessary for a dynamic marketplace. Without sufficient engaged participants, even the best tools for innovation will go unused. But with the right foundation in place, platforms can focus on enabling and incentivizing unpredicted innovation at scale.

Efficient Matching: Balancing Market Clearing with Discovery

The second pillar of the allocation layer addresses a sophisticated design challenge: how to structure the matching process to optimize both the efficiency and the effectiveness of the matching process. This idea is what economists call "non-congestion" – a state where "transaction speed is sufficiently rapid to ensure market clearing but slow enough to allow participants to seek alternatives" (Agrawal et al., 2015, p. 977).

Even marketplaces that appear to operate instantly must carefully orchestrate the temporal dynamics of matching. Consider Uber's apparently instantaneous driver matching. The app actually spends crucial seconds allowing multiple drivers to bid for your ride while letting you evaluate options like price and arrival time. This brief but essential window of discovery and choice enables market efficiency through what we might call "productive friction" – just enough structure to make matching efficient, but sufficient time and space for proper evaluation.

This temporal balancing act becomes particularly critical in marketplaces built around knowledge work and innovation. The matching process must be efficient enough to maintain marketplace momentum but deliberate enough to enable informed decisions. On platforms like Upwork, both sides need adequate time to evaluate fit: clients must review portfolios and compare proposals, while freelancers need to assess potential clients and projects. Yet, when a job ad is posted on Upwork, proposals can start coming in a matter of minutes. By allowing clients to set screening questions, the platform provides a mechanism for clients to weed out irrelevant proposals and find the best matches.

Search and recommendation systems play a crucial role in achieving non-congestion. Comparison mechanisms need to make evaluation straightforward while surfacing the kind of detailed information that can help market participants make matching decisions. The Upwork platform uses its own AI algorithm to suggest best matches, and shows badges on freelancer profiles that have particular accomplishments or success rates. It allows clients to invite keyword-matching freelancers or freelancers they have worked with before to apply for their new job posting in addition to the proposals that come in regularly. The platforms allows clients to short-list and have chat conversations or meetings with potential hires before finalizing a hire. On the other side, freelancers are also shown detailed information about the history of the client, how many hires they have made, and how much money they have spent on the platform.

Trust and Safety: Creating a Secure Space for Innovation

As Kornberger et al. (2017) argue, trust and safety systems form an essential "evaluative infrastructure" that enables both basic market function and generative innovation:
- Rankings and ratings that help participants navigate quality
- Recognition systems that create innovation incentives
- Discovery mechanisms that surface available offerings
- Reputational capital that creators can leverage

The core challenge lies in balancing protection with possibility. Marketplace operators must create enough trust for participants to confidently experiment while avoiding controls that would stifle creativity. The safety and trust infrastructure for generativity requires systems that simultaneously protect and enable innovation.

Building Trust Through Layered Infrastructure
Looking across successful generative marketplaces, we see a number of key trust mechanisms working together:
- **Rules and Standards.** As Tadelis (2016) notes, clear marketplace rules create the predictability participants need to invest in innovation enable. The rules aren't just restrictions – they make experimentation less risky.
- **Identity and Verification.** Authentication systems help alleviate the problem of fake identities, such as agency organizations pretending to be individuals, or other types of misrepresentation.

- **Payment and Settlement Infrastructure.** Secure, reliable payment systems reduce transaction friction and risk.
- **Community-Powered Quality.** Many marketplaces effectively distribute trust-building functions to their communities, leveraging distributed governance.
- **Intellectual Property Protection.** A key motivator for innovators in many cases is to know that the effort they put into their innovations can be protected as a source of advantage at least for a reasonable amount of time. Our study of the Bubble ecosystem platform revealed an interesting trade-off here: Bubble plugin developers learned immensely about how to build plugins for Bubble from "free" plugins that were forced by the platform to be open source but also benefited from keeping the source code closed for plugins that they wanted to sell for profit.

The Generative Power of Trust

When designed thoughtfully, these systems provide the security infrastructure for generativity – the confidence that enables participants to experiment with novel offerings, invest in creating high-quality contributions, try products from unknown creators, build on others' innovations, and share knowledge and best practices.

As marketplaces grow, maintaining trust becomes both more crucial and more challenging. Technology provides powerful tools for building trust at scale through:
- Reputation systems that create ongoing incentives for quality
- Automated monitoring that can quickly detect issues
- Community moderation tools that leverage collective intelligence
- Clear dispute resolution processes that maintain confidence

The most successful marketplaces thoughtfully combine automated systems with human oversight and community participation. However, with the new availability of LLM-driven AI agents, many of these monitoring and moderation mechanisms are being automated in unprecedented ways. For example, on his popular website Nomad List (nomads.com), Pieter Levels has automated the entire process of content moderation on community forums with AI agents, and comments that, as a result, it has never been "so chill and friendly and free of spam as now."[1]

Conclusion: The Allocation Layer as Innovation Infrastructure

The allocation layer provides the fundamental infrastructure that every marketplace needs to function. Market thickness ensures enough participants for meaningful

---

1 https://x.com/levelsio/status/1764416587862303025

transactions. Efficient matching helps participants find and evaluate opportunities without getting overwhelmed. Trust and safety systems create the confidence needed to participate, experiment, and innovate in the market.

Bubble.io's marketplace has made efforts to address market thickness, efficient matching, and trust and safety, with varying degrees of success. To foster market thickness, Bubble has focused on specific segments and supported a diversity of plugins, although this also brings the challenge of managing the quality of these resources. Efficient matching is supported through search and review systems, but there is still room for improvements to aid in discovery of useful solutions. Trust and safety are partially addressed through user ratings and documentation, but there is a lack of formal quality control or IP protection mechanisms, leaving developers to have to take their own measures. In the Bubble.io ecosystem, trust is fostered through a combination of community engagement and user-driven accountability. The platform encourages users to publicly share their work, which fosters a culture of transparency and mutual support. The community ethos is generally to credit and support each other's work, which adds to the culture of trust. The forum serves as a space where users ask for help, share ideas, and build relationships, which also increases trust and mitigates the fear of failure, encouraging more active participation and experimentation

In the next section, we will explore how the generation layer builds on this foundation to actively foster innovation and drive value creation at scale.

The Generation Layer: Spurring Innovation at Scale

The generation layer is where the true magic of marketplace generativity happens. While the allocation layer creates the foundation, the generation layer helps us go beyond the mental model of markets as matching mechanisms and transforms a marketplace into an engine of continuous innovation. This is where users become creators, where ideas collide and combine in unexpected ways, and where a platform can tap into the distributed creativity of thousands or millions of minds.

When economists use the term "knowledge spillovers" (Glaeser et al., 1992, n.p.) to refer to the flow of ideas between people and projects that sparks new innovations, it can sound like something that happens by accident. This terminology is again rooted in the idea that the main function of markets is matching, and anything else that happens is an "externality" or "spillover" effect that wasn't in the original model. But spurring innovation at scale doesn't happen by accident. Successful platform companies that pursue a generativity advantage intentionally design and orchestrate their generation layers to amplify creativity and propagate innovation at scale.

A fundamental insight about the origin of innovations is that they emerge from connecting and recombining existing ideas in novel ways (Johnson, 2011; Pentland,

12

2014). The role of the generation layer is to make these connections more likely and more fruitful. This requires at least two critical elements identified by Nobel laureate Edmund Phelps (2013): The range and diversity of ideas available for combination, and the mechanisms that enable those ideas to interact and combine effectively. These ideas guide the discussion in this section (see Table 7.2).

Table 7.2: Components of the Generation Layer in the Architecture of Generative Marketplaces.

Element and Purpose	Challenges	Key Strategies	Examples
Range and Diversity of Ideas and Participants	– Attracting participants with diverse expertise and perspectives. – Avoiding echo chambers and groupthink.	– Highlight diverse and unique contributions. – Encourage dissent and intellectual debate to refine ideas. – Enable broad participation across use cases. – Embrace outliers and spotlight unconventional ideas.	– Airbnb evolved from air mattresses to unique stays like treehouses and airplanes. – Wikipedia fosters constructive debates through its Talk pages. – Kickstarter and Figma showcase outlier innovations to inspire broader creativity.
Interactivity of Ideas	– Bridging geographic, cognitive, and social distances. – Preventing isolation of ideas while avoiding overload.	– Facilitate interdisciplinary exchanges via forums and structured discussions. – Use robust archiving tools for temporal knowledge. – Encourage structured serendipity with recommendation systems and discovery tools.	– Bubble.io's forums foster organic interactions and unexpected knowledge sharing. – Upwork's tools enhance cross-domain collaborations. – Stack Overflow archives community-generated solutions for reuse and cross-temporal learning.

Table 7.2 (continued)

Element and Purpose	Challenges	Key Strategies	Examples
Experimentation Engine	– Reducing fear of failure. – Capturing insights from both successes and failures. – Managing costs of experimentation.	– Make experimentation accessible and low-cost. – Share aggregated insights and frontier knowledge across the ecosystem. – Create feedback loops for continuous learning.	– OpenAI's custom GPTs enable accessible experimentation. – Shopify shares trend reports and best practices for app developers.
Boundary Resources and Innovation Toolkits	– Making tools accessible to non-developers. – Balancing flexibility with reliability. – Ensuring scalability.	– Develop no-code interfaces and APIs. – Provide libraries of pre-built components for reuse. – Build learning resources to empower users. – Design knowledge-structuring tools to capture and refine insights.	– Android and iOS app SDKs provide developers with the tools to build apps for these marketplaces. – Roblox Studio provides accessible game development tools for non-technical creators.
Standards and Interoperability	– Avoiding fragmentation while encouraging innovation. – Managing evolving standards in the ecosystem.	– Develop clear design guidelines and quality benchmarks. – Treat standards as living documents that adapt to community needs. – Balance creativity and consistency. – Enable combinatorial innovation by ensuring interoperability.	– APIs and SDKs provide standards for developers. – Roblox ensures that whatever is built on the Roblox Studio is compatible with its platform.

Table 7.2 (continued)

Element and Purpose	Challenges	Key Strategies	Examples
Enabling Organization	– Supporting diverse team structures. – Helping teams scale operations while fostering collaboration.	– Provide tools for team collaboration and analytics. – Facilitate onboarding and resource sharing. – Support scalability for organizations within the ecosystem. – Leverage platform knowledge to recommend complementary team members and opportunities.	– Shopify's Partner Program supports agencies and team scaling. – Roblox enables small studios to handle large-scale projects. – Bubble.io provides Team and Enterprise features and pricing.

The Power of Diversity for Innovation

The more user-innovators you have on your platform, the more innovation experiments are being conducted by these users. A larger number of experiments is especially important when the statistical distribution of potential outcomes is heavy-tailed, because it increases the chances of outlier successes (Jamshidi et al., 2025; Keyhani & Jamshidi, 2025; Taleb, 2020). And indeed, phenomena involving entrepreneurship and innovation do typically have heavy-tailed power law distributions (Crawford et al., 2015).

Creating generative thickness is not just a numbers game, although quantity is important. When participants bring different backgrounds, personalities, education, training, and thought processes to the ecosystem, this diversity expands what complexity theorists call the "adjacent possible" – the space of potential new combinations that could emerge from the given state of a system (Kauffman, 1993). In a system richer with diversity, innovative ideas that were previously out of reach become more likely to form from the rich soup of possible connections, fueling the emergence of unforeseen directions in research, collaboration, or design. Over time, this interplay of diverse ideas enriches the collective imagination and paves the way for discoveries, products, and solutions that would have been impossible in a less diverse environment.

The diversity of participants not only enriches the supply side but also the demand side, and these two have a reinforcing effect on each other (Rietveld & Eggers, 2018). With enough diverse participants, creators feel more confident trying novel approaches since there's likely to be some audience interested in their innovations. This reduces the risk of experimentation and creates a virtuous cycle – more diversity leads to more experimentation, which attracts even more diverse participants. When users are willing to try new things, suppliers are more likely to experiment with novel offerings. Conversely, diverse innovations on the supply side expand users' horizons, opening up new possibilities they hadn't considered before.

Airbnb illustrates how this insurance effect works in practice. The platform began with a narrow focus on air mattresses in spare rooms (hence the original name "AirBed & Breakfast"). But by cultivating diversity on both the host and guest sides, they created conditions where hosts felt safe experimenting with increasingly novel offerings, and guests were interested to try them. Today the platform includes everything from treehouses to converted airplanes, each finding their specific audience within the marketplace's diverse user base.

Building this kind of generative diversity requires intentional design choices that sometimes go against traditional marketplace wisdom. Imagine if Uber encouraged the same kind of diversity among its drivers as Airbnb encourages among its hosts. The platform would risk the reliability that users expect from it. While many platforms optimize for rapid matching of the most common use cases, generative marketplaces need to preserve and highlight diversity even when it creates some friction. They need discovery mechanisms that expose participants to different perspectives and possibilities rather than just showing them more of what they already know they want.

The Intellectual Orders of Generativity

One crucial yet underappreciated role of marketplace designers is to harness diversity in such a way that it actively disrupts groupthink and echo chambers that often inhibit creativity (Janis, 2013; Pariser, 2011). This means creating mechanisms for constructive dispute, dissent, and intellectual debate. As Mike (2017) argues, encouraging innovation in an economy depends on creating "intellectual orders" within economic systems—sets of shared rules that enable participants to consult established knowledge, freely test novel ideas, and engage in genuine persuasion when ideas conflict.

Wikipedia exemplifies how this disciplined search can unfold in practice. Though Wikipedia is not a traditional marketplace, it relies on various alternative incentives (e.g., reputational benefits, shared interest in accurate content) and has well-defined rules and norms for debate. Contributors consult an evolving body of articles, propose edits grounded in reliable sources, and discuss contested points on Talk pages to reach some measure of consensus. This process illustrates Mike's (2017, n.p.) emphasis on "consultation" (through existing articles and citations), "competition" (as editors challenge one another's claims), and "persuasion" (when participants negotiate improvements to the content). The systematic structure of Wikipedia's editorial process, combined with ongoing discussions, helps refine knowledge and reduce bias.

Similarly, Twitter's (X.com's) "Community Notes" system—and its prospective adoption by other social media—shows how platforms can encourage constructive disagreement rather than merely amplifying polarized opinions. Community Notes invites users to attach context or corrections to tweets, with the broader community then evaluating whether those notes are helpful. This arrangement echoes Mike's observation that openness and structured dialogue can spur meaningful debate.

Embracing Outliers as Potential Game Changers

Successful marketplaces increasingly recognize the value of outliers and unusual cases. Rather than optimizing solely for the most common or popular use scenarios, dynamic, knowledge-generative platforms create avenues for spotlighting disruptive ideas that can seed major breakthroughs. As Kuhn (2009) argued, anomalies and unexpected observations often serve as the catalysts for paradigm shifts in scientific communities. Translated into marketplace design, these "outliers" can open up new directions of inquiry, revealing untapped sources of value before they become mainstream. Embracing them, therefore, is a deliberate strategy to remain on the frontier of innovation rather than settling into intellectual complacency.

The importance of embracing outliers is greater when the statistical distribution of potential innovations is more heavy tailed. It is well known that contexts involving entrepreneurship and innovation often have heavy-tailed power law distributions (Crawford et al., 2015). In such settings, it is always possible that new outliers may emerge, and that they could be much better than the best outcomes observed so far (Taleb, 2020).

A variety of generative platforms such as Kickstarter, Figma, Notion, Bubble, and others have a section on their website devoted to highlighting various user innovations, and also highlight these in various email communications. These mechanisms can be leveraged to highlight unconventional or experimental approaches that illustrate possibilities of what can be done on the platform that other users may not have thought of. Highlighting the outlier "rock stars" (Booyavi & Crawford, 2023) or "lead users" (Von Hippel, 1986) who often pioneer new solutions ahead of mass adoption is a great practice for embracing outliers. However, platforms would benefit from highlighting a diversity of lead users so as to avoid converging too quickly on ideas around the best use cases and standard design patterns championed by a narrow group of lead users, and to keep the design space open for reimagining possibilities.

Burt's (2010) work on "structural holes" shows how bridging disconnected or marginal networks can spark creative insights, precisely because novel combinations of knowledge emerge where mainstream and fringe perspectives intersect. In parallel, minority influence theory highlights how original viewpoints can persist against consensus to drive deeper exploration (Nemeth & Kwan, 1987). For platform marketpla-ces, building in mechanisms—like specialized forums, public "debate" tools, or discov-erable experimental channels—that amplify 'maverick' ideas can help keep the sys-tem fresh, flexible, and primed for the kind of breakthroughs that sustain both the platform and its participants over the long term.

At the same time, platforms must remain vigilant about disinformation and algo-rithmic manipulation that can hijack the very openness meant to foster innovation. Research suggests that false stories spread faster and further than factual information in networked environments (Vosoughi et al., 2018), underscoring the importance of thoughtful content moderation and community guidelines. Unconstrained digital spaces risk reinforcing filter bubbles, thereby amplifying extreme or misleading con-tent (Pariser, 2011). To strike the right balance, marketplaces can deploy transparent policies and user-driven checks—such as community fact-checking, multi-stakeholder review boards, or iterative feedback loops—that prevent harmful distortions while still encouraging unconventional thinking. This helps ensure that the pursuit of out-lier ideas remains constructive and that the marketplace's generative potential is not undermined by misinformation.

In the end, the arguments in favor of embracing outliers and the clash of ideas in generative platforms are rooted in the same arguments as those in favor of free speech in society. As eloquently stated by John Stuart Mill in his treatise *On Liberty* (1859, p. 33):

> If all mankind minus one, were of one opinion, and only one person were of the contrary opin-ion, mankind would be no more justified in silencing that one person, than he, if he had the power, would be justified in silencing mankind . . . the peculiar evil of silencing the expression of an opinion is, that it is robbing the human race; posterity as well as the existing generation; those who dissent from the opinion, still more than those who hold it. If the opinion is right, they are deprived of the opportunity of exchanging error for truth: if wrong, they lose, what is almost as great a benefit, the clearer perception and livelier impression of truth, produced by its colli-sion with error.

Making Ideas Interactive: The Communication Infrastructure

While diversity creates the potential for innovation, it is the interactions between ideas and people that pave the path for that diversity to bear fruit. The market de-signer has significant control over who talks to who and when—and this control can be leveraged strategically to enhance generativity.

Many platform companies make the mistake of viewing communication features simply as ways to facilitate transactions. They focus on mimicking face-to-face com-munication or providing basic messaging capabilities. But the most successful genera-tive marketplaces recognize that digital communication can actually enhance knowl-edge sharing in ways that in-person interaction cannot.

Consider these unique advantages of digital communication:

1. **Thoughtful Articulation**: Digital formats allow participants to carefully compose and edit their ideas before sharing them, often leading to clearer expression of complex concepts.
2. **Rich Media Integration**: Unlike verbal communication, digital platforms enable the seamless combination of text, images, code snippets, and interactive elements to convey ideas more effectively.
3. **Permanent Record**: Digital communications can be searched, referenced, and built upon long after they occur, creating a growing knowledge base.
4. **Scalable Distribution**: Once captured, knowledge can be shared with any number of participants at near-zero additional cost.

Facilitating the interactivity of ideas can be viewed as bridging distances that otherwise hinder their interaction. We can think of multiple such dimensions of distance (Madhok et al., 2015):

- Geographic Distance: Digital tools enable collaboration across continents, eliminating physical barriers to innovation (Forman & Zeebroeck, 2012).
- Cognitive Distance: Marketplaces can bridge domains of expertise, allowing ideas from different fields to collide and recombine (Hein et al., 2019).
- Temporal Distance: By recording and archiving knowledge, platforms connect today's innovators with past insights and future possibilities (Consoli & Patrucco, 2009).
- Social Distance: Communication tools allow diverse communities and individuals to collaborate, overcoming cultural or social barriers (Bleakley et al., 2022).

Bridging ideas requires a vibrant knowledge sharing ecosystem that not only aggregates existing insights but accelerates the creation of new ones. From community forums and discussion spaces that facilitate the cross-pollination of ideas to comprehensive documentation and tutorials that help with learning curves (van der Geest & van Angeren, 2023), these systems ensure that the collective intelligence of the marketplace is continuously captured, refined, and built upon. By codifying and disseminating knowledge across time and space, they transform the marketplace into a self-reinforcing engine of intellectual growth.

However, this ease of information sharing comes with its own challenges. As Jones, Ravid, and Rafaeli (2004) found in their research, information overload can actually hinder effective knowledge exchange. Successful platforms need mechanisms to help users "separate the wheat from the chaff."

Platform designers face an interesting strategic tension when it comes to communication features. On one hand, limiting communication between parties can help prevent users from side-stepping the platform to avoid fees. On the other hand, these same limitations can severely hinder knowledge flows that drive innovation.

Upwork's evolution illustrates this balance. While the platform maintains certain restrictions to prevent disintermediation, they have created rich communication channels that allow detailed discussion of methods, tools, and approaches between clients and freelancers. These discussions often generate valuable knowledge that benefits the broader community – freelancers learn new techniques, clients better understand best practices, and the overall quality of work on the platform improves.

Social Processes and Serendipitous Discovery

One often-overlooked aspect of generative marketplaces is the role of social processes in driving innovation. Studies show that creativity flourishes when the brain is nudged to connect unexpected dots, often by stepping away from the familiar and encountering new inputs in unfamiliar settings. For example, creativity researchers have found that sudden insights—the "Aha!" moments—often arise when the mind shifts its focus or takes a detour from routine thought patterns (Pentland, 2014). If creative breakthroughs happen when people are exposed to diverse, seemingly unrelated ideas in new contexts, then if you have any control over the environment in which people ideate and innovate, you can try to make these exposures more likely. This is sometimes referred to as enabling "structured serendipity" (Zweig, 2011).

Generative marketplaces can intentionally design for structured serendipity by creating environments where diverse participants and ideas naturally collide. This might mean fostering interdisciplinary exchanges through open forums, affinity spaces (Gee, 2017), curating tools that enable unexpected combinations, or even providing recommendation systems that surface unconventional projects or solutions. Platforms like GitHub and Bubble excel at this, as developers stumble upon coding innovations or modular plugins from unrelated projects that inspire novel applications. By ensuring that participants are exposed to a broad variety of inputs, these marketplaces mimic the process of venturing into new intellectual terrain and uncovering hidden opportunities.

In the digital world, one of the main available types of space for structured serendipity is online forums. Generative platforms can foster community forums that encourage open discussions beyond specific transactions, publishing community-driven stories and insights, integrating gamification elements to make exploration engaging, and linking with social media profiles to enable informal interactions. For instance, Bubble's community forums have become a strategic asset, where users share tips, techniques, and resources and connect with developers and plugin creators, often through organic side-effects of other conversations. As one Bubble user explained, "If I had a question and didn't know how to do something, I would look on the forum. And usually, I would find someone talking about that thing I didn't know how to do."

The Memory Challenge: Building Collective Knowledge

Market economies are themselves mechanisms for the accumulation of knowledge, or as Metcalfe & Ramlogan (2005, p. 661) put it, "a system for standing on the shoulders of giants." Knowledge grows in marketplaces through processes of variation, selection, and refinement—a process fueled by the constant interplay of individual insights and collective sensemaking. When you have the ability to influence the digital communication infrastructure underlying a marketplace, you can take steps to improve these processes and enhance the market's organizational memory system.

Digital platforms can capture, organize, and make searchable the accumulated wisdom of their communities. The key is to design systems where knowledge is actively maintained, improved, and applied. Platforms that excel at this task provide:

- **Searchable archives** that allow users to quickly locate relevant, high-quality information.
- **Knowledge structuring tools** like tagging, categorization, and hierarchy that make vast repositories navigable.
- **Mechanisms for updating and refining knowledge**, so that outdated or inaccurate content doesn't erode trust or utility.
- **Linking capabilities** that connect related information, enabling users to uncover patterns and relationships they might not have anticipated.

Consider Stack Overflow. Its design goes beyond solving individual coding problems. Through its structured Q&A format and reputation system, the platform ensures that accurate and useful information rises to the surface, while conversations and clarifications provide rich context. Over time, this system has captured a growing repository of development knowledge that has effectively captured the collective wisdom of millions of developers in a form that is immediately useful to others.

The Experimentation Engine: From Natural Selection to Active Learning

Digital platforms have a unique opportunity to influence the structure, rules, and features of their ecosystems in ways that amplify the knowledge accumulation process described by Metcalfe and Ramlogan (2005). By designing platforms to actively facilitate the capture, refinement, and dissemination of knowledge, they can accelerate and enhance the knowledge accumulation process. This involves building systems that intentionally channel the natural variation, selection, and refinement processes that drive innovation.

Unlike traditional markets, which rely on organic and often slow mechanisms for coordinating knowledge, digital platforms have direct control over key affordances such as data collection, algorithmic sorting, and user interaction design. This control allows them to lower the cost of experimentation, curate and synthesize insights, and ensure that knowledge is more easily shared and applied across their user base. Platforms that embrace this role as knowledge orchestrators can transform the uneven and unpredictable accumulation of knowledge into a more dynamic, intentionally catalyzed process of innovation. They can collect detailed data about both successes and failures, analyze patterns, and share insights in ways that would be impossible in conventional settings.

A helpful model of how platforms can orchestrate knowledge accumulation in the market is a cycle that can be referred to as the "Experimentation Engine" (see Figure 7.2). In this approach, the platform actively strives to:

1. Make experimentation low-cost and accessible
2. Capture knowledge from both successes and failures
3. Analyze patterns across many experiments
4. Broadcast insights back to the community
5. Enable quick application of learnings to new experiments

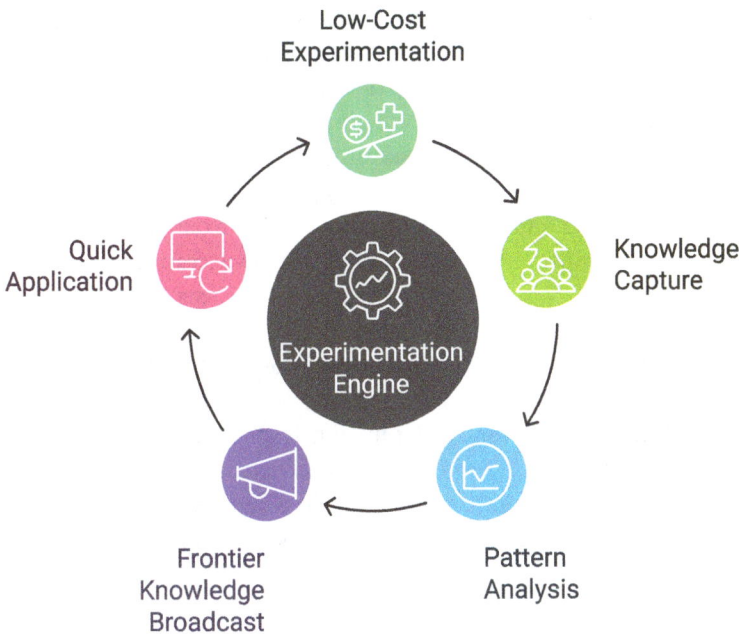

Figure 7.2: The Experimentation Engine.

A strong example of the "Experimentation Engine" in a generative ecosystem is OpenAI's API platform for its GPT models, although many of the same practices are increasingly adopted by other companies in the industry as well (such as Anthropic with its Claude models and Google with its Gemini models). This platform fosters a vibrant ecosystem where developers and businesses can experiment, share insights, and build distributed innovations at scale. The practices of igniting the experimentation engine in this ecosystem include:

1. **Low-cost and accessible experimentation:** OpenAI provides an accessible API that allows developers and companies to quickly integrate AI capabilities into their applications. With flexible pricing tiers and a pay-as-you-go model, it lowers the barriers to experimentation. This encourages a wide range of users—from startups to enterprises—to test new ideas without significant upfront investment.
2. **Capturing knowledge from successes and failures:** The platform collects feedback and usage data from API interactions, capturing insights into what works well and where users encounter challenges. Developers also share their successes and struggles through forums, GitHub projects, and third-party communities like Slack or Discord groups, contributing to a growing knowledge base.
3. **Analyzing patterns across experiments:** OpenAI actively analyzes data across use cases to understand patterns in how the API is being used. This informs improvements to the models (e.g., making them more aligned, versatile, or reliable) and helps surface best practices for building applications with AI. Public examples, like identifying common failure modes of the models, show the platform's ability to extract generalizable insights from distributed experimentation. Anthropic's comprehensive research reports based on anonymized data from user interactions with Claude are also a great example.
4. **Broadcasting insights back to the community:** OpenAI shares knowledge through detailed documentation, case studies, blog posts, and public updates on improvements to its models and best practices for use. For example, it publishes guidelines on prompt engineering or shares examples of successful integrations to inspire the community. This transparency ensures that insights flow back to innovators, helping them refine their approaches.
5. **Enabling quick application of learnings:** OpenAI provides cookbooks with example code snippets in multiple programming languages. These resources enable developers to quickly adopt and implement insights from the platform's broader ecosystem of experiments. By offering clear, practical examples—such as how to fine-tune a model, orchestrate agents, or use structured outputs—OpenAI ensures that users can immediately apply best practices and take advantage of their product's leading edge features.

It is important to note that implementing just one or two parts of the experimentation engine well is not enough. Each element of the cycle depends on the others and if one element is missing or doesn't work well, the circuit breaks.

The Platform's Privileged Knowledge: Broadcasting the Frontier

What makes platform companies uniquely powerful in their ability to foster experimentation engines is their access to market activity data and the ability to aggregate learnings from distributed experiments in real-time and at scale. Unlike governments, which have limited monitoring capabilities, or individual companies, which can only learn from a limited number of experiments, platforms can gather granular data about all experiments in their ecosystem. Not all of them appreciate the strategic value of doing so.

Platform companies have unprecedented access to what economists call "frontier knowledge" (Agarwal & Gaule, 2020) – the latest insights about the leading edge innovations, and about what is working and what is not in their marketplaces. Access to frontier knowledge is of the utmost importance for innovators who want to build on this knowledge and expand the frontier (Iaria et al., 2018). The most successful platforms actively broadcast this knowledge to help their entire community level up more quickly.

They do this through various channels:
– Regular state-of-the-platform updates
– Trend reports and analysis
– Best practice guides
– Highlighting and promoting exemplars
– Case studies of successful innovations
– Analysis of common failure patterns

This approach leverages the position of the platform operator to intentionally spur "knowledge spillover" effects (Agarwal et al., 2007; Glaeser et al., 1992), such that the lessons learned by one participant benefit the entire community. The key is making this knowledge sharing systematic rather than leaving it to chance, taking advantage of the platform owner/operator's privileged knowledge from access to all the market activity data.

The Shopify app marketplace shows how this can work in practice. Their platform:
– Provides developers with detailed analytics about how their apps are being used
– Identifies common user pain points across similar apps
– Highlights emerging opportunities based on user behavior patterns
– Alerts developers to potential issues before they become serious problems

The interesting thing about a platform ecosystem as vibrant as Shopify's, is that the platform does not carry the burden of knowledge orchestration alone. The ecosystem has such strong incentives, that a plethora of websites and online resources have emerged beyond Shopify itself that contribute to knowledge dissemination for Shopify merchants. But these third parties typically do not have access to the privileged knowledge of the platform itself, and so they rely on secondary sources such as interviews, case studies, and observations of trends and patterns that are visible to the public.

Access to frontier knowledge is so coveted by entrepreneurs in profitable marketplaces that third-party tools will step in to provide this knowledge if the platform itself does not. Leaving it to third-party providers may actually be a beneficial strategy if the platform thinks there may not be a single optimal solution that can be developed in-house, and that a variety of approaches may need to be explored. An example of this is the elaborate ecosystem of tools for sellers that have developed around the Amazon platform, such as JungleScout, Helium, SourceMogul, ZonGuru, Keepa, AMZScout, and many others. However, third-party tools can only work if the platform provides them with the APIs to access frontier knowledge.

Boundary Resources and Innovation Toolkits

Building an app for iOS or Android from scratch is a daunting undertaking, even for experienced developers. Without proper development tools and guidelines, creators face overwhelming technical hurdles: managing complex device permissions, handling different screen sizes and hardware capabilities, ensuring security compliance, implementing stable background processes, and maintaining compatibility across multiple OS versions. A simple mistake in any of these areas can lead to crashes, security vulnerabilities, or rejection from the app store. This complexity explains why platforms must provide sophisticated development infrastructure to enable innovation at scale.

At the heart of this infrastructure are what scholars call "boundary resources" – the interfaces and tools that enable external parties to build on top of the platform (Eaton et al., 2015; Ghazawneh & Henfridsson, 2013). The most basic form of these are Application Programming Interfaces (APIs) and Software Development Kits (SDKs). APIs provide structured ways to interact with the platform's core functionality, while SDKs offer pre-built components, testing tools, and implementation examples. Together, these resources dramatically reduce the technical barriers to innovation. For example, rather than having to understand the intricacies of GPS hardware access, location permissions, and background tracking, a developer can use Google Maps' SDK to add location features to their app with just a few lines of code.

While powerful, these developer-focused tools reach only a small fraction of potential innovators. Platforms achieve broader impact by making their capabilities accessible to the general population. If the platform itself does not provide the right boundary resources, there will be an arbitrage opportunity for others to step in and create those resources. This has occurred very notably with no-code app development platforms that allow non-developers to build Android and iOS apps.

Consider OpenAI's journey: The company was initially only developer-focused and offered APIs that thousands of developers used to build AI-powered applications. The introduction of custom GPTs in 2023 marked an attempt to recognize and welcome non-developers as innovators in the OpenAI ecosystem. Anyone could customize and extend ChatGPT's capabilities through a no-code interface for building custom GPTs, without programming knowledge. However, the company initially fell short of

providing the IP protection and monetization capabilities needed for those innovators to be able to pursue serious profit opportunities. Taking non-developer user-innovators seriously as entrepreneurs is no trivial matter.

The concept of boundary resources aligns with the notion of "innovation toolkits" in the user innovation literature (Thomke & Von Hippel, 2002; Von Hippel, 2001). Well-designed innovation toolkits have been described as having four essential elements:

1. They enable complete cycles of trial-and-error learning: Users need to be able to rapidly experiment with all the tools they need from design and prototyping to production and monetization.
2. They offer user-friendly interfaces: The toolkit should allow users to work in the ways that make sense to them, rather than forcing them to learn technical requirements or programming.
3. They include libraries of commonly used components: By providing pre-tested modules, users can focus their creative efforts on the truly novel aspects of their designs.
4. They steer user innovations through production constraints: The toolkit must ensure that user designs can be produced on the platform without requiring significant rework to make them compatible afterwards.

As a highly generative platform with a highly generative marketplace, Roblox provides one of the most successful examples of making innovation toolkits accessible to non-developers, especially young creators. Their Roblox Studio platform offers a comprehensive environment that perfectly illustrates the four elements of well-designed innovation toolkits:

1. Users can rapidly prototype games and game elements with real-time feedback and testing.
2. The interface allows for visual scripting and intuitive building blocks that do not require traditional coding knowledge. Recent AI features make it even easier to build from text prompts.
3. The platform provides an extensive library of pre-built assets, models, and game mechanics.
4. Built-in constraints ensure games will run properly on all supported devices.

Most importantly, Roblox takes its user-innovators seriously as entrepreneurs. The platform has enabled many non-technical and young creators to build sustainable businesses, with some top developers earning millions annually. They've created easy-to-use building tools, proper monetization infrastructure, robust IP protection, and analytics tools to help creators understand and grow their audience. This has resulted in a thriving ecosystem that shows consistent growth year after year.

Standards and Interoperability

Standards play a somewhat dual role in enabling a dynamic ecosystem of innovations. While at first glance we might associate the idea of standards with an inhibition of innovation, resistance to change, and creating barriers to entry, in reality standards also play an important enabling role in spurring the dynamics of innovation at scale (Allen & Sriram, 2000; Blind, 2016). In fact, boundary resources such as APIs and SDKS play an important standardization role by constraining user innovations to certain standards that make them compatible with the platform.

Standards serve multiple crucial functions that enable distributed innovation:

- **Ensuring Interoperability:** Standards ensure that different innovations can work together reliably. This is a foundational aspect, as without interoperability, the value of individual innovations diminishes in a platform ecosystem. Interoperability is key to achieving network effects and avoiding lock-in to old technologies (Blind, 2016). Compatibility standards are crucial for the development of an industry by ensuring seamless connections between products and facilitating the diffusion of innovative products (Zoo et al., 2017).
- **Reducing Complexity:** Standards reduce unnecessary complexity by handling common technical challenges. This allows innovators to focus on unique aspects of their contributions, rather than having to solve basic compatibility issues every time. This is achieved by defining common vocabularies, setting essential characteristics for products or services, and detecting best practices within ecosystems (Shin et al., 2015).
- **Creating Predictability:** Standards create predictable behaviors that users and other innovators can rely on. This predictability reduces uncertainty and risk, encouraging more participation and investment in the ecosystem. By reducing uncertainty and risks associated with new products, minimum quality standards, in particular, build consumer trust (Zoo et al., 2017).
- **Enabling Horizontal Complementarity**: Standards also enable horizontal complementarity, where different innovations can enhance each other's value. In platform ecosystems, this can be understood as the value-creating relationships between complements on a platform, such as an email and calendar application, in which standards can play a role in enabling the interoperability (Thomas et al., 2024). This kind of combinatorial innovation is central to the generative capacity of platforms.

Zoo et al. (2017) provide a useful taxonomy of standards and their effects on innovation:

1. **Variety Reduction Standards**: These standards, by defining specifications of products and services, help firms achieve economies of scale and critical mass.
2. **Minimum Quality Standards**: These standards reduce uncertainty and risks by establishing a baseline level of quality.

3. **Compatibility Standards**: These standards are central to achieving network effects and avoiding lock-ins, allowing different products and services to work together.
4. **Information Standards**: These provide a common understanding of technological knowledge, reducing transaction costs and facilitating trade.

In summary, standards and interoperability are the bedrock of generative platforms, enabling distributed innovation by providing a common language, reducing complexity, and fostering predictability. However, they must be carefully managed to avoid stifling innovation, creating market concentration, or excluding certain participants.

Enabling Organization: The Power of Teams and Organizations in User Innovation

While individual creators can produce remarkable innovations, the most complex and valuable contributions often come from organized teams working together. As innovations become more complex, they often require diverse skills and resources that a single user may not possess. Organization allows for specialization, division of labor, and the combination of diverse skills needed to tackle sophisticated challenges. For example, developing a sophisticated commercially viable product may require expertise in design, engineering, marketing, finance, and legal aspects, which are difficult for an individual to manage effectively. Smart platform companies recognize this reality and build infrastructure to support not just individual innovators but the formation and operation of organizations within their ecosystems. They understand that the highest-value activities in their marketplace – whether developing enterprise-grade software applications, creating comprehensive educational content, or building sophisticated business solutions – are likely to require coordinated effort from multiple contributors. It is crucial here that we are not just talking about enterprise features for large organizations: we are talking about features that enable innovators in the ecosystem to organize, form companies around the value they can create in your ecosystem, and grow.

This dynamic can be seen with many Bubble.io users who have turned their Bubble-made software into viable businesses, and are now managing companies with multiple team members. Bubble provides Team and Enterprise features with specialized pricing for such cases. Similarly, the most successful creators on Roblox aren't individual developers but small game studios that have emerged within the platform's ecosystem. Roblox actively supports this evolution by providing team features and collaboration tools in Roblox Studio.

Platforms that take their user-innovators seriously as entrepreneurs must recognize that high-quality innovations frequently require professional teams and organizational infrastructure. However, platforms should be strategic about where they invest in building support tools – focusing only on areas where they can provide unique value through their data and ecosystem-specific resources. You don't want to reinvent the wheel: there are already lots of third-party tools to help people manage a startup or small business. But those tools don't always integrate with your platform in the ways that your user-innovators need.

For example, while general project management software and CRM systems are readily available, platforms can offer specialized capabilities that generic tools cannot match. A well-designed platform might provide:

– Team Formation Tools: The platform can leverage its unique understanding of user activity patterns, skill profiles, and project histories to create powerful matching systems that connect complementary innovators. Unlike generic professional networks, these recommendations can be based on actual platform-specific experience and demonstrated capabilities.

– Resource Coordination: While teams may use external tools for basic project management, the platform can integrate deeply with its innovation toolkits to enable real-time collaboration. This might include shared workspaces tied directly to the platform's development environment, version control systems optimized for the platform's tools, and resource allocation mechanisms that understand the platform's unique constraints.

– Organization-Level Analytics: The platform has unique access to data about how teams use its tools, interact with customers, and deploy resources. By analyzing this data, platforms can provide teams with insights about their performance, resource utilization, and growth opportunities that would be impossible to get from generic analytics tools.

Consider how Shopify approaches this challenge. While their platform supports individual developers, they have built extensive infrastructure for agencies and development firms. Their Partner Program includes specialized tools for team collaboration, project management, and client relationship handling. This has enabled the emergence of sophisticated Shopify-focused development agencies that can tackle complex projects for major retailers – projects that would be impossible for individual developers to handle alone.

Getting this right is not easy. In our study of the Bubble no-code platform ecosystem we found that many of the most popular and sophisticated Bubble plugins aren't built by lone developers but by small companies that have formed specifically to develop and maintain these tools. They even actively engage in strategic acquisitions of plugins built by others. While Bubble has some support mechanisms for these organizations, most Bubble plugin developers that we interviewed said that the platform still has much room for improvement in providing developer tools and support systems.

The support for organization formation creates a powerful feedback cycle: As platforms make it easier for teams to form and operate effectively, more complex and valuable innovations become possible. These successes attract more talented individuals to the platform, who in turn form new organizations to tackle even more ambitious projects.

This organizational support becomes particularly crucial as platforms mature. While early innovations might come from individual creators, sustained growth often depends on enabling more sophisticated organizational structures that can tackle increasingly complex challenges. Platforms that recognize and support this evolution are more likely to maintain their generative potential over time.

Enabling user innovators to form organizations has other ancillary benefits as well. When users see that other users are able to build profitable businesses with your platform and form professional organizations around those businesses, this is a strong signal that the value creation system is rich enough to allow such activities, and reliable enough to make it a safe-enough bet. Users who are shaping businesses around their innovations with your platform are signaling to the world that they are willing to put skin in your game, and that it is an ecosystem ripe with opportunity.

Engineering Markets for Generativity

In this section on the generation layer of generative marketplaces we have discussed the orchestrating of diversity, interaction, experimentation, and infrastructure, such that distributed creativity can flourish in ways that centralized innovation efforts could never achieve.

What makes the generation layer particularly powerful is the way its elements reinforce one another. Diversity of participants and ideas expands the space of possible innovations, while structured serendipity fosters unexpected connections that lead to breakthroughs. Robust experimentation systems capture insights from both successes and failures, broadcasting these learnings across the ecosystem to accelerate collective progress. Knowledge-sharing infrastructure ensures that the accumulated wisdom of the community remains accessible, usable, and continuously refined. Standards and protocols provide the coherence needed for innovations to build upon each other without stifling creativity. Organization-enabling tools allow small teams to scale their impact and tackle increasingly complex challenges.

At its core, the generation layer embraces outliers and unconventional ideas, recognizing that the most transformative innovations often emerge from the fringes. Platforms that celebrate intellectual diversity and encourage dissent, build systems that disrupt echo chambers and challenge groupthink, enabling paradigm shifts that redefine entire industries. Similarly, by harnessing their privileged position and access to ecosystem data, platforms can act as curators of frontier knowledge, systematically broadcasting insights that help their communities innovate faster and smarter.

Perhaps most importantly, the generation layer fundamentally redefines the role of platform companies. Rather than attempting to predict or control innovation from the center, these platforms focus on engineering the conditions that allow innovation to emerge from anywhere. They build environments that combine structure with openness, empowering participants to create, collaborate, iterate, and build upon each other's ideas. This approach transforms platforms into engines of generativity, where innovation is no longer a byproduct but a deliberate, scalable outcome.

The most valuable innovations come from unexpected combinations of ideas, capabilities, and perspectives that no central planner could have anticipated. The generation layer explicitly architects for this kind of generativity, unlocking new possibilities.

The Appropriation Layer: Capturing Value from Distributed Innovation

While the generation layer enables innovation and the allocation layer facilitates efficient matching, the appropriation layer determines how platform owners can sustainably capture value from the distributed creativity they enable. This is perhaps the most delicate balancing act in designing generative marketplaces. The challenge is to avoid an exploitative mindset and think about a fair distribution of value that nurtures rather than stifles the ecosystem of innovators and the generative potential of the platform.

The literature on multi-sided markets has established that platform business models often defy traditional strategic logic (Rysman, 2009). For instance, it can be optimal to price below marginal cost on one side of the market to generate positive spillover effects on the other side (Rochet & Tirole, 2006). However, most existing research on value capture in platform markets focuses primarily on allocative efficiency rather than generativity. This creates a significant gap in our understanding, as mechanisms designed to extract value from allocative markets may have unintended negative effects on generative capacity.

In this section we discuss some ideas for appropriation mechanisms that support market generativity (see Table 7.3 for a summary).

Innovation-Friendly Pricing and Revenue Models in Generative Marketplaces

The pricing and revenue models a platform adopts fundamentally shape how participants engage with it. Traditional pricing approaches often create barriers that discourage experimentation, pushing participants toward safer, more predictable activities. But thoughtfully designed revenue models can do the opposite – reducing risk, encouraging bold experiments, and creating conditions where breakthrough innovations are more likely to emerge. Several key principles help design innovation-friendly pricing and revenue models:

Table 7.3: Components of the Appropriation Layer in the Architecture of Generative Marketplaces.

Element and Purpose	Challenges	Key Strategies	Examples
Innovation-Friendly Pricing and Revenue Models: Reduce barriers to entry and align platform success with participant success to encourage experimentation and engagement.	– High upfront costs discouraging experimentation. – Risk of pricing models appearing exploitative or unfair. – Balancing revenue capture with fostering generativity.	– Use revenue-sharing models to reduce upfront costs. – Implement freemium tiers for broad access. – Employ dynamic pricing that scales with value creation. – Ensure transparency in fee structures.	– Apple's 70/30 App Store split encourages app development. – AWS's pay-as-you-go model supports gradual scaling. – Spotify uses freemium tiers to attract users and monetize premium subscribers.
Control Points: Establish and evolve control points to guide value flows, sustain competitive advantage, and balance generativity with value capture.	– Avoiding excessive control that stifles ecosystem innovation. – Balancing openness with proprietary advantages to sustain profitability. – Adapting control points dynamically as ecosystems evolve.	– Establish generic control points (modularity, scalability) to enable broad participation. – Develop technical control points (APIs, development frameworks, infrastructure) to steer innovation. – Strengthen strategic control points (brand, customer relationships, orchestration capabilities) to sustain value capture. – Continuously refine control point balance in response to market dynamics.	– Bubble transitioned from strong technical control points (visual programming innovation) to strategic control points (market leadership in no-code, enterprise relationships). – Microsoft Power Platform leveraged existing strategic control points (brand, enterprise relationships, Office ecosystem) to establish new technical control points (visual development, workflow automation).

Table 7.3 (continued)

Element and Purpose	Challenges	Key Strategies	Examples
The Data Advantage: Use aggregated insights to improve platform functionality, empower participants, and drive ecosystem engagement.	– Balancing the use of data for platform advantage with participant trust. – Avoiding monopolistic tendencies in data control. – Ensuring compliance with privacy regulations.	– Share actionable insights to help participants innovate. – Use privacy-preserving data mechanisms like cohort-based advertising. – Provide analytics to refine participant offerings and deepen engagement.	– YouTube provides creators with audience analytics to optimize content. – LinkedIn uses aggregated data to enhance personalization and networking opportunities. – Google Ads matches sellers and consumers using precise data.
Curation and Promotion: Surface and amplify valuable innovations while managing ecosystem health and development.	– Balancing merit vs. strategic needs – Risk of discouraging innovation – Managing competitive dynamics – Maintaining participant trust – Ensuring transparency	– Set clear promotion criteria with strategic flexibility – Surface promising "up and coming" offerings – Fill strategic portfolio gaps – Time promotions to manage ecosystem dynamics – Balance established and emerging contributors	– Notion features innovative templates alongside popular ones – Shopify combines transparent criteria with strategic curation – Webflow showcases both established and breakthrough designers – Stripe balances traditional and innovative fintech tools

Table 7.3 (continued)

Element and Purpose	Challenges	Key Strategies	Examples
Ethical Value Capture: Maintain fairness and trust in value capture to ensure sustained engagement and innovation.	– Managing perceptions of exploitative practices. – Addressing power asymmetries between the platform and participants. – Ensuring equitable sharing of generated value.	– Use transparent pricing models to build trust. – Adopt equitable revenue-sharing structures. – Include contributors in decision-making to balance power dynamics. – Ensure inclusivity for smaller participants.	– Airbnb's proportional service fees foster fairness and trust. – Google offers free tools for small innovators, monetizing through ads. – Etsy's transparent fee structures maintain trust among artisans.
Sustaining Generativity Through Lock-in and Switching Costs: Ensure ecosystem loyalty while fostering generativity and balancing participant dependency.	– Avoiding restrictive practices that stifle generativity. – Managing participant dependency on the platform. – Encouraging sustained innovation within the ecosystem.	– Build unique value propositions through proprietary tools. – Create switching costs via data advantages and relational ties. – Use lock-in strategically to support long-term participant growth.	– Shopify's Partner Program builds loyalty through specialized tools and analytics. – Bubble's plugin developers rely on many users locked in the platform.

Reducing Barriers to Entry and Aligning Incentives

High upfront costs discourage experimentation by steering participants toward proven, less risky ideas. Successful platforms employ various strategies to lower these barriers. This often involves designing pricing models that align their financial success with that of their participants, fostering a mutually beneficial relationship.

– **Revenue Sharing**: By adopting revenue-sharing structures, platforms allow participants to avoid upfront costs and instead pay a percentage of their earnings. Stripe is free to use and build with, but will charge a fee per transaction. Similarly, platforms like Etsy provide a low-cost entry for artisans, enabling them to experiment with unique product ideas without significant initial investment.
– **Freemium or Tiered Models**: Offering free entry-level access allows participants to explore and test their ideas without financial commitment. LinkedIn's free tier attracts millions of users, enabling them to develop their networks, while monetization occurs through premium subscriptions and targeted advertising. This dual

structure creates a pipeline of users who might eventually transition to paid features. GitHub further demonstrates this approach through free public repositories, empowering developers to collaborate and innovate with a low-risk entry point, while monetizing through advanced enterprise tools. Freemium models encourage innovation best when the free tier is good enough for innovators to make significant progress. If too many of the tools they need are in paid or expensive pricing tiers, this is not a very entrepreneur-friendly freemium model. The Tally.so form-builder software provides an example of an entrepreneur-friendly freemium model, where almost all product features are in the free tier, and only a few features important for entrepreneurs who have already reached profitability are in premium pricing tiers.

– **Pay-as-You-Go**: Amazon Web Services' (AWS) pay-as-you-go structure supports innovation by allowing startups and individuals to scale usage and costs incrementally, directly linking resource consumption to value. This model enables a kind of "gradual innovation" where participants can start small, experiment cheaply, and scale up only when they find success. Importantly, if pay-as-you-go options are not available, innovators may have trouble scaling. Replit.com's AI agent for programming initially only allowed a limited number of credits based on your monthly subscription but soon realized that users were demanding to be able to pay to use the product beyond their monthly quotas if they needed to.

Leveraging Cross-Subsidization

Platforms often subsidize certain user groups or activities to drive overall ecosystem growth, recouping costs from complementary revenue streams.

– **Ad-Supported Services**: Google offers free search services, funded through advertising revenue. This model attracts billions of users, creating a rich data ecosystem that fuels advertising innovation. By lowering user costs, platforms can rapidly scale participation while monetizing other aspects of their ecosystem.

– **Freemium to Premium Upgrades**: Spotify entices users with free access while generating revenue through premium subscriptions. This strategy ensures widespread adoption while catering to high-value customers who demand enhanced features. The free tier creates value for artists by building audience reach, which the platform can then monetize through premium subscriptions and advertising.

Ensuring Perceived Fairness and Trust

Trust and fairness in pricing models are pivotal for encouraging sustained engagement and innovation within the marketplace.

– **Transparent Fee Structures**: Platforms like Etsy are known for clearly communicating their transaction fees, which fosters a sense of fairness and reduces user apprehension. Transparent pricing helps ensure that contributors feel valued and not exploited.

- **Equitable Revenue Sharing**: Fair revenue-sharing agreements are essential for maintaining participant trust. Airbnb's model, where hosts pay a percentage of their earnings, is seen as equitable because fees scale with participant success. This proportionality ensures that contributors retain significant rewards from their innovation efforts.

These principles suggest several key strategic considerations for platform leaders:
1. Focus on reducing the cost of failure rather than just rewarding success.
2. Align platform revenue with participant success through revenue sharing.
3. Use free tiers strategically to encourage experimentation and learning.
4. Consider dynamic pricing that scales with value creation.
5. Employ cross-subsidization to build critical mass in key areas.
6. Maintain transparency to build long-term trust.

The ultimate goal is to create revenue models that capture enough value to sustain the platform while minimizing barriers to experimentation and creativity. Getting this balance right is crucial because it shapes not just individual transactions but the overall generative potential of the marketplace.

However, the specific structure of these models matters enormously. If the platform's take is too high, it can still discourage innovation by making it difficult for participants to achieve profitability. Apple and Google's famous ~30% commission fees on apps in their mobile app stores has faced growing criticism from developers who argue it makes many business models unsustainable. The key is finding rates that allow the platform to capture enough value to sustain its operations while leaving participants with sufficient margin to justify continued innovation.

Control Points and Value Capture

The concept of control points emerged from MIT's Value Chain Dynamics Working Group (Trossen & Fine, 2005) as researchers grappled with a fundamental question: How can firms sustainably capture value in rapidly evolving digital industries? Control points refer to "functional areas in a value chain or network where power can be exercised" (Eaton et al., 2010, p. 462). Bohnsack et al. (2024, p. 6) expand the definition of control points to emphasize value capture relative to competitors but with a broadened scope of domains in which they could appear: "a technical or strategic feature in a digital business ecosystem – such as customer access, a unique solution, or an orchestration position – that competitors must navigate, thereby significantly decreasing their bargaining power." Importantly, power and influence can be exercised to steer innovation and profitability, and thinking innovation-first (expanding the pie) is not always fully aligned with thinking profit-first (taking a larger piece of the pie).

Bohnsack et al. (2024) identify three distinct categories of control points that shape value creation and capture in digital ecosystems:

1. **Technical control points** emerge from the platform's technical features – things like APIs, data access, and technical infrastructure that enable or constrain what innovations are possible. These primarily determine value creation potential.
2. **Strategic control points** like brand strength, customer relationships, and orchestration capabilities shape how much value can be captured. Unlike technical control points which can be relatively fluid, strategic control points tend to be more durable sources of advantage.
3. **Generic control points**, particularly modularity and scalability, are table stakes that all ecosystem participants must participate in meaningfully. These enable the basic generative potential of the platform.

Bohnsack et al. describe a "seesaw pattern" where organizations must balance exploiting established control points while developing new ones. This pattern is visible in generative platforms:

1. **Technical to Strategic**: New platforms often start with strong technical control points but must develop strategic ones to ensure sustainable value capture. Bubble's journey from technical innovation in visual programming that allowed them to gain popularity among indie entrepreneurs to gaining recognition as the market leader in no-code/low-code and building enterprise relationships exemplifies this pattern.
2. **Strategic to Technical**: Established companies entering platform markets must translate strategic control points (brand, relationships) into technical ones. Microsoft's Power Platform journey exemplifies this pattern – they leveraged their existing strategic control points (enterprise relationships, Office ecosystem, Azure cloud infrastructure) to enter the no-code/low-code space but had to develop new technical control points around visual development, workflow automation, and citizen development to compete effectively.

A Staged Approach to Control Points

The evolution of control points in digital ecosystems is not a one-time event but a dynamic, staged process. Firms seeking to balance innovation with value capture must carefully navigate the shifting landscape of control points, ensuring that they maintain relevance and competitive advantage as their ecosystems mature. Bohnsack et al.'s framework suggests a four-stage progression that platform leaders can follow to strategically develop and sustain control points over time.

Stage 1 – Establishing Generic Control Points: At the foundational level, every digital platform must first secure basic structural capabilities that enable ecosystem participation. These generic control points do not differentiate a firm but serve as necessary prerequisites for growth and engagement. Two key priorities at this stage are modularity and scalability. Modularity ensures that platform components can be flexibly combined and extended, fostering innovation by allowing third-party developers to build upon the core system. Scalability, on the other hand, ensures that the platform can handle growth without performance bottlenecks. Additionally, firms must establish well-defined interfaces—such as APIs or developer tools—that facilitate ecosystem participation. Without these generic control points in place, a platform lacks the fundamental infrastructure needed to generate sustained value.

Stage 2 – Developing Technical Control Points: Once the foundation is established, firms must shift their focus toward technical control points—distinctive technological capabilities that create value while preserving control. Unlike generic control points, technical ones introduce differentiation, making a platform more attractive relative to competitors. This stage involves the strategic deployment of APIs, development tools, and data access mechanisms that not only enable third-party innovation but also reinforce the platform's influence. Additionally, technical infrastructure must be built to support ecosystem expansion, ensuring reliability and security as the network scales. Firms at this stage also set the technical standards and protocols that define the rules of engagement for ecosystem participants. By controlling the underlying architecture, they shape how value is created and distributed, influencing the direction of innovation.

Stage 3 – Establishing Strategic Control Points: Technical control points alone, however, are rarely sufficient for long-term value capture. As ecosystems mature, firms must transition from merely enabling innovation to strategically orchestrating it. This involves building strong customer relationships, deep industry expertise, and brand positioning—elements that competitors cannot easily replicate. At this stage, network effects become critical. Firms must actively strengthen their position by fostering user interdependencies, ecosystem loyalty, and strategic alliances. Control shifts from the technical infrastructure itself to the ability to orchestrate participants and shape market dynamics. A strong brand, for instance, can serve as a durable strategic control point, ensuring continued influence even as technology evolves.

Stage 4 – Maintaining Dynamic Balance: The final stage is not a static endpoint but an ongoing process of adaptation. Control points are not fixed assets; they must be continuously refined and recalibrated in response to market shifts, competitive pressures, and technological advancements. Firms must monitor ecosystem evolution, identifying emerging threats and opportunities that require adjustments to their control strategy. Some control points may need reinforcement, while others must be relaxed to encourage broader ecosystem participation. Striking the right balance between technical control (which fosters innovation) and strategic control (which ensures value capture) is crucial. Firms that over-index on technical openness may struggle to monetize their platforms, while those that tighten control too aggressively may stifle innovation and alienate partners.

The Data Advantage

One of the most compelling value capture mechanisms in marketplaces stems from the platform owner's unique ability to aggregate, analyze, and deploy data. Platforms accumulate vast amounts of data from interactions, transactions, and user behaviors, transforming these digital footprints into actionable insights. Furthermore, this kind of value capture is usually a win-win outcome for everyone, because the insights produced are valuable for all ecosystem participants but could not have been achieved if not for aggregation at the platform level. Over time, this process creates a self-reinforcing cycle: more participants generate more data, which leads to better insights and improved functionality, attracting even more participants.

This data advantage can lead to a powerful competitive moat for the platform. This advantage is sometimes referred to as "data rents" (Komljenovic, 2021) and involves "assetization" of data, the process where platforms derive long-term value from information flows by transforming raw data into enduring strategic assets. While this enhances the user experience, it also consolidates market power by creating barriers for competitors who lack comparable datasets. When deployed strategically, the data advantage can stimulate distributed innovation by providing ecosystem participants with valuable insights that fuel creativity and experimentation.

Platforms like YouTube exemplify the power of this mechanism. By analyzing viewing patterns and engagement behaviors across billions of users, YouTube gains unique insights into content preferences. These insights inform not only its recommendation algorithms but also empower creators to innovate by providing detailed analytics on audience engagement and preferences. This collaborative feedback loop strengthens the generative ecosystem by helping creators optimize their content, experiment with new formats, and align their innovations with audience needs. YouTube's ability to share data-driven insights fosters distributed innovation, making the platform indispensable for both creators and viewers.

Another obvious benefit of data aggregation is the enabling of targeted advertising. Platforms can efficiently match sellers with consumers by using precise data to target advertisements. Platforms like Google Ads, Facebook Ads, and Amazon rely on such strategies to optimize the relevance of offerings. By steering consumers toward specific products or services, platforms not only drive higher engagement but also create opportunities for distributed innovation. For example, smaller sellers can leverage these insights to refine their offerings and tailor their innovations to meet the precise needs of niche audiences, thus reinforcing the generativity of the marketplace.

Yet this dominance comes with trade-offs. The ability to steer consumer behavior introduces significant power asymmetries between platforms, sellers, and users. As Bergemann and Bonatti (2024) point out, the controlled environment of a platform often restricts sellers' competitive flexibility while simultaneously increasing their dependency. Sellers face a "showrooming constraint"—they must provide competitive off-platform offers to retain consumers who might otherwise use the platform as a discovery tool but purchase elsewhere. This dynamic underscores a critical tension in leveraging the data advantage: balancing appropriation and generativity. Platforms that manage this balance well can encourage ecosystem participants to innovate more freely, knowing they will benefit from the marketplace's broader data-driven insights.

Santesteban and Longpré (2020) provide further clarity on the mechanics of data-driven market power. They emphasize that economies of scale and scope in data aggregation create increasing returns, making it nearly impossible for smaller players to compete effectively. Platforms achieve a compounding advantage as their data troves grow, enabling them to refine algorithms, predict consumer behavior, and optimize resource allocation. However, they also highlight a potential pitfall: platforms that excessively hoard data risk undermining trust and generativity within the ecosystem.

Fast et al. (2023) argue that the scale of data control by platforms like Amazon and Google can entrench monopolistic tendencies. Their analysis underscores the importance of privacy-preserving mechanisms, such as federated learning, which balance the use of data for competitive advantage with consumer trust and regulatory compliance. This perspective aligns with Bergemann and Bonatti's (2024) findings on privacy governance, which suggest that cohort-based advertising—where platforms share aggregated rather than individual data—can enhance consumer surplus without diminishing the platform's ability to create value. By enabling distributed innovation through privacy-preserving data sharing, generative marketplaces can maintain both ecosystem trust and long-term innovation. To fully harness the data advantage, generative marketplaces must navigate the fine line between value creation and overreach.

Curation and Promotion as Strategic Levers

Platforms wield significant influence through their ability to curate and promote content within their marketplaces. This influence extends beyond simply surfacing "best in class" offerings – it serves as a strategic tool for managing the overall health and value of the platform ecosystem. As Rietveld et al. (2019) demonstrate in their study of video game platforms, promotion decisions involve careful orchestration of multiple competing priorities, such as:

1. **Unrealized Potential vs. Established Success:** Rather than simply promoting the highest-performing complements, platforms often focus on "up and coming" offerings that show promise but have not yet reached their full potential. This approach allows platforms to help surface hidden gems and create new stars rather than just amplifying existing successes. For example, mobile app stores may feature promising new apps alongside established favorites to help users discover emerging innovations. Notion's template gallery exemplifies this approach, prominently featuring innovative new use cases alongside popular templates to help users discover emerging workflow innovations.

2. **Portfolio Balance and Ecosystem Gaps:** Platforms strategically promote content to ensure breadth and depth across different categories. If a platform lacks strong offerings in an important category, it may invest extra promotional effort there to help strengthen that part of the ecosystem. This portfolio-level thinking helps platforms maintain comprehensive value propositions for users. Stripe's app marketplace demonstrates this balance, carefully curating a mix of established financial tools and innovative new fintech solutions to ensure their platform serves the full spectrum of modern payment and financial needs.

3. **Timing and Competitive Dynamics:** Promotion timing can be used strategically to boost engagement during slow periods and manage competitive dynamics between complements. Platforms must consider not just which complements to promote but when to promote them to maximize overall ecosystem value. Webflow's showcase strategically times its promotion of both established agencies and breakthrough designers to maintain steady engagement and inspire different segments of their community throughout the year.

4. **Quality Signals and Innovation:** While quality remains a key consideration, platforms look beyond simple metrics to identify truly innovative contributions that advance the state of the art. This helps maintain the platform's competitive position while rewarding genuine innovation. Shopify's app collection process exemplifies this balance, combining transparent quality criteria with strategic curation to surface truly innovative solutions that expand the platform's capabilities.

5. **Platform Loyalty and Strategic Alignment:** Platforms often use promotion to reward and incentivize loyalty from key complement producers. However, this must be balanced against maintaining credible, merit-based promotion criteria that developers trust. For example, while Shopify promotes established app developers who have demonstrated long-term commitment to the platform, they maintain clear paths for new innovators to earn promotion through exceptional quality and innovation.

The power to promote represents both an opportunity and a responsibility for platform sponsors. While they naturally want to use promotion to strengthen their competitive position, they must avoid creating perverse incentives that could discourage innovation or erode trust. Several key tensions must be balanced:

- Supporting established partners versus surfacing new innovators
- Promoting proven successes versus betting on promising newcomers
- Meeting immediate business needs versus long-term ecosystem health
- Using promotion as a strategic lever versus maintaining fair, transparent criteria

The balancing act in practice could take on various forms:

- Establishing clear, merit-based criteria for promotion while maintaining some flexibility for strategic considerations
- Using promotion thoughtfully to shape ecosystem development while avoiding heavy-handed manipulation
- Balancing support for established partners with opportunities for emerging innovators
- Considering both individual complement success and overall portfolio health in promotion decisions

For generative platforms specifically, promotion strategy should align with the goal of encouraging unpredicted innovation at scale. This means maintaining genuinely open pathways for new innovations to gain visibility while still leveraging promotion strategically to strengthen the platform's position.

Ethical Considerations in Profiting from Other People's Innovations

Profiting from the innovations of others on a generative platform is not without ethical complexities. Each innovator has a strong sense of ownership over their creations, and sometimes there can be unresolvable differences of opinion around how much of a claim to contribution the innovator has compared to the platform that made the innovation possible. Ethical challenges for generative platforms revolve around fairness, transparency, and the balance of power between the platform and its contributors. Below are the key ethical challenges and potential solutions, illustrated with real-world examples of platforms that have faced similar dilemmas.

1. **Balancing Value Capture and Fairness:** Platforms must ensure that their revenue models equitably share the value generated by participant innovations. Exploitative practices—such as high commission rates or monopolistic behavior—can erode trust and discourage participation. For instance, criticisms of Amazon's Marketplace have included claims that the platform's fee structures disproportionately benefit Amazon while limiting small sellers' profitability. To address such issues, platforms can adopt revenue-sharing schemes that are transparent and proportional, ensuring contributors retain significant rewards for their innovations.

2. **Maintaining Transparency:** Opaque fee structures or hidden costs can lead to perceptions of exploitation and mistrust among participants. Transparent communication about pricing models is essential. Airbnb's approach to clearly itemizing service fees—including a breakdown of what hosts and guests pay—has been a step in the right direction, fostering trust and encouraging continued engagement.
3. **Addressing Power Asymmetries:** The concentration of decision-making power in platforms can lead to ethical dilemmas, particularly when platforms unilaterally change policies that affect contributors. For example, Etsy's decision to increase seller fees sparked backlash, as many felt the changes were imposed without sufficient consultation. To mitigate such issues, platforms could adopt governance models that involve contributors in decision-making processes, ensuring their voices are heard in policy shifts.
4. **Fostering Inclusive Participation:** Smaller contributors often face significant barriers to participation, particularly if pricing models disproportionately burden them. Google's strategy of offering free tools while monetizing through advertising ensures that even small-scale innovators can engage without upfront costs. This inclusivity broadens participation and fosters a diverse innovation ecosystem.
5. **Encouraging Ethical Data Practices:** Platforms profiting from user data must navigate ethical challenges surrounding privacy and consent. Stemler et al. (2020) emphasize the importance of transparency in data usage and suggest adopting explicit user agreements (a "Code of the Platform") that clarifies how data is monetized and how the platform mediates transactions. Such practices help platforms maintain ethical standards while capturing value from user contributions.

Capturing Value while Spurring Innovation

The appropriation layer must balance the dual imperatives of sustaining the platform's operations and nurturing the creativity that fuels its ecosystem. A well-designed appropriation layer achieves this by combining thoughtful revenue models, strategic control points, and participant-focused mechanisms.

The appropriation layer's success depends on innovation-friendly pricing models. These include revenue-sharing arrangements that lower upfront costs, freemium tiers that encourage broad participation, and dynamic pricing structures that scale with user success. These strategies reduce barriers to entry and incentivize experimentation, creating a vibrant environment for innovation.

Equally important are the mechanisms that sustain long-term engagement and reinforce platform ecosystems. Lock-in effects, such as proprietary tools and data advantages, ensure participants remain committed by offering unique value propositions. Switching costs, whether technical or relational, further solidify participant loyalty by embedding their success within the platform's ecosystem. However, these mechanisms must be employed judiciously. Over-reliance on restrictive practices risks stifling the very generativity the platform seeks to promote.

Many users of the Bubble no-code development platform worry about lock-in and switching costs, and consider these issues before deciding to invest heavily in building with the platform. Since many users do eventually get locked in and face high switching costs, various Bubble developers and Bubble plugin developers benefit from having a thick market of such users. But if the platform is too aggressive about its lock-in practices, it will discourage many users from joining in the first place.

Strategic control points play a pivotal role in capturing value without undermining generativity. Platforms like Apple's App Store or Google Maps leverage technical and strategic control points to steer innovation while maintaining profitability. These points—from APIs to branding—enable platforms to foster distributed creativity while ensuring they benefit from the innovations they enable.

The appropriation layer is also enriched by the platform's ability to harness network effects and data advantages. As participation grows, the ecosystem becomes increasingly valuable, reinforcing its attractiveness to new and existing participants. Platforms that effectively analyze and share data-driven insights empower participants to innovate in ways that align with user needs, deepening engagement and sustaining growth.

Ultimately, the appropriation layer's objective is not only to capture value but to do so in a manner that creates a self-reinforcing cycle of innovation and engagement. By aligning platform success with participant success, leveraging strategic mechanisms like lock-in and switching costs thoughtfully, and maintaining trust through transparency and fairness, generative marketplaces can unlock their full potential. The appropriation layer, when designed with care and foresight, transforms distributed creativity into sustainable competitive advantage.

External Factors: The Broader Context of Generative Markets

While we have focused on the internal architecture of generative marketplaces through our three-layered model, these markets don't exist in isolation. They operate within broader economic, social, and institutional contexts that profoundly shape their potential for generativity. Understanding these external factors is crucial because they can either amplify or constrain a marketplace's generative capacity.

Nobel laureate Edmund Phelps (2013) identifies four critical categories of enabling conditions that determine an economy's capacity for generativity:

1. Economic Institutions: The fundamental frameworks of property rights, financial markets, and inclusive participation
2. Political Institutions: Representative systems that ensure stable and predictable governance

3. Cultural Elements: Societal attitudes toward innovation, entrepreneurship, and change
4. Demographic Factors: Population size and urban concentration that enable knowledge exchange

While marketplace designers cannot directly control these factors, they can amplify their positive effects within their platforms. In the following sections we discuss some elements of these external factors and their implications for generative platforms (see Table 7.4 for a summary).

Table 7.4: The Role of External Factors in the Architecture of Generative Marketplaces.

Element & Purpose	Challenges	Key Strategies	Examples
Cultural Dynamics and Innovation Mindsets: Shaping participant behavior toward experimentation	– Overcoming resistance to experimentation in more conservative or risk-averse cultures – Preventing cultural homogenization within a global platform	– Cultivate a culture that celebrates creative remixing and risk-taking – Design policies and features that reinforce openness to failure and reward innovation	– The remix culture exemplified by the generative video game platforms Minecraft and Roblox (as discussed by Lessig, 2009)
Networks and Knowledge Flows: Facilitating the exchange of ideas both within and beyond the platform	– The risk of closed networks and echo chambers that limit new ideas – Balancing proprietary interests with the benefits of open knowledge exchange	– Organize dedicated media channels and events that expose participants to external insights – Create structured documentation and discussion forums to promote both inbound and outbound knowledge flows	– Shopify's "Masters" podcast series, Stripe's "Indie Hackers" podcast, and HubSpot's podcast network

Table 7.4 (continued)

Element & Purpose	Challenges	Key Strategies	Examples
Educational Institutions and Learning Ecosystems: Partnering to build human capital and experimental testbeds	– Bridging academic theory with practical needs – Aligning platform development cycles with academic timelines – Navigating intellectual property concerns in collaborative projects	– Establish university partnership programs and student initiatives – Support research using platform data and develop dedicated curricula or certification pathways	– GitHub Education, AWS Educate, and partnerships between Shopify and universities
Urban Population Centers and Community Engagement: Tapping into the organic vibrancy of cities	– Balancing digital collaboration with the need for physical, face-to-face interactions – Ensuring inclusivity for regions that may lack urban density – Capturing benefits from informal, local knowledge exchanges	– Organize local meetups, workshops, and hackathons that complement online collaboration – Use physical events to create innovation clusters around the platform	– Webflow's global events page, Shopify's merchant meetups, GitHub's coding workshops and hackathons, and WordPress's WordCamps
Regulatory Navigation: Addressing compliance while preserving innovation	– Adapting to diverse, region-specific regulatory requirements – Balancing the pace of innovation with public interest and legal obligations – Managing the operational costs associated with compliance	– Develop integrated compliance tools that simplify regional regulations – Engage proactively with regulators to shape policy – Create region-specific features to align with local laws	– Airbnb's tailored approaches to local home-sharing regulations and the adjustments made by platforms in response to Europe's GDPR

Cultural Dynamics and Innovation Mindsets

The cultural dimension deserves special attention because it so profoundly shapes how participants engage with generative marketplaces. Cultures that embrace experimentation and tolerate failure tend to generate more breakthrough innovations. Platform companies can actively cultivate these cultural elements within their ecosystems.

While embracing experimentation and failure tolerance are not typical measures of national culture found in the empirical literature, studies using the standard Hofstede dimensions of culture have shown that acceptance of uncertainty (or low uncertainty avoidance), lower power distance, and higher individualism correlate with higher rates of innovation at the national level (Espig et al., 2021; Shane, 1993; Sun, 2009).

In a different and interesting approach to measuring culture, Gelfand et al. (2011) provide a comprehensive examination of cultural "tightness" versus "looseness" across 33 nations. In "tight" cultures, as they describe them, social norms are numerous, clearly defined, and strictly enforced, leaving little room for deviant behavior. By contrast, "loose" cultures are characterized by a weak set of norms and a high tolerance for behaviors that deviate from the norm.

The authors detail how distal factors, such as ecological and historical threats, shape the degree of norm strength within a nation. Societies that have faced challenges such as high population density, resource scarcity, frequent natural disasters, or prolonged territorial conflicts tend to develop tighter norms. These threats create a pressing need for social coordination and order, which is achieved by imposing strict behavioral expectations. Conversely, societies with fewer such pressures tend to exhibit looser norms, allowing for a broader range of acceptable behavior and more flexibility in social interactions.

Gelfand et al. also demonstrate that the tightness or looseness of a culture is reflected in everyday situations and is supported by underlying psychological processes. In nations with strong situational constraints, everyday settings—from classrooms to public parks—exhibit a narrow range of acceptable behaviors. This pervasive normativity influences individual psychological processes, such as a heightened need for structure and stronger self-monitoring, which in turn reinforce the cultural system.

The Minecraft and Roblox generative video game platforms provide an instructive example of how platforms can influence the culture of their own ecosystem. The platforms have deliberately fostered a "remix culture" (Lessig, 2009, n.p.) where building on others' ideas is not just allowed but celebrated. This cultural development has resulted in an explosion of creative game development that might have been stifled in more restrictive environments.

Networks and Knowledge Flows

Research on networks has shown that people are typically part of a limited number of relatively closed networks where they have strong ties with others in those network, but little or no ties with individuals outside of those networks (Burt, 2008, 2010). We often need the trust and safety that comes with network closure. But spending a lot of time with like-minded individuals can lead to echo chamber effects that are not conducive to innovation (Janis, 2013; Pariser, 2011). Instead, it is precisely those weak ties with individuals outside of our typical networks that end up being the sources of the most novel ideas and innovations that we may come up with. This is a phenomenon famously known as "the strength of weak ties" (Granovetter, 1973, n.p.).

Digital platforms can play a vital role in helping their ecosystem participants maintain this crucial balance between strong internal ties and external knowledge connections. Successful innovation networks need to simultaneously enhance knowledge flows among current participants while being open to external connections (Powell & Grodal, 2006). Platforms can facilitate this through features like public-private collaboration spaces, external API integrations, and cross-platform knowledge sharing initiatives. They can also organize events and forums that bring together their core community members with outside experts, academics, and innovators from adjacent fields.

Some platforms have mastered the art of bringing external knowledge to their supply-side participants through dedicated media efforts. Shopify's long-running "Masters" podcast series exposes their merchants to insights from retail experts, successful entrepreneurs, and industry leaders outside the Shopify ecosystem – helping prevent merchants from developing platform tunnel vision. Similarly, Stripe's "Indie Hackers" podcast deliberately seeks out founders using diverse business models and technologies, ensuring their developer community stays connected to broader entrepreneurship trends and opportunities beyond payments. HubSpot has taken this approach even further by building an entire podcast network that brings marketing, sales, and business experts from outside their platform to share knowledge with their users. These platforms recognize that their supply-side participants need more than just platform-specific knowledge to succeed – they need ongoing exposure to external perspectives, emerging trends, and cross-industry insights. By facilitating these knowledge flows through podcasts and other media, they help their ecosystems stay dynamic and innovative rather than becoming closed loops of internal echo chambers.

The relationship between marketplaces and external knowledge flows works in both directions. Inbound knowledge flows can include benefiting from academic research and educational outputs, industry best practices and standards, public discourse and cultural trends and technical innovations from adjacent fields. Outbound knowledge flows can include novel business models that spread to other contexts, technical solutions that find applications elsewhere, organizational innovations that influence broader business practices, and user behaviors that shape social norms.

Educational Institutions and Learning Ecosystems

Educational institutions play a unique dual role in shaping generative marketplaces. They act as knowledge producers through research while serving as knowledge multipliers through teaching. As Phelps (2013) emphasizes, the capacity for innovation in an economy depends heavily on its systems for developing human capital and transmitting knowledge across generations. For platform companies, educational institutions represent crucial partners (whether explicit or not) that can enhance both the breadth and sophistication of innovation within their ecosystems.

The relationship between the ecosystem of user-innovators in generative platforms and educational institutions operates through multiple channels, and is especially important when specialized knowledge and advanced education are needed to produce high quality innovations in the platform's ecosystem.

GitHub's relationship with educational institutions provides an instructive example. Through GitHub Education, the platform offers free access to students and teachers, effectively seeding future developers while gathering insights from educational use cases. This program has evolved beyond simple tool provision to include curriculum resources, teacher training, and student certification pathways. The platform gains valuable insights from the innovative ways educators adapt GitHub for teaching – approaches that frequently influence professional practice.

Similarly, AWS has built extensive educational partnerships through its AWS Educate program, which helps universities integrate cloud computing into their curricula. This is a win-win partnership – universities get access to cutting-edge technology and teaching resources, while AWS cultivates a pipeline of cloud-native developers who will build businesses on their platform. The program demonstrates how educational partnerships can create self-reinforcing cycles of innovation and adoption.

These relationships require careful orchestration. Platform companies must balance their commercial interests with academic freedom, manage intellectual property rights across institutional boundaries, and adapt their typical timelines to academic cycles. However, when managed effectively, educational institutions can become powerful amplifiers of platform generativity. Platform leaders can leverage educational institutions through several key mechanisms:
1. Research partnerships that advance platform technologies
2. Educational programs that train future innovators
3. Experimental testbeds for new platform features
4. Certification programs that build ecosystem expertise
5. Community building through academic networks

Leveraging Urban Population Centers

The role of geographic concentration in innovation, extensively studied by scholars like Glaeser (2012) in his work on the "Triumph of the City," remains crucial even for digital platforms. As Phelps (2013) emphasizes, the agglomeration of populations in cities creates powerful opportunities for knowledge exchange and community building that can accelerate innovation. Rather than trying to replicate these effects purely digitally, successful platforms actively tap into existing urban communities and networks.

Cities naturally foster an environment where diverse talent and a mix of cultural, economic, and creative energies converge. Glaeser (2012) argues that the density of cities is a critical engine for economic growth because it promotes rapid knowledge spillovers. Jane Jacobs (1992) argued long ago that the very design of cities—with their mixed-use neighborhoods and lively streets—cultivates the kind of everyday encounters that underpin community resilience and innovation.

An example of what digital platforms do to allow urban population centers to feed their generativity is to hold a variety of local events in different communities. For example, Webflow maintains an events page that highlights local meetups and community gatherings around the world. This practice not only leverages the inherent advantages of population centers but also reinforces the role of physical, in-person interactions in sustaining a vibrant innovation ecosystem. Similarly, platforms like Shopify organize merchant meetups in major cities, drawing on the natural energy of urban environments to spark collaboration and knowledge sharing among entrepreneurs. GitHub's sponsorship of coding workshops and hackathons is yet another example where digital communities are brought into physical spaces, creating an intersection where ideas can flourish and evolve through direct interaction.

Regulatory Considerations

In many cases, regulatory frameworks are designed to protect consumers and ensure fair competition, yet they can also constrain digital platforms in many ways. Navigating these constraints is not a trivial matter.

Airbnb offers a clear example of a platform that has navigated this terrain by engaging with regulators across diverse jurisdictions. The company has adopted a proactive stance—working with local governments on issues ranging from housing regulations to taxation. Although this approach has sometimes slowed expansion in specific markets, it has ultimately contributed to a more sustainable and trusted business model.

In Europe, the introduction of the General Data Protection Regulation (GDPR) illustrates how comprehensive regulatory frameworks can impact platform operations. GDPR has redefined data privacy standards by mandating greater transparency, stricter consent requirements, and enhanced rights for users over their personal data. As digital platforms adjust to these requirements, they are compelled to integrate robust data protection measures into their business practices. While compliance can introduce additional costs and operational constraints, it also fosters greater consumer trust and ultimately contributes to a more resilient marketplace.

Conclusion: Architecting for Generative Growth

The deliberate design of generative marketplaces represents a profound shift in how we think about market creation in the digital age. While traditional market design focuses primarily on allocation efficiency, we've argued throughout this chapter that unleashing the generative potential of marketplaces requires a more sophisticated architectural approach that spans three interconnected layers: allocation, generation, and appropriation.

The allocation layer provides the essential foundation – creating the thickness, matching efficiency, and trust mechanisms needed for basic market function. But unlike marketplaces that optimize purely for matching, generative marketplaces must design these foundational elements with distributed innovation in mind. However, the matching function must still work well for the marketplace to be able to operate at all. Matching mechanisms need to balance efficiency with discovery. Trust and safety systems must protect while enabling experimentation.

The generation layer transforms this foundation into an engine of continuous innovation. Through carefully orchestrated diversity, rich interaction mechanisms, and robust experimentation systems, this layer enables platforms to tap into what Hayek (2002) called the "distributed knowledge" of market participants. The most successful platforms don't just wait passively for innovation to happen – they actively design for it, creating environments where breakthrough ideas are more likely to emerge and spread. This requires sophisticated infrastructure for knowledge sharing, collaboration, and organizational support.

The appropriation layer completes the architecture by ensuring sustainable value capture without stifling generativity. This involves entrepreneur-friendly revenue models, thoughtful design of control points, data advantages, and curation mechanisms that align platform success with participant success. The most effective platforms find a beautiful structure of incentives that allows them to profit from distributed innovation while maintaining the trust and engagement that drive continued participation.

These layers don't operate in isolation but rather reinforce each other in powerful ways. A well-designed allocation layer creates incentives that drive activity in the generation layer. The generation layer produces innovations that create value, which the appropriation layer can then help distribute in ways that encourage more innovation. When all three layers work in harmony, they create a self-reinforcing system where each layer strengthens the others, enabling sustained innovation at scale. This architecture must also be thoughtfully embedded within broader institutional, cultural, and demographic contexts.

As we wrap up a long section of the book on market generativity, let us circle back to the idea of product generativity, and look into the synergies between product generativity and market generativity in the next chapter.

Chapter 8
The Generativity Flywheel

The most powerful manifestations of generativity occur when generative products and generative markets combine to create self-reinforcing cycles of innovation and value creation. This phenomenon, which we call the "generativity flywheel," explains why companies that successfully harness both forms of generativity—like Apple, Google, and Amazon—have achieved unprecedented scale and durability in their competitive advantages.

Before detailing the product-market generativity framework and the stages of the generativity flywheel, I would like to devote a section to why I have emphasized the value of markets being built on top of generative products and the idea of profitability as a design characteristic of generative products so much in this book. In short, it is because of the high-powered incentives.

Market Incentives as Innovation Accelerant: The Power of Profit

Much of the literature on open innovation, ecosystems, and platform strategy overlooks a fundamental truth: the most powerful way to drive sustained distributed innovation is to help people make money. While discussions often focus on community building, knowledge sharing, and strategic alignment, the simple reality is that profit potential drives both the scale and sophistication of innovation in ways that other incentives cannot match.

The limitations of non-profit-driven approaches are evident in practice. Open source projects, despite their ideological appeal and occasional breakthroughs, often struggle with maintenance, systematic improvement, and user support. Community platforms generate enthusiastic early participation but rarely sustain professional-grade innovation. Even sophisticated ecosystem approaches that emphasize strategic partnerships often falter because they don't create clear paths to profitability for participants.

Market-based incentives fundamentally transform this dynamic. When Shopify opened its app marketplace, it created opportunities for third-party innovation, not just as quirky side-projects but as viable paths to entrepreneurial wealth. Shopify developers can build multi-million dollar businesses around their innovations.

This profit potential justifies significant investments that would be impossible to sustain through other motivations. When an innovator in your ecosystem can profit well, they can engage in activities and investments that turn them into even more capable innovators. For example: hiring specialized talent, conducting extensive market research, developing sophisticated technical solutions, providing enterprise-grade

https://doi.org/10.1515/9783110779639-008

support, maintaining and improving products over years, marketing and customer acquisition, building sales and support teams, etc.

Mobile app stores dramatically illustrate this dynamic. They created thousands of millionaires among app developers, spawned numerous public companies, and enabled countless developers to build sustainable businesses. This profit potential attracted massive talent and investment to mobile app innovation, driving both quantity and quality of apps far beyond what other incentive systems could achieve.

Even in traditionally open source domains, the introduction of profit potential transforms innovation dynamics. While WordPress itself remains open source, its commercial plugin marketplace enables sophisticated innovation through profit incentives. Complex e-commerce, security, and performance optimization plugins command premium prices, enabling their creators to build viable business around their innovations on the WordPress platform. Premium plugins like WooCommerce, Yoast SEO, and Wordfence command prices from hundreds to thousands of dollars annually per customer. These prices support sophisticated development teams and enable continuous innovation. The results – in terms of functionality, reliability, and user experience – far exceed what voluntary contribution models typically achieve.

The market mechanism becomes particularly powerful when combined with product generativity. A generative product creates expansive possibility spaces for innovation, while profit potential directs sustained investment toward valuable opportunities within those spaces. The marketplace acts as a massive parallel search process, using price signals to guide both the direction and intensity of innovation efforts. Unlike approaches that rely primarily on intrinsic motivation or strategic alignment, profit incentives enable focused, sustained investment in innovation while maintaining the advantages of distributed, parallel exploration.

Crucial to this dynamic is ensuring innovators capture a significant portion of the value they create. As discussed previously, well-designed marketplaces enable this through support mechanisms such as:

- Clear monetization mechanisms
- Reasonable platform fee structures
- Intellectual property protection
- Support for premium pricing
- Infrastructure for recurring revenue
- Tools for customer relationship management
- Payment and subscription handling

Failing to provide the right tools to transform your user-innovators to profit-generating entrepreneurs is an unfortunately common mistake among companies with generative products. This is what I call the problem of not taking your users seriously enough as entrepreneurs. Oceans of opportunity have been lost because of this problem.

In our interviews with Bubble plugin developers for example, we found that these developers had many frustrations with the supports provided by the platform.

One plugin developer remarked that "I think this is a complaint that I have about the bubble system . . . So I don't know what the lifetime value of a user is. Because it's like completely anonymous, and just a black box to me . . . I think there's the opportunity to give users our plugin builders a lot more data about their users, so that they can make more intelligent decisions." These power users can provide a rich set of ideas to the platforms for product features that would help them be serious entrepreneurs as user-innovators. For example, this developer went on to say, "One thing that I feel like could be tricky to implement, but could be highly valuable for both the plugin developers and Bubble is opening up an AB testing framework for pricing."

We also found in our interviews that sometimes non-monetary incentives were able to drive plugin developers to contribute despite a lack of profit. One developer said, "it was mainly out of curiosity, but I also saw it as a way to market myself," and another remarked that "being part of a community makes you do things for reasons other than making money." However, while these curiosity incentives may drive some innovators in the early stages, they cannot sustain long-term effort. Simply put, curiosity does not pay the bills.

Sustaining Innovation Through Career-Level Commitment

The most powerful manifestation of profit-driven innovation occurs when participants can build entire careers and organizations around your platform. This transforms their relationship with the platform from occasional contribution to deep, long-term commitment. When innovators can reliably shape their professional futures around your ecosystem, they invest in ways that transcend typical platform participation.

Consider the ecosystem that has evolved around Bubble's no-code platform. Numerous companies exist solely to develop and maintain plugins for Bubble. These aren't just individual developers creating side projects—they're full-fledged businesses with dedicated teams, professional development practices, and long-term growth strategies. Some plugin developers have built substantial companies, completed strategic acquisitions of other plugins, and shaped entire careers around extending Bubble's capabilities. Zeroqode, a company built entirely around building and maintaining plugins for the Bubble no-code platform, lists more than 50 employees on their website as of the time of writing.

This career-level commitment enables a number of crucial dynamics:
1. Deep Platform Expertise: Participants invest years mastering platform intricacies.
2. Long-term Innovation Planning: Development roadmaps extend months or years ahead.
3. Specialized Skill Development: Teams cultivate unique platform-specific capabilities.
4. Customer Relationship Building: Organizations develop lasting user relationships.
5. Ecosystem Investment: Participants contribute to platform growth and evolution.

6. Knowledge Accumulation: Deep expertise gets codified and shared.
7. Professional Networks: Specialized communities of practice emerge.

This emphasis on profit-driven innovation and career-level commitment doesn't preclude other motivations. Open source, community contribution, and strategic partnership all play valuable roles. But profit potential uniquely enables the scale, sophistication, and sustainability of innovation that a truly generative platform requires. Platform leaders who truly understand this don't just tolerate participant profits or think of them as amusing side-effects—they actively help innovators in their ecosystems build profitable, sustainable businesses and careers.

The Product-Market Generativity Framework

To understand the interplay between product and market generativity, we can think of a two by two framework that categorizes companies based on their levels of product generativity (the capacity of a product to enable user-driven innovation) and market generativity (the ability of a marketplace to harness distributed innovation). Each quadrant provides insights into different innovation dynamics and strategic pathways (see Figure 8.1).

Quadrant 4: High Product, Low Market Generativity

These companies excel in creating products with significant generative potential but initially lack a structured marketplace for user-driven innovations. Over time, many transition to Quadrant 1 by building marketplaces around their products. And in the meantime, unofficial or third-party marketplaces sometimes arise to address the gap.

Examples:
- **Raspberry Pi**: Initially designed as a flexible computing tool for education and DIY projects, with no formal ecosystem for sharing or selling add-ons.
- **Notion**: A modular workspace that allows extensive customization but lacked a marketplace for templates or extensions in its early stages.
- **LEGO (Pre-LEGO Ideas)**: Empowered creativity through its building blocks but for many years there was no way for users to profit from their innovations with LEGO in a marketplace.
- **Coda (Before Packs Marketplace)**: Enabled users to create custom workflows but lacked a formalized platform for sharing or monetizing these innovations.

Quadrant 3: Low Product, Low Market Generativity

Companies in this quadrant offer products and marketplaces that are relatively closed to external innovation. Their growth typically relies on internal innovation and efficiency rather than distributed creativity.

Examples:
- **Uber**: Focused on matching supply and demand (drivers and riders), with limited user-driven customization or broader ecosystem innovation.
- **Hermès**: A luxury brand offering meticulously crafted products through tightly controlled distribution channels, emphasizing internal craftsmanship and tradition rather than external innovation or marketplace dynamism.
- **Peloton**: A fitness platform with tightly controlled content, offering little room for user or developer innovation.

Quadrant 2: Low Product, High Market Generativity

Platforms in this quadrant build vibrant marketplaces or ecosystems without inherently generative core products. They rely on enabling contributors to create value through the marketplace rather than the product itself. However, sometimes they try to create generative products or innovation toolkits that allow more people to participate more easily in their marketplaces. Other times a third-party product may enter the game to take advantage of the opportunity when high demand exists to participate in a dynamic marketplace.

Examples:
- **Etsy**: Provides a generative marketplace for artisans and small businesses but does not offer a particularly generative product.
- **Amazon Marketplace**: While Amazon has created a highly dynamic marketplace with millions of third-party sellers, its core marketplace product remains primarily a transaction and distribution platform. Amazon has leveraged this marketplace to build more generative products (see section below on "Building Generative Products from Generative Markets.")
- **eBay**: Offers a vibrant marketplace with extensive opportunity for sellers to innovate in what they offer and how they present it, but its core product focuses on facilitating transactions rather than providing generative tools. eBay's platform doesn't enable users to build new functionalities or extend its core capabilities in unpredictable ways—it primarily optimizes the buying and selling process.

Quadrant 1: High Product, High Market Generativity

This quadrant represents the most generative systems, where companies combine open, innovative products with ecosystems that foster distributed creativity and innovation. This synergy creates flywheel effects, accelerating growth and innovation potential.

Examples:
- **Google and Apple (Smartphones & App Stores)**: Combines generative hardware and software with a marketplace that empowers developers to innovate and monetize.
- **Roblox**: Allows users to create games and monetize them within a thriving ecosystem, fostering both product and market generativity.
- **Minecraft**: Offers an open-ended creative platform and supports mods and marketplaces for user-generated content.
- **WordPress**: A highly flexible Content Management System (CMS) with a robust ecosystem of themes, plugins, and professional services.
- **YouTube**: Enables content creation through advanced tools and a marketplace that allows creators to monetize and experiment.

Product-Market Generativity Framework

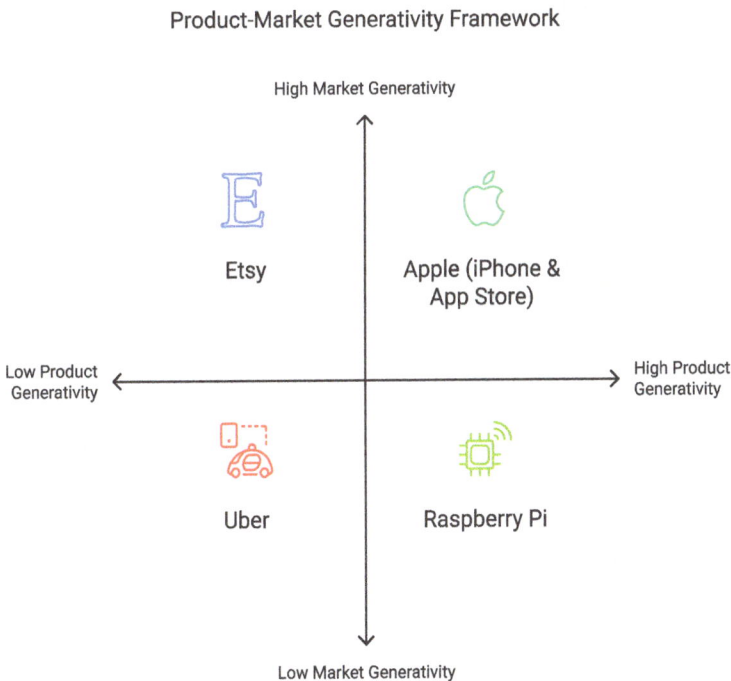

Figure 8.1: The Product-Market Generativity Framework with Examples.

Building Generative Markets from Generative Products

Some companies begin in Quadrant 4—focused on highly generative products—and later evolve to Quadrant 1 by building ecosystems and marketplaces around their products. This is a very natural pattern because a generative product provides the ideal conditions for the formation of a generative marketplace.

The potential is so high that if the company itself does not create and manage a marketplace around its generative product, unofficial marketplaces will naturally form to take advantage of the arbitrage opportunity. This is the case for example with templates for Microsoft Excel. Millions of users around the world innovated for years with these templates but Microsoft never created a managed marketplace to help these innovators profit from their work. While some users have found workarounds and sell Excel templates on Etsy or Gumroad or Shopify, it is possible that many more users could have contributed to a generative marketplace if Microsoft had decided to explicitly create one.

However, the custom GPT marketplace saga has demonstrated that creating marketplaces is not easy. Many companies enjoyed growth through product generativity for years before being able to set up a marketplace around their product. Some examples include:

Raspberry Pi: From DIY Innovation to Ecosystem of Tools and Add-Ons

Raspberry Pi began as a generative product—a low-cost, flexible computing platform designed for educational and hobbyist use. Early adopters leveraged its adaptability to create a vast range of projects, from home automation systems to robotics. Initially, there was no formalized marketplace around Raspberry Pi, and users had to rely on forums and informal channels for components and project ideas.

Raspberry Pi eventually fostered an ecosystem that included accessory marketplaces, official hardware extensions (e.g., cameras and sensors), and a thriving network of distributors offering compatible products. The foundation also supports platforms for sharing project designs and educational resources, solidifying its position as both a generative product and a market.

Notion: From Customizable Workspace to Template Marketplace

Notion started as a highly generative product—a flexible, modular workspace allowing users to create tailored solutions for note-taking, project management, and more. However, for a long time, it lacked a formal marketplace to share or monetize these innovations.

Recognizing the potential of its user-generated templates, Notion launched a template gallery and later encouraged users to monetize their creations. The marketplace provides a structured environment for sharing workflows and templates, turning individual customizations into communal resources.

LEGO: From Blocks to Collaborative Design and Monetization

LEGO has always been a generative product, empowering users to create virtually anything with its iconic building blocks. Historically, however, LEGO operated within a product-centric model, with limited engagement in user-driven design beyond fan communities.

LEGO embraced market generativity through initiatives like the LEGO Ideas platform, where fans can submit designs that, if selected, are turned into official sets with revenue-sharing opportunities. This move created a marketplace of co-creation, harnessing the creativity of its user base to fuel product development and engagement.

Coda: From All-In-One Document Tool to Packs Marketplace

Coda was designed as a generative product—a tool allowing users to create custom workflows, applications, and collaborative documents. Initially, it lacked a marketplace for users to share or monetize these innovations.

Coda launched its Packs marketplace in July 2022, nearly four years after it had introduced the concept of packs as a way to integrate third-party apps into Coda. In 2022, the Packs marketplace finally allowed users to make money from the Packs they made, and an easy-to-use Pack Studio product was also launched to help users make those Packs.

Building Generative Products from Generative Markets

Although this is a less common pattern, it is possible to start from a generative marketplace, and gradually create products that make it easier for more people to participate more easily in that marketplace.

An illustrative example here is Amazon. Already having a dynamic and rich marketplace, the company has made various forays into products that make it easier for people to become profit-generating merchants. Examples include:

1. **Fulfillment by Amazon (FBA):** By transforming warehouse management and logistics into a generative product, Amazon dramatically lowered the barriers to entry for small sellers. FBA enabled entrepreneurs to experiment with different inventory management strategies and compete at an enterprise scale without massive capital investments. This innovation spawned entirely new business models, from retail arbitrage to private label brands, and created opportunities for an ecosystem of tools and services focused on FBA optimization.

2. **Kindle Direct Publishing (KDP):** This product transformed the publishing industry by turning the entire publishing process into an easy do-it-yourself process. Authors gained the ability to experiment with pricing, marketing, and content strategies in ways that traditional publishing never allowed. This flexibility en-

abled new genres and formats to emerge, supported rapid iteration and market testing, and ultimately led to the growth of an entire independent publishing ecosystem.

3. **Amazon Merch on Demand:** This product converted merchandise creation into a generative product. By eliminating inventory risk, the platform enabled designers to experiment with different concepts and rapidly test new niches. This created opportunities for design-focused entrepreneurs who previously lacked the resources to enter the merchandise market, and fostered the development of specialized design tools and services.

Similar to the case of building markets on top of generative products, if you have a generative market that could benefit from a generative product or some sort of user toolkit to make it easier to participate in the product, then it will make sense for such a thing to exist. If you do not build it yourself, someone else may beat you to it. You may in fact desire this if you think an ecosystem of third-party providers will be better than one centrally controlled system, or that there is no reason to compete with already existing third-party tools that enable innovations in your marketplace. For example, while Amazon has itself built "Amazon Merch on Demand," Shopify and Etsy have not built such platforms for their users. However, users have found third-party options like Printful or Printify that can integrate with Shopify or Etsy, and provide the full "merch on demand" pipeline that makes it easy for new entrepreneurs to start selling merchandise on these platforms.

Similarly, mobile app marketplaces provided a ripe opportunity for Google or Apple to provide no-code app building tools to users. Despite a number of efforts, no products by either company succeeded in attracting a large number of non-developer users to the app-making process. An entire industry of no-code software development platforms was created to address this gap.

The Six Stages of the Generativity Flywheel

Product generativity and market generativity create powerful chain reactions when they work together effectively. A generative product first attracts innovative users who see its creative potential. These users, supported by market mechanisms and incentives, begin exploring and expanding the product's possibility spaces through novel applications. As these innovations demonstrate new value and attract broader user segments, the market provides ways for innovators to capture value from their creations. This in turn attracts more innovative users and inspires new ways of using the product, leading to further expansions of the possibility space. This mutually reinforcing cycle creates what we call the "generativity flywheel" – a self-sustaining engine of innovation that continuously expands both what is possible and what is profitable (see Figure 8.2).

The Generativity Flywheel

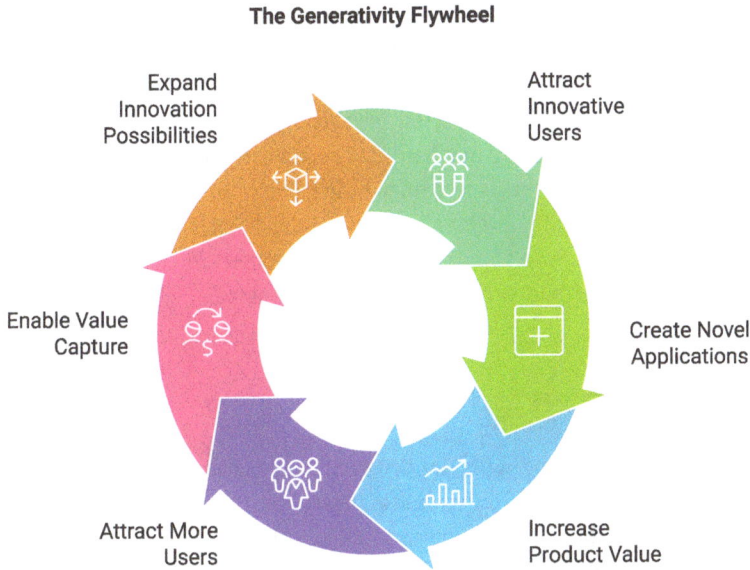

Figure 8.2: The Generativity Flywheel.

While the generativity flywheel might superficially resemble network effects, it represents a fundamentally different mechanism. Network effects, as theorized by Katz and Shapiro (1994), describe how a product becomes more valuable as more people use it. The generativity flywheel, however, creates value not just through increased adoption but through the expansion of possibility spaces. This creates combinatorial growth patterns where innovations can build on each other in exponentially increasing ways. The market effectively functions as a massive parallel experimentation engine, testing countless combinations simultaneously.

Consider Roblox, the gaming platform. Traditional network effects make Roblox more valuable because more players mean more people to play with. But the generativity flywheel goes further: each successful game on Roblox potentially inspires new game mechanics, virtual economy innovations, or social features that expand what is possible on the platform. This continuous expansion of possibilities creates a form of strategic advantage that is particularly difficult for competitors to replicate.

We can break down the generativity flywheel into six interconnected stages that create a powerful engine of continuous innovation and value creation.

Stage 1: Attract Innovative Users

The flywheel begins when a product's generative potential attracts users who see possibilities beyond its obvious applications. These users are drawn to products with accessible entry points but deep possibility spaces—paths that invite experimentation and are rich with opportunity. These users recognize latent potential in the product's design and are motivated by the opportunity to create novel solutions.

Consider how Minecraft initially attracted technically sophisticated users who saw beyond its simple block-building mechanics. These early adopters—modders, server operators, and content creators—recognized the game's potential as a platform for creativity well before it became a global phenomenon. Their early innovations, from custom server modifications to elaborate in-game computers, demonstrated possibilities that Mojang (Minecraft's creator) hadn't itself recognized.

Stage 2: Create Novel Applications

As innovative users begin working with the product, they create applications that demonstrate the breadth of its possibility space. These aren't just new features—they're fundamental expansions of what the product can do. Each novel application serves as a proof-of-concept that inspires others to imagine even more possibilities.

The history of spreadsheet software provides a compelling example. While Visi-Calc was initially designed for financial calculations, users quickly adapted it for everything from project management to game design. Each novel application demonstrated the platform's flexibility and inspired others to imagine new possibilities.

Stage 3: Increase Product Value

Novel applications expand the product's value proposition in two crucial ways. First, they create immediate utility by solving specific user needs. More importantly, they demonstrate entirely new categories of use that expand the product's perceived possibility space. This expansion attracts new user segments who previously didn't see the product as relevant to their needs.

Apple's App Store perfectly illustrates this dynamic. Each innovative app—whether it is a revolutionary photo editing tool or a groundbreaking augmented reality application—not only serves existing users but also attracts new users who previously saw no value in smartphones. The platform becomes more valuable not just because it has more apps, but because it continuously reveals new possibilities.

Stage 4: Attract More Users

As the product's possibility space expands, it attracts an increasingly diverse user base. Each new user segment brings distinct needs, perspectives, and creative approaches, further accelerating the expansion of possibilities. This diversity creates a compound effect where innovations from one domain inspire applications in others, leading to unexpected combinations and novel use cases.

Consider how Roblox evolved from a children's gaming platform to a sophisticated ecosystem for digital experiences. As it attracted older users, professional developers, and educational institutions, each group brought new ideas about what the platform could become, further fueling its generative potential.

Stage 5: Enable Value Capture

For the flywheel to maintain momentum, the platform must help innovators transform their creations into sustainable ventures. User-innovators must be taken seriously as entrepreneurs. Successful platforms provide tools for business management, customer relationship building, and market expansion, treating user-innovators as serious entrepreneurs.

Shopify exemplifies this stage effectively. Beyond providing tools for building online stores, it creates multiple pathways for value capture: app developers can monetize through the app store, theme designers can sell templates, and experts can offer services through the Shopify Partners program. This rich ecosystem of value capture opportunities ensures continued investment in innovation.

Stage 6: Expand Innovation Possibilities

The final stage—which feeds directly back into attracting innovative users—involves systematically expanding the possibility space for future innovations. Successful platforms achieve this by converting proven innovations into accessible building blocks, creating tools that lower barriers to innovation, and establishing knowledge sharing mechanisms that accelerate creative recombination.

At this stage, successful innovations become building blocks for future creativity. When Stripe demonstrated how to simplify online payments through APIs, it didn't just solve one problem—it created a foundation for countless financial technology innovations. Each expansion of possibilities attracts new innovative users, completing one cycle of the flywheel while setting the stage for the next.

Conclusion

The generativity flywheel represents a fundamental shift in how we think about innovation and value creation in the digital age. When product generativity and market generativity work in concert, they create something more powerful than either force alone: a self-reinforcing engine of innovation that continuously expands what is possible while ensuring that valuable possibilities are discovered and developed. This dynamic explains why platforms that master both forms of generativity—like Apple's App Store, Roblox's gaming ecosystem, or WordPress's publishing platform—achieve unprecedented scale and durability in their competitive advantages.

The ideas of product-market generativity and the generativity flywheel provide thinking tools for platform strategy. Whether starting with a generative product and building market mechanisms around it, or beginning with a marketplace and developing tools to enhance participation, success requires careful attention to both sides of the generativity equation. The product-market generativity framework provides a roadmap for this journey, helping companies understand their current position and chart a path toward fuller realization of generative potential.

Chapter 9
Generativity in Practice: The Trade-offs and Challenges of Generativity

The allure of generativity lies in its promise: the ability to unlock a practically boundless ecosystem of profit-generating innovation. But while the generativity advantage is enticing, its implementation is far more complex and fraught than it initially seems. Firms embarking on this journey soon realize they must navigate a labyrinth of tensions, trade-offs, and dilemmas. OpenAI discovered this with the "laundry buddy" saga discussed in the opening of this book. Even with their core product ChatGPT that took the world by storm, there was no shortage of people mocking or undermining the technology, calling it a "stochastic parrot" (Bender et al., 2021) or "glorified tape recorder" (Cao, 2023).

Steve Jobs was initially hesitant to allow third-party apps on the iPhone, preferring to maintain control and a high bar for quality. Microsoft never created a managed marketplace for Excel templates. The Bubble no-code platform hasn't yet provided proper documentation to its plugin developers on how to build plugins. Google's Gemini large language models had APIs that were so notoriously more difficult to use than those of OpenAI that they had to simplify them after community backlash. It took years for Coda to establish a marketplace around its extremely generative product. In short, achieving a generativity advantage is not easy, and not something to be taken for granted.

These cases are no accidents—they result from the qualities embedded in the very DNA of generative ecosystems which thrive on openness, collaboration, and distributed innovation. Yet these same qualities clash directly with the traditional imperatives of control, predictability, and operational efficiency in business strategy. The pursuit of generativity is not a linear path, nor is it a guaranteed formula for success. It demands that organizations step into uncharted territory, often embracing ambiguity and risk. It forces firms to confront uncomfortable questions: How much control should they relinquish? What inefficiencies are they willing to tolerate? How do they balance the needs of their core operations with the demands of innovation at the edges?

This chapter focuses on the tensions and trade-offs that typically arise as organizations strive to pursue a generativity advantage in practice. See Table 9.1 for a summary. Drawing on both scholarly insights and real-world examples, we explore these tensions in depth, offering actionable remedies to help firms navigate this challenging yet rewarding terrain. Implementing generativity may be easier said than done, but for those who embrace its complexities, the rewards can be transformative.

https://doi.org/10.1515/9783110779639-009

Table 9.1: Key tensions and trade-offs on the path to a generativity advantage.

Tension	Description	Real-World Example	Potential Remedies
Control vs. Generativity	The balance between maintaining control over a platform (for quality, security, and strategic alignment) and fostering generativity (openness, innovation, user participation). Too much control stifles innovation.	Apple's initial tight control over iOS development, later relaxed to allow more third-party apps.	– Use boundary resources (APIs, SDKs) to structure interaction. – Implement governance mechanisms (guidelines, incentives). – Establish processes for dynamic adaptation based on feedback.
Stability vs. Flexibility	The need for a stable, predictable platform (for reliability and developer confidence) versus the need for flexibility to adapt to new technologies and user needs. Too much stability leads to stagnation.	Google's Android fragmentation due to its open nature, leading to developer challenges and inconsistent user experience.	– Employ modular design for independent updates. – Implement version control for different use cases. – Foster collaborative governance to involve stakeholders in platform evolution.
Variety vs. Utility	The challenge of balancing a wide variety of complements (to attract diverse users) with the actual utility those complements provide. More variety doesn't always mean more value, especially for experiential goods.	Video game consoles: early-stage generativity (new game types) increases satisfaction, but later-stage generativity can lead to lower quality and decreased satisfaction.	– Aim for quality generativity with screening mechanisms. – Offer incentives for high-quality content. – Improve discoverability of high-utility complements. – Adapt governance over time as the platform matures.
Originality vs. Remixing	The balance between encouraging original content creation and allowing remixing of existing content. Remixing can drive innovation but may hinder the emergence of truly novel works.	The Scratch Online Community: while remixing is encouraged, issues of originality and superficial adaptations arise.	– Design features that encourage transformative remixing. – Promote visibility of original content. – Implement recognition and rewards for originality. – Educate users on creative contributions and copyright.

Table 9.1 (continued)

Tension	Description	Real-World Example	Potential Remedies
Ecosystem Boundaries vs. Product Boundaries	The tension between expanding the network of platform participants (ecosystem) and expanding the platform's features and functions (product). These can be synergistic but also conflicting, especially when product expansion competes with ecosystem innovations.	LLM providers like OpenAI: initial focus on API access for ecosystem growth, later expansion into features like multi-modality and code interpretation, creating uncertainty for some developers.	– Establish clear feedback loops between ecosystem and product development. – Implement mechanisms for complementors to propose new features. – Develop policies for handling competition with ecosystem innovations. – Focus on user experience.
Openness vs. Value Capture	The conflict between maximizing a platform's accessibility and collaborative potential (openness) and ensuring sufficient economic benefits for the platform and its stakeholders (value capture). Particularly challenging for open-source platforms.	The WordPress ecosystem: open-source core software enables a vast plugin ecosystem, but value capture relies on indirect mechanisms like premium plugins and complementary services.	– Create and control strategic control points within the ecosystem. – Implement curation and promotion strategies. – Leverage the data advantage while respecting privacy. – Foster a symbiotic relationship between the platform and its ecosystem.

Control Versus Generativity

The tension between control and generativity is a fundamental paradox that must be dealt with in any effort to implement or pursue a generativity advantage. The openness characteristic of generative systems fuels innovation, attracts users, and expands the platform's reach, forming a self-reinforcing dynamic. However, this very openness creates a challenge for the platform owner who also seeks to maintain a level of control over the ecosystem (Tilson et al., 2010). Control becomes necessary to ensure quality, security, and strategic alignment with the platform's vision. The tension arises because control can stifle the very generativity it seeks to harness, leading to a potential decrease in innovation (Cennamo & Santaló, 2019). The platform owner must carefully balance these competing forces to maximize the platform's potential.

The challenge is that generativity requires some level of decentralization, allowing various actors to innovate in an uncoordinated fashion. This differs from traditional, hierarchical management structures where control is centralized, and innovation is managed from within the firm. The platform owner has to relinquish some of its command and control over the platform's evolution, and instead has to rely on external actors to drive the platform in unforeseen directions (Eaton et al., 2011). This creates a risk that the platform might evolve in ways that are not aligned with the owner's strategic goals. Conversely, over-controlling the platform can inhibit the flow of ideas and dampen the enthusiasm of external developers, reducing the platform's potential for expansion. The platform owner is thus in a constant balancing act, seeking to optimize the level of control and to leverage the power of the crowd for innovation while protecting the platform's key assets. This constant adjustment and recalibration is a key feature of managing digital platforms.

Real-World Example: Apple's Shifting Stance on iOS Development

Apple's journey with the iOS platform offers a compelling case study of the tension between control and generativity (Eaton et al., 2015). Initially, Apple adopted a highly controlled approach, requiring all applications to be approved through their App Store. This curation ensured a high level of quality and security, but it also limited the range of applications and the autonomy of developers. The company's policy also restricted the use of certain technologies, such as Adobe Flash, for reasons of security and performance. This control generated friction with the developer community who often felt that their innovative efforts were being stifled. The result was a tension between Apple's desire to control the user experience and developers' desire to create innovative apps. However, over time, Apple has gradually relaxed some of its restrictions, allowing more apps to be developed and distributed, and introducing more flexible development tools. The move was clearly influenced by the need to leverage the creativity and distributed innovation of external developers. This highlights the dynamic nature of the control-generativity tension, requiring platforms to adapt to the shifting needs of their users and their ecosystems.

Apple's initial stance on Voice over Internet Protocol (VoIP) apps provides another example of this dynamic. At first, Apple restricted VoIP applications on its platform, likely due to concerns about competition with its telecommunications partners. This created tensions with third party developers who wanted to offer innovative alternatives to established telecommunication providers. However, under pressure from the user and developer communities, and with increasing competitive pressures, Apple eventually relaxed its position, allowing VoIP apps while establishing certain parameters for their functionality. These examples illustrate how control is not simply an on/off switch but rather a strategic choice that needs to be adjusted in response to the dynamics of the ecosystem.

Potential Remedies: Balancing Control and Generativity

The tension between control and generativity cannot be resolved by choosing one over the other; rather, it calls for finding a delicate balance. One key strategy involves using boundary resources to structure the interaction between the platform and its ecosystem (Ghazawneh & Henfridsson, 2013). We have talked about boundary resources earlier in this book but did not emphasize one key feature: they are modular interfaces that allow external actors to develop complementary innovations while ensuring that the core architecture of the platform remains under the control of the platform owner. Application Programming Interfaces (APIs) and Software Development Kits (SDKs) act as such boundary resources by enabling third parties to build on the platform without having direct access to the core source code. Boundary resources, therefore, offer a way to channel external creativity while still safeguarding the platform's strategic objectives. The design of these resources is key as it determines the types of innovation that are possible on the platform. Therefore, careful calibration of these boundary resources is needed to both promote innovation and protect platform integrity.

Another effective approach is to use governance mechanisms, which establish clear rules, guidelines, and incentives for ecosystem participants, while maintaining a degree of flexibility. Governance mechanisms can include things such as transparent review processes for applications, guidelines that foster positive network effects, and well-designed user feedback mechanisms that offer developers crucial information. Effective governance helps align the actions of external actors with the overall goals of the platform by establishing clear and predictable behavioral boundaries. By making the rules explicit and providing channels for feedback, platform owners can encourage responsible innovation and mitigate the risk of uncontrolled development. This approach recognizes that control does not have to be top-down but can be a process of guiding and coordinating the actions of the ecosystem as a whole. The key is to shift the mindset from control as a mechanism of restriction to control as a tool for enabling and coordinating a vibrant ecosystem.

Finally, the platform owner needs to establish processes for dynamic adaptation by regularly evaluating the effectiveness of its control mechanisms and adjusting them as required (Eaton et al., 2011). This involves monitoring the ecosystem for disruptive innovations and using a variety of channels to collect feedback from ecosystem participants, and responding to this feedback by adapting the platform's boundary resources and governance mechanisms. Furthermore, platform owners can facilitate this by creating a culture of experimentation that welcomes failure as a learning opportunity. By staying responsive and agile, platform owners can adapt to the constantly evolving needs of their ecosystems, and by constantly tuning their control mechanisms, they can prevent the stifling of generativity. This constant evolution highlights the importance of a flexible mindset when it comes to balancing control and generativity, and the need to adapt to the dynamic nature of digital ecosystems.

By carefully calibrating boundary resources, governance mechanisms, and adaptive processes, platform owners can effectively manage the inherent tensions between control and generativity, fostering a vibrant ecosystem that creates value for all stakeholders involved.

Stability Versus Flexibility

The tension between stability and flexibility is another core paradox that platform owners must navigate to foster successful ecosystems (Tilson et al., 2010). While generativity provides the potential for unbounded innovation, platforms also require a degree of stability to function predictably and reliably. Stability in a digital platform context refers to the consistency of the platform's core functions, interfaces, and rules, ensuring that the platform remains a reliable foundation for innovation. This stability allows developers to build on the platform with a degree of confidence, knowing that their work will not be disrupted by unforeseen changes. However, this very need for stability can create inertia and hinder the platform's ability to adapt to new technological trends and user needs (Lyytinen et al., 2017). Therefore, platform owners must balance this need for stability against the need for flexibility, which is the capacity of the platform to evolve in response to changing conditions. This includes the ability to incorporate new technologies, respond to user feedback, and adapt to changing market conditions. Too much stability can lead to stagnation, while too much flexibility can create chaos and make the platform difficult to use and develop for. The tension, therefore, is to strike a balance between predictability and change, between a solid foundation and the ability to adapt.

This paradox manifests itself in different ways. For example, platform owners need to maintain stable APIs so that developers' applications continue to work as the platform evolves. However, these same APIs might need to be updated or even replaced to support new features and technologies. Every time OpenAI or Anthropic update the capabilities of their Large Language Models, scores of developers have to update their code. The challenge is to make changes to the platform without disrupting the work of the ecosystem, or the user experience. This is a key aspect of digital platform evolution, where changes can have far-reaching consequences for all users and stakeholders. Furthermore, a stable platform attracts developers by providing a predictable environment for innovation, while a flexible platform ensures that the platform remains competitive and relevant in a fast-paced digital world. This inherent duality requires a dynamic balancing act where platform owners are constantly adapting their strategy to maintain a balance between stability and flexibility.

Real-World Example: Google's Android Fragmentation

The Android operating system provides an example of the challenges associated with managing the stability-flexibility tension in a real-world setting. Android's open nature allows for significant customization by device manufacturers, which promotes flexibility and innovation. However, this flexibility also leads to a fragmented ecosystem, with different versions of the operating system running on different devices, causing significant challenges for developers, and often a suboptimal experience for end users. This fragmentation makes it difficult for developers to target all Android users effectively, as their apps may behave differently on various devices and versions of the operating system. The need to test across multiple Android versions often creates additional costs for developers which impacts innovation. In a sense, the high degree of flexibility in the Android ecosystem created a lack of platform stability, making it a challenge to provide a seamless user experience, which impacted negatively on the platform's potential and value capture. This highlights the inherent challenges of managing a platform ecosystem where flexibility and stability are at odds with each other.

The tension between stability and flexibility on the Android platform is evident in Google's attempts to address the fragmentation issue. While Google encourages innovation and customization, they have also implemented measures to ensure a minimum level of consistency across the ecosystem. For example, Google has introduced compatibility requirements for devices to run Google's suite of apps. This was intended to create a core level of stability, while still allowing device manufacturers a degree of freedom to innovate. These efforts show that even with the advantages of an open and flexible platform, there is a need to maintain a certain level of stability to guarantee a smooth, consistent, user experience, and to enable a thriving developer ecosystem. The ongoing need to balance these conflicting needs shows that this is a constant challenge for the platform owners.

Potential Remedies: Modular Design and Versioning

One way to navigate the stability-flexibility tension is through modular design, where the platform is built using independent, interchangeable modules (Pil & Cohen, 2006). This approach allows platform owners to update specific parts of the platform without affecting other parts of the system. For example, new features can be introduced as separate modules which can be integrated into the platform without requiring extensive changes in the core. This minimizes the risk of disruption from changes while allowing for incremental improvements and innovation. The modular design approach, therefore, promotes flexibility by enabling change to be introduced without compromising the overall stability of the platform.

Another strategy is to implement version control mechanisms, providing different versions of the platform for different use-cases or user segments. This allows for new features and technologies to be tested in controlled environments before being rolled out to the entire ecosystem. It also allows platform owners to support legacy applications while gradually migrating to new versions of the platform. Versioning, therefore, can be used as a way to provide both flexibility and stability at the same time.

Variety Versus Utility

As platforms embrace generativity, they often face a critical tension between the variety of complements offered and the utility that those complements provide to users (Cennamo & Santaló, 2019). While a greater variety of complements can attract a wider user base by catering to diverse needs and preferences, not all complements are created equal. Some may be of low quality, poorly designed, or simply not very useful, thus diminishing the overall value proposition of the platform. The core challenge, then, is that while generativity can lead to greater variety, it does not automatically guarantee that such variety will be high in utility. This is especially true in the case of "experiential" goods, such as software applications or games, where the user needs to consume the complement to determine its true value. Therefore, the platform owner must find ways to incentivize the creation of high-utility complements while also fostering a diverse ecosystem. Moreover, an increase in variety can also lead to a greater variance in user satisfaction with complements, making the overall platform experience less predictable and potentially damaging to the platform's reputation. This is because, as more complements are created, it becomes more difficult for users to find high-quality options, and some users may have negative experiences that color their perception of the platform as a whole.

This tension is not merely a theoretical concern. It has very practical implications for platform owners and complementors. When user satisfaction is a critical driver for platform adoption and usage, the presence of low-quality complements can undermine the entire ecosystem. This creates a free-rider problem, where some complementors benefit from the overall reputation of the platform without investing in the quality of their own offerings. As the platform matures, this problem may become more pronounced, as the initial positive spillover effect of generativity is outweighed by the negative free-rider effect. This can reduce the incentives for complementors to invest in innovation, thus diminishing the overall value of the platform (Cennamo & Santaló, 2019). Therefore, platform owners need to consider how their approach to generativity will evolve over time, especially as the platform matures, and address this variety-utility tension.

Real-World Example: Video Game Consoles

The video game console market provides a compelling example of the variety-utility tension (Cennamo & Santaló, 2019). In the early stages of a console's lifecycle, greater generativity, as measured by the introduction of new game types, positively affects user satisfaction with games. This is because new games, especially in new genres, provide a wider range of experiences, which attract a diverse base of users. However, as the console matures and the number of available games increases, the positive effect of generativity on user satisfaction diminishes and eventually turns negative. This is because, with greater generativity and variety, there is also a higher chance of free-riding and lower-quality games being released. As more games enter the marketplace, users' average satisfaction declines because there is also a greater variance in quality and the abundance of options makes it harder to find the best titles. Thus, while the increase in the number of games can appeal to a wider audience, the games that are introduced later in a console's lifecycle are associated with declining average user satisfaction.

Potential Remedies: Balancing Variety and Utility

To address the variety-utility tension, platform owners can implement a variety of strategies that seek to balance the two. First, rather than maximizing variety per se, they should aim for quality variety. This means implementing more robust screening mechanisms to filter out low-quality complements and creating a more curated experience. These mechanisms can involve setting minimum quality standards for inclusion in the platform, providing support and resources to developers to help them improve their products, and even offering direct marketing support to complementors. Additionally, the platform owner can also offer incentives for complementors to produce high-quality content. This can be achieved through a combination of direct financial incentives, reduced royalty fees, or higher placement in the discovery mechanisms. The platform owner can also make it easier for consumers to identify and find high-quality complements through its promotion and curation privileges, by implementing recommendation systems, user review systems, and curated lists of "best" complements.

Another approach is to focus on the platform's architecture and design to promote complements that provide specific types of utility. For example, a platform owner might design APIs and SDKs that make it easier to create certain types of complements (Ghazawneh & Henfridsson, 2013). This approach can guide the ecosystem towards certain areas of innovation. However, they must also allow for flexibility for complementors to innovate in unexpected ways. For example, a platform may have a developer program that encourages a particular kind of application but still allows others to participate in the ecosystem.

Finally, it is important to understand that the variety-utility tension can change as the platform matures. Platform owners must evolve their governance mechanisms over time, adapting to the changing dynamics of the ecosystem. This may involve shifting from a more open approach in the early stages of the platform's lifecycle to a more curated approach as the platform matures. Ultimately, the key is to find a balance that allows for both variety and utility, ensuring that the platform ecosystem remains vibrant and valuable for all participants.

Originality Versus Remixing

The tension between originality and remixing arises from the inherent nature of digital platforms as spaces for both collaboration and creation (Hill & Monroy-Hernández, 2013). While generativity often involves the remixing and re-appropriation of existing content (Lessig, 2009), this process can sometimes hinder the emergence of truly original works. The ease with which content can be copied, modified, and redistributed can inadvertently lead to superficial adaptations rather than genuine creative transformations. Given that remix culture can be very conducive to generativity, platform designs must carefully balance the generative potential of remixing with the need to foster original contributions that push the boundaries of creative expression.

This tension is further complicated by the fact that certain features that promote the generativity of a work also tend to decrease the originality of the resulting remixes (Hill & Monroy-Hernández, 2013). For example, works created by prominent authors tend to be remixed more often, but these remixes often maintain a high degree of recognizability with the original, limiting the originality of the derivative work. Similarly, works that are already remixes themselves are more likely to be remixed further, but these subsequent remixes tend to be less original, becoming increasingly refined rather than transformative. Recent debates around AI art illustrate this phenomenon: many artists refuse to even recognize AI-generated images as art, and consider resemblance to the work of real artists to be a form of theft (Goetze, 2024). This highlights the complexity of managing a platform's creative ecosystem as features and designs that promote increased user engagement through remixing may come at the cost of diminished originality and lead to superficial content.

Real-World Example: The Scratch Online Community

The Scratch Online Community, a platform where young people create and share interactive animations and games, provides a concrete illustration of this tension (Hill & Monroy-Hernández, 2013). In this community, remixing is explicitly encouraged, with every project licensed under Creative Commons, allowing for reuse, and the platform features prominent download buttons for easy access. The platform also features ways for users to communicate with each other, as well as "love" projects which promote creator visibility. Despite this encouragement, the data from Scratch shows that only a small portion of projects are ever remixed, and issues of originality often emerge. Users react negatively to visibly similar remixes and accuse others of a lack of originality. Hill and Monroy-Hernandez (2013) found that while moderate complexity, creator prominence, and cumulativeness increased generativity in Scratch, these very qualities were associated with decreased originality in the resulting remixes. These dynamics highlight the challenges that platform designers face when trying to encourage both remixing and originality.

Potential Remedies: Balancing Generativity and Originality

Addressing the tension between originality and remixing requires a multi-faceted approach that goes beyond simply encouraging user contributions. First, it is necessary for designers to recognize the impact of their design choices on the creative output of their users. For instance, platform features should not overemphasize or reward the mere act of remixing, which can unintentionally incentivize superficial adaptations over original work. Platform designers should aim to provide an environment that encourages more transformative remixing. This approach may include offering tools and features that enable users to go beyond the mere copying of existing content and create novel outputs with unique value.

Second, it is important to promote the visibility of new original content alongside remixes to provide a more balanced ecosystem. Platforms can highlight original works through dedicated sections or reward systems, ensuring that they are not drowned out by the sheer volume of remixes. It is important to support and promote the authors of original works and make them visible in the community. Moreover, platforms might consider mechanisms for recognizing and rewarding originality, such as badges, rankings, or other forms of recognition that encourage users to create novel content. These methods can counter the bias towards remixing by emphasizing and rewarding unique creations. Additionally, education about copyright and creative contributions could help users understand the difference between a transformative remix and mere copying, which might address negative user reactions.

Ecosystem Boundaries Versus Product Boundaries

The generativity advantage is about being able to benefit from the innovations of others outside your firm. But your firm is likely in a position of privileged access to the platform, in such a way that it would be a market leader if it pursued some innovations with the platform on its own. So the question becomes: which innovations to pursue internally and which innovations to leave to the external ecosystem?

The expansion of ecosystem boundaries and the expansion of product boundaries represent two distinct yet interconnected pathways for platform growth and evolution. The expansion of ecosystem boundaries refers to the broadening of the network of actors participating in a platform, including complementors, developers, and users. This expansion involves increasing the diversity of participants, their skills, and their motivations for engaging with the platform. In contrast, the expansion of product boundaries pertains to increasing the variety of content, services, and functions offered on a platform, reflecting the technological and functional evolution of the platform itself (Fürstenau et al., 2023).

This tension is complicated by both synergistic and adversarial relationships between these forms of expansion. On the synergistic side, expanding product boundaries by adding new features and capabilities often attracts new users who may become complementors themselves. These new complementors can then leverage the expanded product capabilities to create even more innovative solutions, creating a virtuous cycle of growth. For instance, when a platform adds new API capabilities, it not only enhances the product's functionality but potentially attracts developers specializing in those capabilities, who then create innovations that draw more users to the platform.

However, these two forms of expansion do not always reinforce each other linearly. While a larger ecosystem can provide more diverse ideas and contributions, the social interactions required for that collaboration may not directly translate into new product features if there is no process for those ideas to be incorporated. Furthermore, the pursuit of expanding product boundaries by introducing new categories of content or services can sometimes dilute the focus of the platform, making it more difficult for new complementors to identify their niche or contribution, potentially creating a "too much choice" problem for users (Cennamo & Santaló, 2019; Fürstenau et al., 2023).

A particularly challenging aspect emerges when platforms expand their product boundaries in ways that directly compete with ecosystem innovations. This creates significant uncertainty for complementors, who must weigh the risk of their innovations potentially becoming core platform features against their investment in development. When platforms absorb successful ecosystem innovations into their core product, it can effectively eliminate entire categories of complementary businesses, and the looming threat of such a thing can deter complementary innovators in the first place.

Real-World Example: LLM Platforms

Large Language Model (LLM) providers like OpenAI offer a compelling example of the tension between ecosystem and product boundary expansion. These platforms initially focused on providing access to powerful LLMs through APIs, enabling a broad ecosystem of developers to build applications and services. This strategy prioritizes the expansion of the ecosystem, empowering third-party developers to generate diverse use cases and applications.

However, as the platforms evolve, a tension emerges between the initial focus on ecosystem growth and the desire to expand product boundaries. OpenAI, for example, has introduced numerous features such as custom GPTs, multi-modality (the ability to process different types of data like text and images), "canvas" (a document-editing workspace), "code interpreter" (which allows the LLM to execute code), web search (allowing the LLM to search the internet), and Deep Research (allowing reasoning LLMs to search deep in the internet and compile detailed reports). All of these are efforts to expand the platform's product boundary. Each new feature creates opportunities for innovative applications, potentially attracting new users who might become complementors themselves. For instance, the addition of image processing capabilities has drawn in developers specializing in visual AI applications, expanding both the ecosystem and the range of possible innovations.

Yet this same product expansion can create uncertainty for existing complementors, who face uncertainty around whether or not their product is going to become "just another feature" on ChatGPT. When OpenAI introduced custom GPTs with the ability to process specific document types or execute specialized tasks, it effectively reduced the value and posed a competitive threat to many third-party "LLM wrapper" applications built on its API (Stokel-Walker, 2023). This expansion of product boundaries, while beneficial to some platform users, might not align perfectly with the needs of all developers in the ecosystem, and can also add complexity to the core platform, increasing the learning curve for developers and potentially detracting from the initial goal of ease of use that made the platform attractive to them in the first place. There is a risk that a platform owner could over-extend the core product, leading to a "feature bloat" that detracts from its original purpose while simultaneously undermining the business models of ecosystem participants who had invested in building similar functionalities.

Potential Remedies: Aligning Ecosystem and Product Expansion

To effectively manage the tension between ecosystem and product boundary expansion, platform designers need to adopt a more integrative and dynamic approach. First, it is crucial to establish clear feedback loops between the ecosystem and the product development processes. This can involve creating mechanisms for the platform's community to directly contribute to decisions about the platform's features and functionality. For instance, platforms can use open forums, surveys, or co-creation events to gather insights from the community about their needs and preferences. These insights can then be used to guide the expansion of the product's features, ensuring that it aligns with the needs of the ecosystem.

Platforms might also consider establishing a formal system for complementors to propose new platform components or features (Fürstenau et al., 2023). This could include a standardized process for submitting, evaluating, and implementing new ideas, fostering an environment of collaborative growth. Transparent product roadmaps can be provided to allow the ecosystem to better anticipate changes in product boundaries. However, in a highly competitive market, releasing too much information about future plans may not be the right strategic move.

A crucial consideration is how to handle situations where platform evolution might compete with ecosystem innovations. Some platforms address this through clear policies about which areas they consider "core" versus open for ecosystem innovation, or by establishing fair compensation or acquisition strategies when absorbing successful ecosystem innovations. For example, Salesforce often acquires successful ecosystem companies rather than simply replicating their functionality, creating positive exit opportunities for complementors while maintaining ecosystem trust.

Openness Versus Value Capture

The tension between openness and value capture is a critical challenge for platform ecosystems, and it manifests uniquely in the context of open-source platforms like WordPress (Um et al., 2013). In essence, this tension highlights the inherent conflict between maximizing the accessibility and collaborative potential of a platform (openness) and ensuring that the platform and its key stakeholders can derive sufficient economic benefits from the ecosystem they have created (value capture). Openness, in this context, is characterized by the free availability of the platform's core code, which allows anyone to build on, modify, and redistribute it. This fosters a rich ecosystem where third-party developers contribute to the platform's functionality, enhancing its overall value and appeal. However, this inherent openness makes direct value capture from the core platform challenging, since the core platform is essentially free. As a result, platform owners and ecosystem participants must find indirect mechanisms for value capture, such as complementary services, premium plugins, or data-driven insights. The challenge is in ensuring that value capture mechanisms align with, and do not undermine, the open and collaborative nature of the platform that is the source of its value in the first place.

The tension between openness and value capture, therefore, is about how to create a business model that is both sustainable and promotes, or at least does not hinder, the collaborative nature of the open platform. This involves balancing the need to monetize the platform with the need to maintain the level of openness that fuels the platform's ecosystem and network effects.

Real-World Example: The WordPress Ecosystem

The WordPress ecosystem exemplifies the complex interplay of openness and value capture. WordPress.org is an open-source platform, and its core software is freely available to all. This openness has enabled a vibrant community of third-party developers to create over 22,000 plugins, vastly extending the platform's functionality (Um et al., 2013). However, this has also created a complex dynamic where the platform owners do not directly capture value from the core platform but instead rely on indirect mechanisms, including commercial offerings through WordPress.com, as well as various forms of value capture by third party plugin developers. For example, some developers offer free plugins and other paid premium versions of the same plugins that provide additional features. In addition, the open nature of WordPress has led to the emergence of a large number of vendors offering complementary services like premium themes, website hosting, and other forms of platform support. The core platform's openness enables all of these vendors to grow by leveraging the WordPress platform's vast popularity and user base. Although WordPress is an open platform, the platform owners exercise extensive control over the evolution of the ecosystem through their APIs. In turn, the third-party developers utilize both the platform's internal and external APIs to extend its functionality. This highlights how the inherent openness of the core WordPress platform is both a value driver and a source of tension in the ecosystem. This tension exists because the core platform is open, and yet the various actors in the system are attempting to capture value through various indirect channels. This tension, however, is fundamental to the generativity of the platform and the diverse ecosystem that surrounds it.

Potential Remedies: Balancing Openness and Value Capture

Addressing the tension between openness and value capture requires a multifaceted approach. One potential remedy is to focus on creating and controlling critical resources or "control points" within the ecosystem (Bohnsack et al., 2024; Eaton et al., 2010). In the WordPress ecosystem, these control points can include the core APIs, documentation, or community forums. By maintaining some control over these resources, the platform owners can influence the direction of innovation, encourage positive contributions, and ensure a degree of quality and consistency. This approach balances the desire for value capture with the platform's generative potential. Furthermore, platform owners can adopt a strategy of "curation and promotion" to incentivize and reward high-quality contributions, while also addressing potential ecosystem gaps. This approach not only promotes valuable additions but also helps the platform maintain trust and avoid biases in curation that could undermine the overall ecosystem. This can involve promoting high-quality, innovative content transparently, while also balancing exclusivity with inclusivity.

Another important aspect of managing this tension is to recognize and leverage the data advantage that can be gained from the platform's activity (Komljenovic, 2021). The platform can collect valuable insights from user interactions and plugin usage, which can then be used to provide valuable feedback to the ecosystem participants, while also improving the platform itself. This data advantage can create a virtuous cycle, where data-driven insights fuel innovation and encourage participation. However, it is equally important to balance data capture with privacy and ensure that data is used in a way that does not undermine user trust or the generativity of the platform. For instance, the platform could share aggregated data to enhance the user experience, while also protecting the individual privacy of its users. In the case of WordPress, this might involve sharing information about how plugins are used, while also ensuring that individual user data is not exposed. By carefully managing data flows and usage, platform owners can align value capture with generative capabilities of the platform.

Conclusion: Embracing the Paradoxes of Generativity

The tensions we've explored in this chapter can be viewed as challenges to be managed but also barriers to competition and strategic opportunities to be embraced. Like a tightrope walker maintaining dynamic balance, successful platforms continuously adjust their position across multiple dimensions of tension.

What makes these tensions particularly fascinating is how they emerge naturally from the very qualities that make generativity powerful. The openness that enables distributed innovation creates control challenges. The flexibility that allows platforms to evolve can undermine their stability. The variety that attracts diverse users can dilute quality. These aren't bugs in the system—they're essential features of generative environments.

The examples we've examined—from Apple's evolving app store policies to WordPress's open ecosystem, from Android's fragmentation challenges to OpenAI's expansion dilemmas—reveal that even the most successful platforms grapple with these tensions continuously. Their success lies in developing sophisticated mechanisms for dynamic adjustment and patient evolution.

Several key principles emerge from our analysis:

1. **Embrace Opportunities**: Rather than viewing tensions as problems to solve, see them as spaces where innovative solutions can emerge. This means developing governance structures that can harness opposing forces productively.

2. **Practice Strategic Patience**: Particularly around monetization and value capture, resist the urge to optimize too early. Build trust and ecosystem health before implementing more robust revenue models.

3. **Employ Data-Driven Adaptation**: Use metrics and analytics to understand eco-system health and guide adjustments. This empirical foundation helps platforms make more informed trade-offs.
4. **Layer Your Approach**: Use multiple complementary mechanisms to address each tension. For example, combining technical boundary resources with social governance systems to manage the control-generativity balance.
5. **Enable Discovery**: Rather than rigidly maintaining a predefined value proposition, create conditions where new forms of value can emerge from user innovations. Let the platform's vision evolve in dialogue with its community's discoveries.

Perhaps most importantly, platform owners must recognize that these tensions will evolve as their platforms mature. What works in the early stages of platform development may need significant adjustment as the ecosystem grows and becomes more complex.

The rewards for those who master these challenges are transformative. By creating environments that enable and channel distributed innovation while maintaining platform integrity, organizations can tap into creative potential far beyond their own boundaries. The generativity advantage offers firms the ability to scale innovation beyond traditional limits, co-create value with diverse stakeholders, and shape the future of their industries.

Chapter 10
Celebrating the Shared Potential of Humanity

Generative products and marketplaces, at their core, are celebrations of possibility—an invitation for humanity's collective ingenuity to transform uncertainty into opportunity. A generative system is a catalyst, not a conclusion. It is designed to invite and amplify the creativity of others, opening spaces where solutions and possibilities multiply. Designing for generativity is about building platforms where new grammars of innovation emerge—languages of creativity that empower users to express and solve in ways the original creators could never have imagined.

No-code platforms like Bubble and Zapier illustrate this principle powerfully. Bubble enables users without coding expertise to build fully functional web applications, while Zapier allows non-technical users to automate workflows by connecting various tools. Many users who experienced these platforms for the first time had a sudden sense of delight and empowerment, like they were given new tools and languages they never had before, that allowed them to build things they could never build before. These platforms do not merely solve problems; they create environments where users can invent new solutions, often exceeding the vision of the platform's creators. They provide the scaffolding for creativity and innovation, allowing individuals and small teams to scale their ideas without needing vast technical resources.

More recently, LLMs and platforms like OpenAI's ChatGPT and Anthropic's Claude have created this sense of delight and empowerment once again among millions of user-innovators. You must have felt it, too, the first time you use an LLM platform like ChatGPT: a sense of magic and the opening of entire new worlds of possibilities. These platforms have enabled a new wave of applications, from personalized assistants to creative tools for writers and educators. The generativity of these platforms lies in their ability to adapt to countless scenarios, driven by user creativity and problem-solving.

I have personally felt the magic of Generative AI several times since the popularization of LLMs in 2023. Most recently, the ability to build my own game app (called "Match Beat") and offer it on the Google play store using a combination of Claude, Cursor, and Replit made me feel like I could do things I never thought I could. I then pushed myself to build a full-fledged Software-as-a-Service (SaaS) list curation platform that I've always wanted to build. Using Replit's AI agent and assistant tools for hundreds of hours, I was able to build Lstr.cc, one of the world's most comprehensive list curation platforms, with AI features galore! For many years I thought I would have to recruit a team of software developers to build this, but now I was able to do it myself. I now teach my students to use AI coding or "vibe coding" tools in similar ways, and encourage them to completely rethink their capability sets.

https://doi.org/10.1515/9783110779639-010

The generativity advantage is not just valuable for the business leaders who pursue it; it is valuable precisely because it empowers others to create and capture value of their own. In building generative platforms, leaders craft the foundations for a new grammar of progress—one that embraces unpredictability and prizes the contributions of many over the control of the few.

Generativity operates as a compounding force, hence the "generativity flywheel," where each turn accelerates the next. Each innovation begets more innovation, each discovery catalyzes new possibilities. These cycles of creativity not only sustain momentum but also amplify the range and depth of what is achievable. Generativity feeds itself, not through central planning but through distributed ingenuity.

LLMs provide a particularly striking example of the generativity flywheel in action. The release of GPT-4 and Claude, coupled with APIs and development tools, created an explosion of possibilities that continues to accelerate. Each innovative application—whether it's an AI writing assistant, a coding companion, or a specialized research tool—demonstrates new possibilities that inspire others to imagine and build. Custom GPTs and AI agents built on these platforms spawn entire new categories of applications, which in turn suggest new ways to leverage the underlying technology. Developer platforms like Replit, Vercel, and Cursor combine LLMs with other tools to create even richer possibility spaces. The profit potential attracts serious entrepreneurs who make sustained investments in building sophisticated applications, while marketplace mechanisms help these innovators capture value from their creations. This virtuous cycle has turned LLMs from powerful but abstract technologies into engines of practical innovation, spawning thousands of applications that their creators could never have envisioned.

Embracing the Unknowable

Generative systems are rooted in the embrace of uncertainty. They thrive not by dictating outcomes but by cultivating the conditions for serendipity. These systems reject the notion that every innovation can or should be planned. Instead, they create frameworks where the unexpected can flourish, where solutions to problems yet unknown can emerge from the creativity of others.

Platforms like Zapier have flourished because they embrace this principle. Zapier's simplicity and adaptability allow users to connect applications in novel ways, automating tasks that were previously time-consuming or impossible. Each unexpected connection made by users expands the platform's value, revealing possibilities the original developers never envisioned. Similarly, OpenAI's API ecosystem thrives on the unknown. Developers are using it to create tools for niche markets, from healthcare diagnostics to legal document automation—solutions that emerged not from OpenAI's vision but from the imagination of its users.

The generativity advantage requires leaders to relinquish the illusion of complete control. It asks them to accept that the most transformative uses of their systems may arise from directions they never anticipated. By embracing the unknowable, businesses can transcend traditional limits and enable the kind of innovation that defines eras.

Pursuing generativity is not for the timid. It demands a deliberate choice to prioritize openness and long-term value over short-term gains and rigid control. It involves navigating trade-offs between enabling innovation and maintaining strategic coherence. For platforms like no-code tools and automation systems, this balance is essential—supporting creativity without allowing chaos to erode the user experience.

The leaders of generative systems understand that their role is not to dictate outcomes but to design ecosystems that thrive on their own. These ecosystems must be robust enough to support distributed innovation while capturing value sustainably. The generativity advantage is not about micromanaging every interaction; it is about enabling countless contributors to create, explore, and redefine the boundaries of what is possible.

The generativity advantage is not just valuable for the business leaders who pursue it; it is valuable precisely because it empowers others to create and capture value of their own, and that those innovations of others do not need to be predicted in advance. It requires patience, humility, and a commitment to fostering environments where creativity thrives.

I wrote in an earlier chapter that generativity "requires the humility to acknowledge that the most valuable uses of your creation may come from directions you never anticipated." This means that a platform like Bubble would have to be prepared for the possibility that one of the apps built on the platform ends up being even more profitable than Bubble itself. Someone may discover the "killer" use case for Bubble and it may be something that the company itself did not predict. Already, Bubble's co-CEO boasts that internet traffic to Bubble apps is roughly ten times higher than traffic to Bubble's own website.[1]

An example of this has recently happened with Anthropic, the maker of one of the leading Large Language Models, whose Claude 3.5 Sonnet was the best AI programmer for many months, and almost single handedly spawned the AI coding reovlution. While the company has a consumer facing app at Claude.ai that users can use for a variety of tasks, Sonnet has found its most demanded use case outside of the consumer app, where its services are employed through the API as a software coding assistant. Two of the most popular coding assistants are Replit.com and Cursor.com, and indications are that users of these platforms are using Claude so much that Anthropic is running out of capacity to deliver its services.[2] In other words, a single use

---

1 https://x.com/estraschnov/status/1928524402741616880
2 https://x.com/artificialguybr/status/1879402029061378171

case for Anthropic's generative product was found by other companies (not Anthropic) and is so popular that Anthropic is running out of capacity to satisfy demand. When I say that generativity requires the humility to embrace the unknowable I mean that a company like Anthropic should be prepared for outcomes like this, and should feel no shame in not having been the ones to find the most popular or profitable use case themselves.

The Anthropic case gives us the opportunity to note once again that applying conventional approaches to strategy and entrepreneurship may not be the right approach for generative products. With the lean startup philosophy of "pivoting" until you find "Product-Market Fit" (PMF), a company like Anthropic may decide that since the strongest PMF for their product is currently in AI coding, then that means they should refocus all their efforts on becoming an AI coding company. For generative products, this approach is ill-advised, and would lead to a weakened generativity advantage by creating unnecessary focus and locking the company out of a world of unforeseen possibilities. A rule of thumb for a generativity strategy is to choose the path that involves the least need for both prediction and control of other people's innovations around your platform.

AI Agents and the Future of Generativity

Generativity points to a future defined by collaborative invention and expanding possibilities. The next generation of platforms will not just connect users or distribute tools; they will amplify human potential by enabling co-creation on a massive scale. These systems hold the promise of democratizing innovation, allowing more voices to participate in shaping solutions to global challenges.

Increasingly, AI agents will play a significant role in this future. LLM-driven agents are evolving from passive tools to autonomous contributors within generative digital platforms. Research has already demonstrated their capacity to produce good ideas (Girotra et al., 2023), and recent advancements have enabled these agents to incorporate memory, specialized knowledge, and autonomous planning capabilities (Sumers et al., 2024). They can already control a mouse and keyboard and will soon be able to act like any other innovator in generative ecosystems. Users of Bubble have already employed LLMs with computer use capabilities to autonomously build with the Bubble platform,[3] and Bubble has recently released an AI app builder agent as well.

When LLMs take care of certain intellectual tasks, including ones that involve creativity, the role of humans may move to a higher meta-level in the process. But the key takeaway for generative platforms at the dawn of the generative AI age is that

---

3 https://x.com/chris_strobl/status/1882934972409053677

they must prepare their platforms not only for humans but also for AI agents. Both humans and AIs should be able to interface with the platform, and contribute ideas and innovations. All generative platforms need to rethink their product interface to allow AI agents to become idea-contributing agents in their user-innovation workflows. If you don't do it yourself, someone will build the alternative to your platform that does it.

Take for example, the rise of Lindy.ai and similar platforms like Gumloop and n8n that are now challenging Zapier. Despite being a very AI-forward company and rapidly adding AI features, Zapier was still not allowing AIs to contribute in every way so humans could contribute ideas to the design of no-code automations. Lindy.ai has essentially re-created the Zapier interface and mechanics, with the key difference that for any field that you can enter as a human in Zapier, you can ask an AI to determine what to put in that field in Lindy, and you can do so every single time the automation flow runs.

This is a sign of things to come for every software platform out there, and specifically for generative platforms: you need to expand the sources of unpredicted ideas to include AI agents.

A Challenge to You

In closing, I would like to issue a challenge and an invitation to you, the reader. To entrepreneurs and leaders: appreciate the value of designing systems that amplify possibility by enabling the masses (not just developers) to innovate and profit from their innovations. To policymakers and academics: champion frameworks that protect and nurture generativity, as it results in patterns of growth that benefit society as a whole. To creators and users: look for the products and platforms that not only have an extensive range of functionality you can play with but are also made by companies that take you seriously as an innovator and entrepreneur, and help you profit fairly from your innovations. Continue to push the boundaries of these systems and expand what they can achieve.

Generativity is not confined to business applications; it is conducive societal progress. By empowering distributed innovation—including the contributions of intelligent AI agents—generative systems hold the key to unlocking solutions to the world's most pressing problems. They enable us to move beyond incremental change and toward transformative leaps that redefine industries, economies, and societies.

The Generativity Advantage is a call to celebrate the shared potential of humanity in whatever your next project is. It is based on a timeless truth: the most powerful innovations are those that empower others to innovate.

References

Agarwal, R., Audretsch, D., & Sarkar, M. B. (2007). The process of creative construction: Knowledge spillovers, entrepreneurship, and economic growth. *Strategic Entrepreneurship Journal, 1*(3–4), 263–286. https://doi.org/10.1002/sej.36

Agarwal, R., & Gaule, P. (2020). Invisible Geniuses: Could the Knowledge Frontier Advance Faster? *American Economic Review: Insights, 2*(4), 409–424. https://doi.org/10.1257/aeri.20190457

Agrawal, A., Cockburn, I., & Zhang, L. (2015). Deals not done: Sources of failure in the market for ideas: Deals Not Done. *Strategic Management Journal, 36*(7), 976–986. https://doi.org/10.1002/smj.2261

Akerlof, G. A. (1970). The Market for "Lemons": Quality Uncertainty and the Market Mechanism. *The Quarterly Journal of Economics, 84*(3), 488–500.

Alchian, A. A., & Demsetz, H. (1972). Production, information costs, and economic organization. *The American Economic Review, 62*(5), 777–795.

Allen, R. H., & Sriram, R. D. (2000). The role of standards in innovation. *Technological Forecasting and Social Change, 64*(2–3), 171–181. https://doi.org/10.1016/S0040-1625(99)00104-3

Backhouse, R. E., & Medema, S. G. (2009). Defining economics: The long road to acceptance of the Robbins definition. *Economica, 76*, 805–820.

Baldwin, C. Y., & Woodard, C. J. (2009). The architecture of platforms: A unified view. In A. Gawer (Ed.), *Platforms, Markets and Innovation*. Edward Elgar Publishing. https://doi.org/10.4337/9781849803311.00008

Barney, J. B. (2001). Resource-based theories of competitive advantage: A ten-year retrospective on the resource-based view. *Journal of Management, 27*(6), 643–650.

Baumol, W. J. (2002). *The free-market innovation machine: Analyzing the growth miracle of capitalism.* Princeton University Press.

Beinhocker, E. D. (2007). *The origin of wealth: Evolution, complexity, and the radical remaking of economics.* Random House.

Bender, E. M., Gebru, T., McMillan-Major, A., & Shmitchell, S. (2021). On the Dangers of Stochastic Parrots: Can Language Models Be Too Big? 🦜. *Proceedings of the 2021 ACM Conference on Fairness, Accountability, and Transparency*, 610–623. https://doi.org/10.1145/3442188.3445922

Bergemann, D., & Bonatti, A. (2024). Data, competition, and digital platforms. *American Economic Review, 114*(8), 2553–2595. https://doi.org/10.1257/aer.20230478

Blank, S., & Dorf, B. (2020). *The startup owner's manual: The step-by-step guide for building a great company.* Wiley.

Bleakley, A., Rough, D., Edwards, J., Doyle, P., Dumbleton, O., Clark, L., Rintel, S., Wade, V., & Cowan, B. R. (2022). Bridging social distance during social distancing: Exploring social talk and remote collegiality in video conferencing. *Human–Computer Interaction, 37*(5), 404–432. https://doi.org/10.1080/07370024.2021.1994859

Blind, K. (2016). The impact of standardisation and standards on innovation. In J. Edler, P. Cunningham, A. Gök, & P. Shapira (Eds.), *Handbook of Innovation Policy Impact*. Edward Elgar Publishing. https://doi.org/10.4337/9781784711856.00021

Bohnsack, R., Rennings, M., Block, C., & Bröring, S. (2024). Profiting from innovation when digital business ecosystems emerge: A control point perspective. *Research Policy, 53*(3), 104961. https://doi.org/10.1016/j.respol.2024.104961

Booyavi, Z., & Crawford, G. C. (2023). Different, but same: A power law perspective on how rock star female entrepreneurs reconceptualize "gender equality." *Journal of Business Venturing Insights, 19*, e00374. https://doi.org/10.1016/j.jbvi.2023.e00374

Brousseau, E., & Penard, T. (2007). The economics of digital business models: A framework for analyzing the economics of platforms. *Review of Network Economics, 6*(2). https://doi.org/10.2202/1446-9022.1112

https://doi.org/10.1515/9783110779639-011

Bubeck, S., Chandrasekaran, V., Eldan, R., Gehrke, J., Horvitz, E., Kamar, E., Lee, P., Lee, Y. T., Li, Y., Lundberg, S., Nori, H., Palangi, H., Ribeiro, M. T., & Zhang, Y. (2023). *Sparks of Artificial General Intelligence: Early experiments with GPT-4* (arXiv:2303.12712). arXiv. https://doi.org/10.48550/arXiv.2303.12712

Burt, R. S. (2008). *Brokerage and closure: An introduction to social capital* (Reprint). Oxford Univ. Press.

Burt, R. S. (Ed.). (2010). *Structural holes: The social structure of competition*. Harvard University Press.

Cagan, M. (2017). *INSPIRED: How to create tech products customers love* (Second edition). Wiley.

Cao, S. (2023, August 15). *A.I. Today Is a 'Glorified Tape Recorder,' Says Theoretical Physicist Michio Kaku*. Observer. https://observer.com/2023/08/michio-kaku-ai-chabot/

Cennamo, C., & Santaló, J. (2019). Generativity Tension and Value Creation in Platform Ecosystems. *Organization Science*, *30*(3), 617–641. https://doi.org/10.1287/orsc.2018.1270

Chen, A. (2021). *The cold start problem: How to start and scale network effects* (First edition). Harper Business, an imprint of HarperCollinsPublishers.

Chesbrough, H. (2006). *Open innovation: A new paradigm for understanding industrial innovation*. Oxford University Press.

Chomsky, N. (1961). Some methodological remarks on generative grammar. *Word*, *17*(2), 219–239.

Consoli, D., & Patrucco, P. P. (2009). Innovation Platforms and the Governance of Knowledge: Evidence from Italy and the UK. In *Technology Infrastructure*. Routledge.

Crawford, G. C., Aguinis, H., Lichtenstein, B., Davidsson, P., & McKelvey, B. (2015). Power law distributions in entrepreneurship: Implications for theory and research. *Journal of Business Venturing*, *30*(5), 696–713. https://doi.org/10.1016/j.jbusvent.2015.01.001

D'Aveni, R. A., Dagnino, G. B., & Smith, K. G. (2010). The age of temporary advantage. *Strategic Management Journal*, *31*(13), 1371–1385. https://doi.org/10.1002/smj.897

de Reuver, M., Sørensen, C., & Basole, R. C. (2018). The digital platform: A research agenda. *Journal of Information Technology*, *33*(2), 124–135. https://doi.org/10.1057/s41265-016-0033-3

Dierickx, I., & Cool, K. (1989). Asset stock accumulation and sustainability of competitive advantage. *Management Science*, *35*(12), 1504–1511. https://doi.org/10.1287/mnsc.35.12.1504

Do Rosario, A. (2024, January 25). *Got GPT? Put it behind a paywall!* https://generativeai.pub/got-gpt-put-it-behind-a-paywall-9fb349533adf

Dohmke, T., Iansiti, M., & Richards, G. (2023, June 26). *Sea change in software development: Economic and productivity analysis of the AI-powered developer lifecycle*. arXiv.Org. https://arxiv.org/abs/2306.15033v1

Eaton, B. D., Elaluf-Calderwood, S. M., & Sørensen, C. (2010). *The role of control points in determining business models for future mobile generative systems*.

Eaton, B. D., Elaluf-Calderwood, S., Sorensen, C., & Yoo, Y. (2011). *Dynamic structures of control and generativity in digital ecosystem service innovation: The cases of the Apple and Google mobile app stores* (Monograph 183; Issue 183). London School of Economics and Political Science. http://www.lse.ac.uk/management/research/academic-groups/information-systems-and-innovation/home.aspx

Eaton, B. D., Elaluf-Calderwood, S., Sørensen, C., & Yoo, Y. (2015). Distributed Tuning of Boundary Resources: The Case of Apple's iOS Service System. *MIS Quarterly*, *39*(1), 217–244.

Eck, A., & Uebernickel, F. (2016). *Untangling generativity: Two perspectives on unanticipated change produced by diverse actors*.

Eck, Alexander; Uebernickel, Falk; and Brenner, Walter, "*The Generative Capacity of Digital Artifacts: A Mapping of the Field*" (2015). Proceedings of the Pacific Asia Conference on Information Systems (PACIS). 231. http://aisel.aisnet.org/pacis2015/231

Eisenhardt, K. M. (1989). Agency theory: An assessment and review. *Academy of Management Review*, *14*(1), 57–74.

Eloundou, T., Manning, S., Mishkin, P., & Rock, D. (2023). *GPTs are GPTs: An early look at the labor market impact potential of large language models* (arXiv:2303.10130). arXiv. https://doi.org/10.48550/arXiv.2303.10130

Epstein, R. (1999). Generativity theory. *Encyclopedia of Creativity, 1,* 759–766.

Erikson, E. H. (1963). *Childhood and society* (Vol. 2). Norton New York.

Espig, A., Mazzini, I. T., Zimmermann, C., & Carvalho, L. C. de. (2021). National culture and innovation: A multidimensional analysis. *Innovation & Management Review, 19*(4), 322–338. https://doi.org/10.1108/INMR-09-2020-0121

Fama, E. F. (1980). Agency problems and the theory of the firm. *Journal of Political Economy, 88*(2), 288–307.

Fast, V., Schnurr, D., & Wohlfarth, M. (2023). Regulation of data-driven market power in the digital economy: Business value creation and competitive advantages from big data. *Journal of Information Technology, 38*(2), 202–229. https://doi.org/10.1177/02683962221114394

Forman, C., & Zeebroeck, N. V. (2012). From wires to partners: How the internet has fostered R&D collaborations within firms. *Management Science, 58*(8), 1549–1568. https://doi.org/10.1287/mnsc.1110.1505

Foster, R., & Kaplan, S. (2011). *Creative Destruction: Why companies that are built to last underperform the market—And how to success fully transform them.* Crown Currency.

Friedman, M. (2009). *Capitalism and freedom* (40. anniversary ed., [Nachdr.]). University of Chicago Press.

Fürstenau, D., Baiyere, A., Schewina, K., Schulte-Althoff, M., & Rothe, H. (2023). Extended generativity theory on digital platforms. *Information Systems Research, 34*(4), 1686–1710.

Garud, R., Jain, S., Tuertscher, P. (2009). Incomplete by Design and Designing for Incompleteness. In: Lyytinen, K., Loucopoulos, P., Mylopoulos, J., Robinson, B. (eds) Design Requirements Engineering: A Ten-Year Perspective. Lecture Notes in Business Information Processing, vol. 14. Springer, Berlin, Heidelberg. https://doi.org/10.1007/978-3-540-92966-6_7

Gee, J. P. (2017). Affinity spaces and 21st century learning. *Educational Technology, 57*(2), 27–31. JSTOR.

Gelfand, M. J., Raver, J. L., Nishii, L., Leslie, L. M., Lun, J., Lim, B. C., Duan, L., Almaliach, A., Ang, S., Arnadottir, J., Aycan, Z., Boehnke, K., Boski, P., Cabecinhas, R., Chan, D., Chhokar, J., D'Amato, A., Subirats Ferrer, M., Fischlmayr, I. C., . . . Yamaguchi, S. (2011). Differences between tight and loose cultures: A 33-nation study. *Science, 332*(6033), 1100–1104. https://doi.org/10.1126/science.1197754

Ghazawneh, A., & Henfridsson, O. (2013). Balancing platform control and external contribution in third-party development: The boundary resources model. *Information Systems Journal, 23*(2), 173–192. https://doi.org/10.1111/j.1365-2575.2012.00406.x

Girotra, K., Meincke, L., Terwiesch, C., & Ulrich, K. T. (2023). *Ideas are dimes a dozen: Large language models for idea generation in innovation* (SSRN Scholarly Paper 4526071). https://doi.org/10.2139/ssrn.4526071

Glaeser, E. L. (2012). *Triumph of the city: How our greatest invention makes us richer, smarter, greener, healthier, and happier.* Penguin Books.

Glaeser, E. L., Kallal, H. D., Scheinkman, J. A., & Shleifer, A. (1992). Growth in cities. *Journal of Political Economy, 100*(6), 1126–1152. https://doi.org/10.1086/261856

Goetze, T. S. (2024). AI art is theft: Labour, extraction, and exploitation: Or, on the dangers of stochastic pollocks. *The 2024 ACM Conference on Fairness, Accountability, and Transparency,* 186–196. https://doi.org/10.1145/3630106.3658898

Granovetter, M. S. (1973). The strength of weak ties. *American Journal of Sociology, 78*(6), 1360–1380. https://doi.org/10.1086/225469

Gupta, S., Shrivastava, V., Deshpande, A., Kalyan, A., Clark, P., Sabharwal, A., & Khot, T. (2024). *Bias runs deep: Implicit reasoning biases in persona-assigned LLMs* (arXiv:2311.04892). arXiv. https://doi.org/10.48550/arXiv.2311.04892

Hall, D. (2007). Fail fast, fail cheap. *Business Week, 32,* 19–24.

Hartwick, J., & Barki, H. (1994). Hypothesis testing and hypothesis generating research: An example from the user participation literature. *Information Systems Research, 5*(4), 446–449.

Hayek, F. (1945). The use of knowledge in society. *American Economic Review, 35*(4).

Hayek, F. (2002). Competition as a discovery procedure. *Quarterly Journal of Austrian Economics, 5*(3), 9–23.

Hein, A., Setzke, D. S., Hermes, S., & Weking, J. (2019). *The influence of digital affordances and generativity on digital platform leadership*. International Conference on Interaction Sciences. https://www.semanti cscholar.org/paper/The-Influence-of-Digital-Affordances-and-on-Digital-Hein-Setzke /6c162d8aec85f66b79c7b69027dc7ec1623e30de

Helfat, C. E., & Raubitschek, R. S. (2018). Dynamic and integrative capabilities for profiting from innovation in digital platform-based ecosystems. *Research Policy, 47*(8), 1391–1399. https://doi.org/10.1016/j. respol.2018.01.019

Hill, B. M., & Monroy-Hernández, A. (2013). The remixing dilemma: The trade-off between generativity and originality. *American Behavioral Scientist, 57*(5), 643–663. https://doi.org/10.1177/0002764212469359

Hodges, A. (2014). *Alan Turing: The enigma*. Princeton University Press.

Iaria, A., Schwarz, C., & Waldinger, F. (2018). Frontier knowledge and scientific production: Evidence from the collapse of international science*. *The Quarterly Journal of Economics, 133*(2), 927–991. https://doi. org/10.1093/qje/qjx046

Jacobs, J. (1992). *The death and life of great American cities* (Vintage books ed). Vintage Books.

Jacobs, J. (2000). *The nature of economies*. Random House Canada.

Jaech, A., Kalai, A., Lerer, A., Richardson, A., El-Kishky, A., Low, A., Helyar, A., Madry, A., Beutel, A., Carney, A., Iftimie, A., Karpenko, A., Passos, A. T., Neitz, A., Prokofiev, A., Wei, A., Tam, A., Bennett, A., Kumar, A., . . . Li, Z. (2024). *OpenAI o1 System Card* (arXiv:2412.16720; Version 1). arXiv. https://doi.org/ 10.48550/arXiv.2412.16720

Jamshidi, Z., Keyhani, M., & Choi, K. J. (2025). *The value of random experimentation*.

Janis, I. L. (2013). *Groupthink: Psychological studies of policy decisions and fiascoes* (2. ed., [Nachdr.]). Wadsworth.

Jaume, G. (2022, July 20). *Power your business with the new Pack ecosystem*. Coda. https://coda.io/@glenn/ power-your-business-with-the-new-pack-ecosystem

Johnson, S. (2011). *Where good ideas come from: The natural history of innovation* (1. paperback ed). Riverhead Books.

Jones, Q., Ravid, G., & Rafaeli, S. (2004). Information overload and the message dynamics of online interaction spaces: A theoretical model and empirical exploration. *Information Systems Research, 15*(2), 194–210. https://doi.org/10.1287/isre.1040.0023

Kamruzzaman, M., Shovon, M. M. I., & Kim, G. L. (2024). *Investigating subtler biases in LLMs: Ageism, beauty, institutional, and nationality bias in generative models* (arXiv:2309.08902). arXiv. https://doi.org/ 10.48550/arXiv.2309.08902

Katz, M. L., & Shapiro, C. (1994). Systems competition and network effects. *Journal of Economic Perspectives, 8*(2), 93–115.

Kauffman, S. A. (1993). *The origins of order: Self-organization and selection in evolution*. Oxford University Press.

Keyhani, M. (2023). The logic of strategic entrepreneurship. *Strategic Organization, 21*(2), 460–475. https://doi.org/10.1177/14761270211057571

Keyhani, M., Hemmati, H., & Salgado, L. (2023, November 21). *Why student experiments with generative AI matter for our collective learning*. The Conversation. http://theconversation.com/why-student-experiments-with-generative-ai-matter-for-our-collective-learning-210844

Keyhani, M., & Jamshidi, Z. (2025). *Random experimentation and exceptional outcomes in entrepreneurship*. *Academy of Management Perspectives*.

Keyhani, M., & Mohaghegh-Neyshabouri, S. (2025). The Rise of generative AI: Capabilities and potential for higher education. In S. Sabbaghan (Ed.), *Navigating generative AI in higher education: Ethical, theoretical and practical perspectives* (n.p.). Edward Elgar.

Knetsch, J. L. (1989). The endowment effect and evidence of nonreversible indifference curves. *The American Economic Review, 79*(5), 1277–1284. JSTOR.

Komljenovic, J. (2021). The rise of education rentiers: Digital platforms, digital data and rents. *Learning, Media and Technology, 46*(3), 320–332. https://doi.org/10.1080/17439884.2021.1891422

Kornberger, M., Pflueger, D., & Mouritsen, J. (2017). Evaluative infrastructures: Accounting for platform organization. *Accounting, Organizations and Society, 60*, 79–95. https://doi.org/10.1016/j.aos.2017.05.002

Kuhn, T. S. (2009). *The structure of scientific revolutions* (3. ed., [Nachdr.]). Univ. of Chicago Press.

Lehmann, J., & Recker, J. (2019, November 11). Offerings that are "ever-in-the-making": Post-launch continuous digital innovation in late-stage entrepreneurial ventures. *ICIS 2019 Proceedings*. https://aisel.aisnet.org/icis2019/innov_entre/innov_entre/11

Lessig, L. (2009). *Remix: Making art and commerce thrive in the hybrid economy*. Penguin Books.

Levinthal, D. A., & March, J. G. (1993). The myopia of learning. *Strategic Management Journal, 14*(S2), 95–112. https://doi.org/10.1002/smj.4250141009

Lynch, B. (2024, May 8). *OpenAI's CTO breaks down the top 3 unexpected outcomes of ChatGPT's launch*. CCW Digital. https://www.customercontactweekdigital.com/tools-technologies/articles/openai-chatgpt-launch

Lyytinen, K., Sørensen, C., & Tilson, D. (2017). Generativity in digital infrastructures: A research note. In *The Routledge companion to management information systems* (pp. 253–275). Routledge.

Madhok, A., Keyhani, M., & Bossink, B. (2015). Understanding alliance evolution and termination: Adjustment costs and the economics of resource value. *Strategic Organization, 13*(2), 91–116. https://doi.org/10.1177/1476127015580309

Mehrotra, S. (2024, December 18). *Q&A with Shishir Mehrotra: Uniting coda and grammarly* [Interview]. https://www.grammarly.com/blog/company/meet-shishir/

Metcalfe, J. S., & Ramlogan, R. (2005). Limits to the economy of knowledge and knowledge of the economy. *Futures, 37*(7), 655–674. https://doi.org/10.1016/j.futures.2004.11.006

Metcalfe, J., & Shimamura, A. P. (Eds.). (1996). *Metacognition: Knowing about knowing* (1. MIT Press paperback ed). MIT Press.

Metz, R. (2024, October 1). *OpenAI lets anyone use its new voice assistant in third-party apps*. BNN Bloomberg. https://www.bnnbloomberg.ca/business/technology/2024/10/01/openai-lets-anyone-use-its-new-voice-assistant-in-third-party-apps/

Mike, K. (2017). The intellectual orders of a market economy. *Journal of Institutional Economics, 13*(4), 899–915. https://doi.org/10.1017/S1744137417000029

Mill, J. S. (with Mississauga – University of Toronto). (1859). *On liberty*. London, J.W. Parker. http://archive.org/details/onlibertyxero00milluoft

Minaee, S., Mikolov, T., Nikzad, N., Chenaghlu, M., Socher, R., Amatriain, X., & Gao, J. (2024). *Large Language Models: A survey* (arXiv:2402.06196). arXiv. https://doi.org/10.48550/arXiv.2402.06196

Morris, M. R., Sohl-dickstein, J., Fiedel, N., Warkentin, T., Dafoe, A., Faust, A., Farabet, C., & Legg, S. (2024). *Levels of AGI for operationalizing progress on the path to AGI* (arXiv:2311.02462). arXiv. https://doi.org/10.48550/arXiv.2311.02462

Murphy, M. (2014). Boundary jumping: Understanding the value of modest anarchy in entrepreneurial networks. *Silicon Flatirons Center*.

Nambisan, S. (2017). Digital entrepreneurship: Toward a digital technology perspective of entrepreneurship. *Entrepreneurship Theory and Practice, 41*(6), 1029–1055.

Navigli, R., Conia, S., & Ross, B. (2023). Biases in large language models: Origins, inventory, and discussion. *Journal of Data and Information Quality, 15*(2), 10:1–10:21. https://doi.org/10.1145/3597307

Nemeth, C. J., & Kwan, J. L. (1987). Minority influence, divergent thinking and detection of correct solutions. *Journal of Applied Social Psychology, 17*(9), 788–799. https://doi.org/10.1111/j.1559-1816.1987.tb00339.x

Nicoli, M., & Paltrinieri, L. (2019). Platform cooperativism: Some notes on the becoming "common" of the firm. *South Atlantic Quarterly, 118*(4), 801–819. https://doi.org/10.1215/00382876-7825624

Osterwalder, A., Pigneur, Y., Bernarda, G., & Smith, A. (2015). *Value proposition design: How to create products and services customers want.* John Wiley & Sons.

Ouyang, L., Wu, J., Jiang, X., Almeida, D., Wainwright, C. L., Mishkin, P., Zhang, C., Agarwal, S., Slama, K., Ray, A., Schulman, J., Hilton, J., Kelton, F., Miller, L., Simens, M., Askell, A., Welinder, P., Christiano, P., Leike, J., & Lowe, R. (2022). *Training language models to follow instructions with human feedback* (arXiv:2203.02155). arXiv. https://doi.org/10.48550/arXiv.2203.02155

Pariser, E. (2011). *The filter bubble: What the Internet is hiding from you.* Penguin Press.

Parker, G. G., Van Alstyne, M. W., & Choudary, S. P. (2016). *Platform revolution: How networked markets are transforming the economy and how to make them work for you.* WW Norton & Company.

Pentland, A. (2014). *Social physics: How good ideas spread-the lessons from a new science.* The Penguin Press.

Phelps, E. S. (2013). *Mass flourishing.* Princeton University Press. https://doi.org/10.1515/9781400848294

Phelps, E. S. (2015). Hayek's new ideas and present-day ones. *The Review of Austrian Economics, 28*(3), 253–256. https://doi.org/10.1007/s11138-015-0308-x

Phelps, E. S., Bojilov, R., Hoon, H. T., & Zoega, G. (2020). *Dynamism.* Harvard University Press. https://doi.org/10.4159/9780674246683

Pil, F. K., & Cohen, S. K. (2006). Modularity: Implications for imitation, innovation, and sustained advantage. *Academy of Management Review, 31*(4), 995–1011. https://doi.org/10.5465/amr.2006.22528166

Powell, W. W., & Grodal, S. (2006). *Networks of innovators.* Oxford University Press. https://doi.org/10.1093/oxfordhb/9780199286805.003.0003

Rachitsky, L. (2023, February 28). *How to kickstart and scale a marketplace business – Part 4: Cracking the chicken-and-egg problem 🐣 – Growing initial demand (plus a bonus!).* https://www.lennysnewsletter.com/p/how-to-kickstart-and-scale-a-marketplace-2e5

Remneland-Wikhamn, B., Ljungberg, J., Bergquist, M., & Kuschel, J. (2011). Open innovation, generativity and the supplier as peer: The case of iphone and android. *International Journal of Innovation Management, 15*(1), 205–230.

Ries, E. (2011). *The lean startup: How today's entrepreneurs use continuous innovation to create radically successful businesses* (1st ed.). Crown Business.

Rietveld, J., & Eggers, J. P. (2018). Demand heterogeneity in platform markets: Implications for complementors. *Organization Science, 29*(2), 304–322. https://doi.org/10.1287/orsc.2017.1183

Rietveld, J., Schilling, M. A., & Bellavitis, C. (2019). Platform strategy: Managing ecosystem value through selective promotion of complements. *Organization Science, 30*(6), 1232–1251. https://doi.org/10.1287/orsc.2019.1290

Rochet, J.-C., & Tirole, J. (2003). Platform competition in two-sided markets. *Journal of the European Economic Association, 1*(4), 990–1029. https://doi.org/10.1162/154247603322493212

Rochet, J.-C., & Tirole, J. (2006). Two-sided markets: A progress report. *The RAND Journal of Economics, 37*(3), 645–667. https://doi.org/10.1111/j.1756-2171.2006.tb00036.x

Romer, P. M. (1990). Endogenous technological change. *Journal of Political Economy, 98*(5, Part 2), S71–S102.

Ross, S. A. (1973). The economic theory of agency: The principal's problem. *The American Economic Review, 63*(2), 134–139.

Roth, A. E. (2008). What have we learned from market design? *The Economic Journal, 118*(527), 285–310.

Rumelt, R. (2011). *Good Strategy/Bad Strategy: The difference and why it matters.* Profile Books.

Rysman, M. (2009). The economics of two-sided markets. *Journal of Economic Perspectives, 23*(3), 125–143. https://doi.org/10.1257/jep.23.3.125

Santesteban, C., & Longpre, S. (2020). How big data confers market power to big tech: Leveraging the perspective of data science. *The Antitrust Bulletin, 65*(3), 459–485. https://doi.org/10.1177/0003603X20934212

Sarasvathy, S. D. (2001). Causation and effectuation: Toward a theoretical shift from economic inevitability to entrepreneurial contingency. *Academy of Management Review, 26*(2), 243–263.

Schoffelen, J., & Huybrechts, L. (2013). *Sharing is caring. Sharing and documenting complex participatory projects to enable generative participation.* https://documentserver.uhasselt.be//handle/1942/18329

Schumpeter, J. A. (2013). *Capitalism, socialism and democracy* (5th ed.). Routledge. https://doi.org/10.4324/9780203202050

Shah, S. K., & Tripsas, M. (2007). The accidental entrepreneur: The emergent and collective process of user entrepreneurship. *Strategic Entrepreneurship Journal, 1*(1–2), 123–140. https://doi.org/10.1002/sej.15

Shane, S. (1993). Cultural influences on national rates of innovation. *Journal of Business Venturing, 8*(1), 59–73. https://doi.org/10.1016/0883-9026(93)90011-S

Shapiro, C., & Varian, H. R. (1999). *Information rules: A strategic guide to the network economy.* Harvard Business Press.

Shin, D.-H., Kim, H., & Hwang, J. (2015). Standardization revisited: A critical literature review on standards and innovation. *Computer Standards & Interfaces, 38*, 152–157. https://doi.org/10.1016/j.csi.2014.09.002

Smith, A., & Butler-Bowdon, T. (2010). *The wealth of nations: The economics classic; a selected edition for the contemporary reader.* Capstone.

Smithson, M. (1989). *Ignorance and uncertainty.* Springer. https://doi.org/10.1007/978-1-4612-3628-3

Stemler, A., Perry, J., & Haugh, T. (2020). The Code of the Platform. *Georgia Law Review, 54*(2). https://digitalcommons.law.uga.edu/glr/vol54/iss2/5

Stier, B. G. (2024). Applying Steve Jobs's insights on innovation, leadership, and technology toward an Apple-Inspired law school. *Notre Dame Journal of Law, Ethics & Public Policy, 38*(1), 217–282.

Stokel-Walker, C. (2023, December 4). *OpenAI's GPT store might not have killed the company – But it could still threaten AI startups.* Fast Company. https://www.fastcompany.com/90991188/openais-gpt-store-might-not-have-killed-the-company-but-it-could-still-threaten-ai-startups

Sumers, T. R., Yao, S., Narasimhan, K., & Griffiths, T. L. (2024). *Cognitive architectures for language agents* (arXiv:2309.02427). arXiv. https://doi.org/10.48550/arXiv.2309.02427

Sun, H. (2009). A meta-analysis on the influence of national culture on innovation capability. *International Journal of Entrepreneurship and Innovation Management, 10*(3/4), 353. https://doi.org/10.1504/IJEIM.2009.025678

Surowiecki, J. (2004). *The wisdom of crowds: Why the many are smarter than the few and how collective wisdom shapes business, economies, societies, and nations* (1. ed). Doubleday.

Tadelis, S. (2016). Reputation and feedback systems in online platform markets. *Annual Review of Economics, 8*(1), 321–340. https://doi.org/10.1146/annurev-economics-080315-015325

Tajedin, H., Madhok, A., & Keyhani, M. (2019). A theory of digital firm-designed markets: Defying knowledge constraints with crowds and marketplaces. *Strategy Science, 4*(4), 323–342.

Taleb, N. N. (2020). *Statistical consequences of fat tails: Real World preasymptotics, epistemology, and applications: papers and commentary.* STEM Academic Press.

Tamkin, A., Brundage, M., Clark, J., & Ganguli, D. (2021). *Understanding the capabilities, limitations, and societal impact of large language models* (arXiv:2102.02503). arXiv. https://doi.org/10.48550/arXiv.2102.02503

Teece, D. J., Pisano, G., & Shuen, A. (1997). Dynamic capabilities and strategic management. *Strategic Management Journal, 18*(7), 509–533.

Terwiesch, C., & Xu, Y. (2008). Innovation contests, open innovation, and multiagent problem solving. *Management Science, 54*(9), 1529–1543. https://doi.org/10.1287/mnsc.1080.0884

Teubner, T., Flath, C. M., Weinhardt, C., van der Aalst, W., & Hinz, O. (2023). Welcome to the era of ChatGPT et al. *Business & Information Systems Engineering, 65*(2), 95–101. https://doi.org/10.1007/s12599-023-00795-x

Thomas, L. D. W., Ritala, P., Karhu, K., & Heiskala, M. (2024). Vertical and horizontal complementarities in platform ecosystems. *Innovation*, 1–25. https://doi.org/10.1080/14479338.2024.2303593

Thomas, L. D. W., & Tee, R. (2022). Generativity: A systematic review and conceptual framework. *International Journal of Management Reviews*, *24*(2), 255–278.

Thomke, S., & Von Hippel, E. (2002). Customers as innovators: A new way to create value. *Harvard Business Review*, *80*(4), 74–81.

Tikhonov, A., & Yamshchikov, I. P. (2023). *Post turing: Mapping the landscape of LLM Evaluation* (arXiv:2311.02049). arXiv. https://doi.org/10.48550/arXiv.2311.02049

Tilson, D., Lyytinen, K., & Sørensen, C. (2010). Digital infrastructures: The missing IS research agenda. *Information Systems Research*, *21*(4), 748–759. https://doi.org/10.1287/isre.1100.0318

Tiwana, A. (2013). *Platform ecosystems: Aligning architecture, governance, and strategy*. Newnes.

Trossen, D., & Fine, C. (2005). Value chain dynamics in the communication industry. *MIT Communications Future Programme*. MIT.

Turing, A. M. (1950). Computing machinery and intelligence. *Mind*, *LIX*(236), 433–460. https://doi.org/10.1093/mind/LIX.236.433

Um, S., Yoo, Y., Wattal, S., Kulathinal, R., & Zhang, B. (2013, December 18). The architecture of generativity in a digital ecosystem: A network biology perspective. *ICIS 2013 Proceedings*. https://aisel.aisnet.org/icis2013/proceedings/BreakthroughIdeas/15

van der Geest, C., & van Angeren, J. (2023). Architectural generativity: Leveraging complementor contributions to the platform architecture. *California Management Review*, *65*(2), 71–92.

Varian, H. R. (2010). Computer mediated transactions. *American Economic Review*, *100*(2), 1–10. https://doi.org/10.1257/aer.100.2.1

Vaswani, A., Shazeer, N., Parmar, N., Uszkoreit, J., Jones, L., Gomez, A. N., Kaiser, Ł. ukasz, & Polosukhin, I. (2017). Attention is all you need. *Advances in Neural Information Processing Systems*, *30*. https://proceedings.neurips.cc/paper_files/paper/2017/hash/3f5ee243547dee91fbd053c1c4a845aa-Abstract.html

Von Hippel, E. (1986). Lead users: A source of novel product concepts. *Management Science*, *32*(7), 791–805. https://doi.org/10.1287/mnsc.32.7.791

Von Hippel, E. (2001). User toolkits for innovation. *Journal of Product Innovation Management*, *18*(4), 247–257. https://doi.org/10.1111/1540-5885.1840247

Vosoughi, S., Roy, D., & Aral, S. (2018). The spread of true and false news online. *Science*, *359*(6380), 1146–1151. https://doi.org/10.1126/science.aap9559

Warsh, D. (2006). *Knowledge and the wealth of nations: A story of economic discovery*. WW Norton.

Wikipedia Contributors. (2025). Coda (document editor). In *Wikipedia*. https://en.wikipedia.org/w/index.php?title=Coda_(document_editor)&oldid=1267021247

Wolfers, J., & Zitzewitz, E. (2004). Prediction markets. *Journal of Economic Perspectives*, *18*(2), 107–126.

Yang, C., & Foster, W. (2021, November 25). *Interview with Wade Foster, co-founder and CEO of Zapier* [Podcast]. https://stationf.co/news/interview-with-wade-foster-co-founder-and-ceo-of-zapier

Yoo. (2010). Computing in everyday life: A call for research on experiential computing. *MIS Quarterly*, *34*(2), 213. https://doi.org/10.2307/20721425

Yoo, Y. (2013). The Tables have turned: How can the information systems field contribute to technology and innovation management research? *Journal of the Association for Information Systems*, *14*(5), 227–236. Business Source Complete.

Zarifhonarvar, A. (2024). Economics of ChatGPT: A labor market view on the occupational impact of artificial intelligence. *Journal of Electronic Business & Digital Economics*, *3*(2), 100–116. https://doi.org/10.1108/JEBDE-10-2023-0021

Zihnioglu, N., & Zhao, I. (2020, November 26). Why Notion is loved by users: Customization and quality. *DNX Ventures Blog*. https://medium.com/dnx-ventures/why-notion-is-loved-by-users-customization-and-quality-f4bde5e38663

Zittrain, J. (2006). The generative internet. *Harvard Law Review*, *119*(7), 1974–2040. JSTOR.

Zittrain, J. (2008). *The future of the internet: And how to stop it*. Yale University Press.

Zoo, H., De Vries, H. J., & Lee, H. (2017). Interplay of innovation and standardization: Exploring the relevance in developing countries. *Technological Forecasting and Social Change, 118*, 334–348. https://doi.org/10.1016/j.techfore.2017.02.033

Zweig, J. (2011, January 18). Structured serendipity. *Jason Zweig*. https://jasonzweig.com/structured-serendipity/

Zynda, M. R. (2013). The first killer app: A history of spreadsheets. *Interactions, 20*(5), 68–72.

About the Author

Mohammad Keyhani is an Associate Professor at the Haskayne School of Business, University of Calgary, where he teaches courses on generative AI and no-code technology for entrepreneurs. Mohammad's research has been published in leading journals and presented in international conferences where he has received multiple best paper and best reviewer awards. Mohammad is co-founder of www.Honeybee Logic.com, and maker of www.Lstr.cc. He has been an advisor to multiple startups, and has held roles as Lab Strategist at the Creative Destruction Lab Rockies, and David Rockefeller Fellow at the Trilateral Commission. He holds a doctorate in strategic management from York University, and M.Sc. and B.Sc. degrees from the University of Tehran. His blog and projects can be found at www.DigitVibe.com.

https://doi.org/10.1515/9783110779639-012

List of Figures

Figure 1.1 Jeremy Howard's tweet in disapproval of custom GPTs like Laundry Buddy —— 6
Figure 2.1 The Components of Generativity Advantage —— 13
Figure 3.1 An Extended Model of Profit-Driven Generativity —— 31
Figure 4.1 The co-founder of Bubble being surprised by a user's innovation —— 37
Figure 4.2 Yoo's Seven Properties of Digital Artifacts —— 46
Figure 5.1 Generative products vs. specific-use products —— 57
Figure 5.2 Pros and cons of generative products —— 58
Figure 5.3 A new mindset for managing generative products —— 63
Figure 7.1 A suggested Architecture for Generative Marketplaces —— 72
Figure 7.2 The Experimentation Engine —— 89
Figure 8.1 The Product-Market Generativity Framework with Examples —— 125
Figure 8.2 The Generativity Flywheel —— 129

https://doi.org/10.1515/9783110779639-013

List of Tables

Table 5.1 Examples of how a generative product (Coda.io) is described in the press —— **59**
Table 7.1 Components of the Allocation Layer in the Architecture of Generative Marketplaces —— **73**
Table 7.2 Components of the Generation Layer in the Architecture of Generative Marketplaces —— **80**
Table 7.3 Components of the Appropriation Layer in the Architecture of Generative Marketplaces —— **99**
Table 7.4 The Role of External Factors in the Architecture of Generative Marketplaces —— **112**
Table 9.1 Key tensions and trade-offs on the path to a generativity advantage —— **134**

https://doi.org/10.1515/9783110779639-014

List of Tables

Index

accessibility 14, 25–29, 38, 43–44, 135, 146
Adalo 11, 35, 56, 75
adaptability 14, 29, 38, 42, 126, 151
Airbnb 83, 110, 117
AirTable 35, 56
Alibaba 10
allocation layer
– components 72, 73
– generative power of trust 78
– innovation infrastructure 78–79
– layered infrastructure 77–78
– market thickness 74
– matching, efficient 76–77
– robust participation mechanisms 75
– strategic approaches 74–75
– strategic growth management 75–76
– trust building 77–78
– Uber 72
Amazon 10, 16, 48, 53, 65, 92, 109, 120, 124, 128
Amazon Web Services' (AWS) 102, 116
Android operating system 11, 35, 43, 92, 139, 148
Apple Inc. 3, 5–6, 10–13, 19, 20, 23, 26, 136
– App Store 65–67, 75, 111, 130
– Google and 125
– intuitive interface 43
– iOS Development 136
application programming interfaces (APIs) 1, 50, 92
– boundary resources 94
– connector tools 35
– developers' applications 138
– and development tools 151
– ecosystem evolution 147
– Google services 11
– GPT models 89
– integrations 115
– large language models 133
– OpenAI 3
– and SDKs 39, 43, 81, 137
– software coding 152
appropriation layer 98–101
– control points and value capture 103–104
– curation and promotion 107–109
– data advantage 106–107
– freemium 101–102
– innovation-friendly pricing and revenue models 98
– leveraging cross-subsidization 102

– pay-as-you-go 102
– perceived fairness and trust 102–103
– profiting 109–110
– revenue sharing 101
– spurring innovation 110–111
– staged approach 104–106
architectural generativity 31–32
artificial general intelligence (AGI) 1, 5
artificial intelligence (AI) 1, 5, 27, 78, 90, 142, 150–154. *See also* OpenAI
– algorithm 77
– applications 145
– coding platforms 28, 153
– generative AI 150
– generative/generativity 8
– Replit.com 102
– revolution 7
– vibe coding 36

Baumol, W. J. 65
Beinhocker, E. D. 23
Bergemann, D. 107
Blank, S. 61, 62
Bohnsack, R. 103, 104
Bolt.New 28, 36, 52
Bonatti, A. 107
bounded generativity 32–33
Bubble (programming language) 9, 20, 24, 35, 54, 62, 95, 150
– AB testing framework 122
– ecosystem 79
– generative platform 27–28
– generativity flywheel 27
– inverse generativity 33
– marketplace 79–80
– no-code software 74, 111, 122, 133
– plugin developers 78
– product to product-market 25–26
– strategic trade-offs 26
Burt, R. S. 84

career-level commitment 30, 122–123
ChatGPT 1, 3–7, 51, 92, 133, 150
Chomsky, N. 8
co-architects 32
Coda 32, 35, 36, 53–54, 56, 58–59, 75, 76, 127
collective intelligence 67, 78, 86

https://doi.org/10.1515/9783110779639-015

CompuServe 29
cultural dynamics 113–114, 142
Cursor 36, 52, 150–152
customer relationship management (CRM) 40, 41, 96, 121
custom GPTs 4–6, 18, 74, 81, 126, 145, 151

decoupling 42
DeepSeek 3
digital artifacts 46
– addressability 47–48
– associability 53–54
– communicability 50
– leveraging 54–55
– memorizability 51–52
– programmability 46–47
– sensibility 49
– traceability 52–53
digital communication 85, 86, 88
digital platforms 2, 9, 39, 48, 69, 88, 115, 117–118, 132, 146, 153
Dorf, B. 61, 62

ease of mastery 14, 29, 38, 43
eBay 124
entrepreneurship 2, 14, 17
– conventional approaches 153
– fee structures 39–40
– and innovation 59, 84
– intellectual property protection 40
– monetization 39
– payment and subscription 40–41
– premium pricing 40
– problem-solving 45
– residual claimancy 38–39
– user-innovators 39–41
Epstein, R. 8
Erikson, E. H. 8
Etsy 18, 101, 102, 110, 124, 126, 128
external factors, generative markets
– cultural dynamics and innovation mindsets 113–114
– educational institutions and learning ecosystems 116
– networks and knowledge flows 114–115
– regulatory considerations 117–118
– urban population centers 117

Facebook 10, 73, 75, 106
face-to-face communication 85
Fast, V. 107
feedback, customer 27, 40, 51, 61–63, 81, 90, 96, 134, 137, 145, 148
Figma 80, 84
Flappy Bird (game app) 5, 6, 12
Flutter 11
Foster, R. 23–24
Foster, W. 37–38
freelancers 74, 76, 77, 87
freemium models 68, 99, 101, 102, 110
Fulfillment by Amazon (FBA) 127
Fürstenau, D. 32

Gelfand, M. J. 114
General Data Protection Regulation (GDPR) 117
generation layer 79–82
– boundary resources 92–93
– communication infrastructure 85–87
– experimentation engine 88–90
– fundamental pillars 72
– innovation toolkits 92–93
– intellectual orders 83–84
– memory challenge 88
– organization 95–98
– outliers value 84–85
– privileged knowledge 90–92
– serendipitous discovery 87
– social processes 87
– standards and interoperability 94–95
– user-innovators 82–83
generative pretrained transformer (GPT) 3, 7.
    See also ChatGPT
– API platform 89
– GPT-4 38, 151
generative products 34–35
– API connector tools 35
– designing patterns 41–45
– digital artifacts 46–55
– entrepreneurship 38–41
– general-purpose toolkits 14
– management 56–64
– and marketplaces 2
– no-code app tools 35–36
– product management 9
– profitability 30–31
– vs. specific-use products 56, 57

generativity 2–3, 24–28, 153–154. *See also*
    marketplaces, generativity
– AI-based generation 8
– components 13
– in computer science 7–9
– control *vs.* 135–138
– definition 10–13
– ecosystem *vs.* product boundaries 143–146
– embrace of uncertainty 151–153
– entrepreneurship 24
– governance mechanisms 137
– marketplace 21–23
– network effects 20
– openness *vs.* value capture 146–148
– originality *vs.* remixing 142–143
– profitability to generativity 30–31
– profit-generating innovation 133
– self-reinforcing cycles 19–20
– stability *vs.* flexibility 138–140
– sustainability 22
– trade-offs 133–135
– variety *vs.* utility 140–142
generativity flywheel (six stages) 13, 19–20
– Bubble 27
– innovation possibilities 131
– innovative users, attracting 129–130
– market incentives 120–123
– more users, attracting 130–131
– novel applications 130
– product-market 123–128
– product value 130
– value capture 131
generativity theory 2, 8, 9
– architectural generativity 31–32
– bounded generativity 32–33
– extensions 32
– inverse generativity 33
GitHub 44, 52, 87, 90, 102, 113, 116, 117
Glaeser, E. L. 117
The Good Life™ 3
Google 10–12, 20, 52, 120, 125, 139
Google Ads 12, 100, 106
GPT-4 38, 151
GPT Wrappers 3
Gumloop 154
Gumroad 18, 40, 126

Hayek, F. 16, 67–69, 118
Hermès 124

Hill, B. M. 143
Howard, J. 5, 6
HubSpot 112, 115
Huybrechts, L. 62
hypothesis 61

innovation toolkits 39, 81, 92–93, 96
Instagram 19, 51
interoperability 81, 94–95
inverse generativity 33

Jacobs, J. 117
Jobs, S. 133
Jones, Q. 86

Kaplan, S. 23–24
Katz, M. L. 129
Kickstarter 80, 84
killer apps 14, 57
Kindle Direct Publishing (KDP) 127–128
knowledge spillovers 79, 91, 117
Kornberger, M. 77
Kuhn, T. S. 84

Large Language Models (LLMs) 4, 7, 8, 144, 145,
    150, 151, 153
– AI agents 78
– chatbot 38
– ChatGPT 150
– Claude 3.5 Sonnet 152
– fine-tuning 51
– generative AI 38
– sensory capability 49
Laundry Buddy concept 4–6, 133
LEGO 18, 35, 123, 127
Lehmann, J. 34, 159
leverage 9, 14, 29, 38, 41–42, 53–55, 75–78, 91, 111,
    126, 136
– cross-subsidization 102
– urban population centers 117
Lindy.ai 154
lock-in effects 22, 26, 28, 94, 101, 110, 111
Longpre, S. 107
Lovable.dev 28, 36
Lstr.cc 150

machine learning 5, 7, 11, 51
Make.com 35
market-based incentives 120–122

market design 16, 70–72, 85, 118
marketplaces, generativity 2, 5, 9, 15–18, 20, 22, 24, 68–69
– agency problem 66
– allocation layer 71–79
– appropriation layer 98–111
– architecture of 70–71, 112–113
– collective intelligence 67
– computer science 7–9
– digital platforms 67
– external factors 111–118
– generation layer 79–98
– innovation machine 65–66
– internal layers 71
– law of large numbers 66–67
– as learning systems 67–68
– mapping 17
– matching and transactions 74
– often-overlooked aspect 87
– self-identify 66
– well-designed allocation layer 71
Metcalfe, J. S. 88
Microsoft 10, 18, 38, 104, 126, 133
Mike, K. 83–84
Mill, J. S. 85
Minecraft (video game) 12, 58, 59, 114, 125, 130
modular design 42, 134, 139–140
monetization 30, 39, 41, 92–93, 101, 121, 127, 148
Monroy-Hernández, A. 143
Murati, M. 1

Netflix 17, 48, 51
no-code software tools 9, 11, 24, 26–28, 35, 43, 74, 92, 122, 150
Nomad List 78
Notion (software company) 18–19, 35, 37, 46, 47, 54, 56, 84, 108, 123, 127

one size fits all approach 48
On Liberty (Mill) 85
OpenAI 1, 92
– API interactions 90
– ChatGPT 5, 74
– custom GPTs 4, 145
– ecosystem 92
– generativity 3, 6
– GPT marketplace 4
– laundry buddy 133
– multiple programming languages 90

– software development kits (SDKs) 43
– transparency 90

Peloton 124
Phelps, E. S. 7, 65, 68, 80, 111, 116, 117
portfolios 73, 76, 108, 109
pretrained component 7–8
price signals 30, 67, 121
product generativity 9, 14–15, 17, 19, 20, 69, 119, 121, 126, 128, 131. See also generative products
Product-Market Fit (PMF) 153
product-markets, quadrants 17–19, 120
– Coda 127
– generative markets from generative products 126
– generative products from generative markets 127–128
– high product, high/low market generativity 123, 125
– LEGO 127
– low product, high/low market generativity 124
– Notion 126
– Raspberry Pi 126
products management (generative). See also generative products
– hypothesis 61
– meta problem-solving 60
– patient play 60
– thick documentation 62–63
– user tinkering 61–63
profitability 9, 12–14, 27, 30, 31, 45, 103, 109, 120
profit-driven model 13, 30, 31, 122, 123. See also market-based incentives

Rafaeli, S. 86
Ramlogan, R. 88
Raspberry Pi 14, 18, 57, 123, 126
Ravid, G. 86
Recker, J. 34, 159
recurring revenue 40, 41, 121
remix culture 112, 114, 142
Replit 28, 36, 52, 102, 150–151
Retool.com 35
revenue sharing 4, 101, 103, 109, 127
Rietveld, J. 107
Roblox (online game) 12, 18, 48, 81, 82, 93, 95, 114, 125, 129, 131–132
Romer, P. M. 65, 68

Santesteban, C. 107
Schoffelen, J. 62
Schumpeter, J. A. 21
The Scratch Online Community 142–143
self-attention 7
self-refueling systems 65, 68, 70, 71
self-reinforcing cycles 20, 111, 116, 118, 120, 131, 135
self-sustaining value-creating systems 17, 128
sensors 49, 66, 126
Shapiro, C. 129
Shopify 42, 81, 91, 101, 108, 113, 115, 120, 126, 131
Silicon Valley 11
Slack.com 35
Software-as-a-Service (SaaS) 150
software development kits (SDKs) 4, 11, 43, 137
SparkFun Electronics 14, 57
Spotify 48, 51, 53, 102
staged process, control points
– dynamic balance 105–106
– generic control points 104–105
– strategic control points 105
– technical control points 105
Stemler, A. 110
structured serendipity 24, 80, 87, 97, 151
Surowiecki, J. 67

Tadelis, S. 77
thick documentation 62–63
TikTok 51
trade-offs 2, 9, 17, 107
– innovation 152
– navigating strategic 26
– tensions and 133–135
transferability 14, 27, 29, 44, 50, 51
Turing, A. M. 7, 60

Turing Test 7, 60
Twitter 84

Uber 3, 16, 19, 36, 65, 75, 76, 83, 124
"unknown unknowns" idea 66
user-innovators 2, 4, 22, 41, 45, 93, 95, 96, 116, 121, 131, 150

v0.dev AI tool 36, 52
van Angeren, J. 31
van der Geest, C. 31
Vercel 151
vibe coding 36, 150
VisiCalc 14, 34, 57
Voice over Internet Protocol (VoIP) 136

Webflow 73, 75, 100, 108, 113, 117
WooCommerce 121
Wordfence 121
WordPress 6, 12, 35, 40, 42, 121, 125, 132, 147–149

Yang, C. 37–38
Yoast SEO 121
Yoo, Y. 2, 46
YouTube 36, 100, 106, 125

Zapier 35, 37, 50, 56, 150, 154
Zeroqode 27, 122
Zhao, I. 18–19, 35, 37
Zihnioglu, N. 18–19
Zittrain, J. 8–10, 14, 31, 69
– definitions of generativity 68
– generative technologies 35
– generativity conceptualization 29–30, 33
Zoo, H. 94